AMERICANISM CONTRASTED WITH FOREIGNISM, ROMANISM, AND BOGUS DEMOCRACY IN THE LIGHT OF REASON, HISTORY, AND SCRIPTURE

LECTOR HOUSE PUBLIC DOMAIN WORKS

HAPPY READING!

AMERICANISM CONTRASTED WITH FOREIGNISM, ROMANISM, AND BOGUS DEMOCRACY IN THE LIGHT OF REASON, HISTORY, AND SCRIPTURE

WILLIAM GANNAWAY BROWNLOW

ISBN: 978-93-90387-85-4

Published: 1856

LECTOR HOUSE LLP
E-MAIL: lectorpublishing@gmail.com

REV. W. G. BROWNLOW.

Very Respectfully, &c.

W. G. Brownlow

AMERICANISM CONTRASTED WITH FOREIGNISM, ROMANISM, AND BOGUS DEMOCRACY, IN THE LIGHT OF REASON, HISTORY, AND SCRIPTURE;

IN WHICH CERTAIN DEMAGOGUES IN TENNESSEE, AND ELSEWHERE, ARE SHOWN UP IN THEIR TRUE COLORS.

BY

WILLIAM G. BROWNLOW

EDITOR OF "BROWNLOW'S KNOXVILLE WHIG."

"——Go to your bloody rites again:
Preach—perpetuate damnation in your den;
Then let your altars, ye blasphemers, peal
With thanks to Heaven, that let you loose again,
To practice deeds with torturing fire and steel,
No eye may search, no tongue may challenge or reveal!"

THOMAS CAMPBELL.

1856.

DEDICATION.

TO THE YOUNG MEN OF AMERICA.

Young Gentlemen:—Almighty God has conferred on you the peculiar honor and the eminent responsibility of preserving and perpetuating the liberties of this country, both civil and religious. That the American people are on the eve of an eventful period, will not be doubted by any sane man, who can discern the "signs of the times." Indeed, it is an every-day remark, that, as a nation, we are in the midst of a crisis. If, however, a crisis ever did exist in the affairs of this Nation, since its independence was first achieved, which called upon the NATIVE AND LEGAL VOTERS of the country to watch with sleepless vigilance over their blood-bought liberties, that crisis must be dated in the year of our Lord, ONE THOUSAND EIGHT HUNDRED AND FIFTY-SIX! The great Commonwealth of Humanity, in behalf of the momentous interests of Truth, Liberty, and Religion, calls upon the present generation of YOUNG MEN, who will have the issues of a coming revolution to meet, to qualify themselves for the task.

There never was a time known, since the dark days of the Revolution, when the civil and religious liberties of this country were so much endangered as at the present time. This danger we are threatened with from *Foreign influence*, and the rapid strides of *Romanism*, to which we may add *Native treachery*, connived at, as they are, by certain leading demagogues of the country, and a powerful and influential political party, falsely called *Democrats*, who seek the Foreign and Catholic vote, and are willing to obtain it at the expense of Liberty, and the sacrifice of the Protestant Religion!

The great criminal of the nineteenth century, the PAPAL HIERARCHY, is now on trial before the bar of public opinion, having been arraigned by the AMERICAN PARTY. You are called on to decide, YOUNG MEN, as you wield the balance of power, whether this Criminal, arraigned for treason against God, and hostility to the human race, deserves the execrations of all honest and patriotic men, and avenging judgments of a righteous God! In order to decide this grave question, YOUNG *Gentlemen of the Nineteenth Century*, you are to consider the inevitable tendency of the principles of the Church of Rome—the actual results of these tendencies as embodied in history—the indictment brought in by the AMERICAN PARTY, and the testimony of the witnesses. When you have intelligently considered the part the self-styled *Democratic Party* has acted in this infamous drama, you will feel it to be your duty to indict the corporation claiming the right to be called the Great Democratic Party, as *accessory* to the treason, crimes, and infamy, of the aforesaid Papal Hierarchy!

To you, then, Gentlemen, is this brief work most affectionately inscribed by

THE AUTHOR.

PREFACE.

For the last twenty-five years, the writer of this work has employed much of his time in the reading and study of the controversy between Roman Catholics and Protestants. And those who have been subscribers to the paper he has edited and published for the LAST SEVENTEEN YEARS, will bear him witness that he has kept up a fierce and unceasing fire against that dangerous and immoral *Corporation*, claiming the right to be called the HOLY CATHOLIC CHURCH. This he has done, and still continues to do, because he believes firmly that the system of Popery, as taught in the standards of the Church of Rome, as enforced by her Bishops and Priests, and as believed and practised by the great body of Romanists, both in Europe and America, is at war with the true religion taught in the Bible, and is injurious to the public and private morals of the civilized world; and, if unchecked, will overturn the civil and religious liberties of the United States. Such, he believes, is its tendency and the design of its leaders.

Popery is deceitful in its character; and the design of this brief work is, in part, to drag it forward into the light of the middle of the nineteenth century, to strip the flimsy vizor off its face, and to bring it, with all its abuses, corruptions, and hypocritical Protestant advocates, before the bar of enlightened public opinion, for judgment in the case. Roman Catholics misrepresent their own creed, their Church, and its corrupt institutions. The most revolting, wicked, and immoral features of their *holy and immutable system*, are kept out of sight by its corrupt Clergy, and Jesuitical teachers; while, with a purpose to *deceive*, a *Protestant sense* is attached to most of their doctrines and peculiarities. By this vile means, they designedly *misrepresent themselves*, and impose on the public, by inducing charitable and uninformed persons to believe that they are not as profligate as they are represented to be. This game has been played with a bold hand in *Knoxville*, for the last twelve months, and it is being played in every city and town in the South and West, where Romanism is being planted. One object, then, of this *epitomized* work, setting forth the boastings, threats, and disclosures of leading Catholic organs and Bishops, as to their real principles and designs upon this country, suffered to go forth in their more excited moments, or unguarded hours, is, to spread before the people, in a cheap form, true Popery, and to strip it of its *Protestant garb*, which it has for the time being assumed.

An additional reason for bringing out this publication, at this particular time, is, to expose a corrupt bargain entered into by the leaders of the Catholic Church, and the leaders of a corrupt and designing political party, falsely called the Democratic party. One of the most alarming "signs of the times" is, that while Protestant ministers, of different persuasions, only two brief years ago, could preach with power and eloquence against the dogmas and corrupting tendencies of *Romanism*, and pass out of the doors of their churches, receiving the compliments and extravagant praises of their entire congregations, let one of them now dare to hold up this Corporation as a dangerous foreign enemy—let him warn his charge against the influence of Popery, or but only designate the Catholic Hierarchy as the "man of sin" described in the Scriptures, and one half of his congregation are grossly insulted: they charge him with meddling in politics; and, by way of resentment, they will either not hear him again, or they will starve him out, by refusing to contribute to his support!

The hypocritical and profligate portion of the Methodist, Presbyterian, Baptist, and Episcopal membership in this country, are not so much misled by Popery, as they are influenced by *party politics*, and are in love with the *loose moral code* of Romanism. It lays no restraints on their lusts, and gives a loose rein to all their unsanctified passions and desires. Backslidden, unconverted, or unprincipled members of Protestant Churches, find in Popery a *sympathizing irreligion*, adapted to their vicious lives; and hence they fall in with its disgusting superstitions and insulting claims. They are, therefore, ensnared with the delusions of Popery, of *choice*. In other words, Popery is a system of mere human policy; altogether of Foreign origin; Foreign in its support; importing Foreign vassals and paupers by multiplied thousands; and sending into every State and Territory in this Union, a most baneful Foreign and anti-Republican influence. Its old *goutified*, immoral, and drunken Pope, his Bishops and Priests, are *politicians*; men of the world, earthly, sensual, and devilish, and mere men of pleasure. Associated with them for the purpose, in great State and National contests, of securing the Catholic vote, are the worst class of American politicians, designing demagogues, selfish office-seekers, and bad men, calling themselves *Democrats* and "Old-Line Whigs!" These politicians know that Popery, as a system, is in the hands of a Foreign despotism, precisely what the Koran is in the hands of the Grand Turk and his partisans. But corrupt and ambitious politicians in this country, are willing to act the part of traitors to our laws and Constitution, for the sake of profitable offices; and they are willing to sacrifice the Protestant Religion, on the ancient and profligate altar at Rome, if they may but rise to distinction on its ruins!

The great Democratic party of this country, which has degenerated into a *Semi-Papal Organization*, for the base purposes of power and plunder, now fully partakes of the intolerant spirit of Rome, and is acting it out in all the departments of our State and General Governments. What Romanism has been to the Old World, this Papal and Anti-American organization seeks and promises to be to this country. What is Popery in Roman Catholic Europe? It is as intolerant in politics as in religion: it taxes and oppresses the subjects and citizens of every country; it interdicts nations; dethrones governors, chief magistrates, and kings; dissolves civil governments; suspends commerce; annuls civil laws; and, to gratify its unsanctified lust of ambition, it has overrun whole nations with bloodshed, and thrown them into confusion. So it is with this *"Bogus"* Democracy: it wages a war of extermination against the freedom of the press, and against the liberty of speech, the rights of human conscience, and the liberties of man: hence its indiscriminate proscription of all who dare to unite with the Americaｎ Party, or openly espouse their cause. Popery aims at universal power over the bodies and souls of all men; and history proclaims that its weapons have been dungeons, racks, chains, fire, and sword! The *bastard* Democracy of the present age has united with the Prelates, Priests, Monks, and Nuns of Romanism, and is daily affiliating with hundreds of thousands of the very off-scourings of the European Catholic population—stimulating them to deeds of violence, and to the shedding of blood! To-day, they sustain a *Baker* in the foul murder of a *Poole*, in New York, because he was a member of the so-called Know-Nothing party, which had just routed, in an election, this Foreign Locofoco party! To-morrow, we find this same vile party, its editors and orators, sustaining a Foreign Catholic Mob in Louisville, Ky.; and the members of the same party, in surrounding States, exulting over the murder of Protestant Americans! And in the next breath, as it were, we find these sons of Belial, falsely called *Democrats*, after reaching the power they lusted after in Philadelphia, sending up shouts over the lawless deeds of a Foreign Catholic riot, which made the ears of every American citizen to tingle!

Under the guidance of an All-wise Providence, the Protector of our Republic, and of the Protestant Religion, it is in the power of the free and independent voters of these United States to cause this enemy's long *"arm to be clean dried up, and his right eye to be utterly darkened,"* by elevating to the two first offices within the gift of the world, Millard Fillmore and Andrew J. Donelson!

I am, candid Reader, your fellow-citizen,

W. G. BROWNLOW.

Knoxville, July, 1856.

CONTENTS

Page

AMERICANISM CONTRASTED WITH FOREIGNISM, ROMANISM, AND BOGUS DEMOCRACY.

INTRODUCTORY CHAPTER.

The Creed of the American Party—The Platform misrepresented by Mr. Watkins—Official Vote on the adoption of the new Platform—What the Abolitionists and Democrats say of the Platform—Seceders from the Nominating Convention, and their Address.

Lord Byron, just as the war of Greece approached, said: "It is not one man, nor a million, but the *spirit of liberty* which must be spread;" and, carrying out the same bold idea of liberty, he continues, "It is time to act;" or, in the language of the Know Nothing salutation, "It is time for work;" for "what signifies *self*, if a single spark of that genius of liberty worthy of the past, can be bequeathed unquenchably to the future?" In the language of a fair poetess:

—"Our country is a whole,
Of which we all are parts; nor should a citizen
Regard his interests as distinct from hers:
No hopes or fears should touch his patriot soul,
But what affects her honor or her shame."

The civilization—the nationality—the institutions, civil and religious—and the mission of the United States, are all eminently American. Mental light and personal independence, constitutional union, national supremacy, submission to law and rules of order, homogeneous population, and instinctive patriotism, are all vital elements of American liberty, nationality, and upward and onward progress. Foreign immigration, foreign Catholic influence, and sectional factions nourished by them—and breeding demagogues in the name of *Democracy*, by a prostitution of the elective franchise—have already corrupted our nationality, degraded our councils, both State and National, weakened the bonds of union, disturbed our country's peace, and awakened apprehensions of insecurity and *progressive deterioration*, threatening ultimate ruin! To rescue and restore American institutions—to maintain American nationality, and to secure American birthrights, is the mission and the sole purpose of the AMERICAN PARTY—composed of conservative, patriotic, Protestant, Union-loving, native-born citizens of every section, and of every

Christian denomination—self-sacrificing patriots, who prefer their country, and the religion of their fathers, and of the Bible, to a factious name, a plundering political organization, and an infamous Papal hierarchy!

The paramount and ultimate object of our AMERICAN ORGANIZATION is to save and exalt the Union, and to preserve and perpetuate the rights and blessings of the Protestant religion. We contend that American principles should mould American policy; that American mind should rule American destiny; that all sectional parties, such as a party *North*, or a party *South*, should be renounced; that all sectional agitations, such as are kept up by Abolitionists, Free Soilers, and Black Republicans, should be resisted; that Congress should never agitate the subject of domestic slavery, in any form or for any purpose, but leave it where the Constitution fixes it; that as the destiny of the country depends on the mind of the country, intelligence should rule; that the ballot-box should be purified, and corrupt Romanism and foreign influence checked; that any allegiance "to any foreign prince, potentate, or power"—to any power, regal or pontifical, should be rebuked as the most fatal canker of the germ of American independence; that every citizen should be encouraged to exercise freely his own conscience; and that the popular mind should be enlightened, and the popular heart rectified, by proper and universal Christian education. This is the essence of the American creed; and when methodized into a Political Decalogue, it constitutes the *Ten Commandments* of the American party.

In this connection, and at this point, we will give the much-abused Platform of the American party, adopted at the session of the National Council, February 21, 1856. Examine the Platform, and answer to your conscience the question: What true American head can disapprove—what pure American heart can revolt? Can men taking their stand on this Platform be the enemies of civil and religious liberties? Can either civil or religious liberties rest secure on any other grounds? And must not those "Bogus" Democrats and Anti-Americans, therefore, who wage war against this citadel of American birthrights, act as enemies to the Federal Constitution, enemies to the Union, to the mental independence of American citizens—enemies to the Protestant religion, and enemies, consequently, "to civil and religious liberty?"

PLATFORM OF THE AMERICAN PARTY.

1st. An humble acknowledgment to the Supreme Being for his protecting care vouchsafed to our fathers in their successful Revolutionary struggle, and hitherto manifested to us, their descendants, in the preservation of the liberties, the independence, and the union of these States.

2d. The perpetuation of the Federal Union, as the palladium of our civil and religious liberties, and the only sure bulwark of American Independence.

3d. *Americans must rule America*, and to this end, *native*-born citizens should be selected for all State, Federal, and municipal offices, or government employment, in preference to all others: nevertheless,

4th. Persons born of American parents residing temporarily abroad, should be entitled to all the rights of native-born citizens; but,

5th. No person should be selected for political station, (whether of native or foreign birth,) who recognizes any allegiance or obligation of any description, to any foreign prince, potentate, or power, or who refuses to recognize the Federal and State constitutions (each within its sphere) as paramount to all other laws, as rules of political action.

6th. The unqualified recognition and maintenance of the reserved rights of the several States, and the cultivation of harmony and fraternal good-will between the citizens of the several States; and to this end, non-interference by Congress with questions appertaining solely to the individual States, and non-intervention by each State with the affairs of any other State.

7th. The recognition of the right of the native-born and naturalized citizens of the United States, permanently residing in any Territory thereof, to frame their constitution and laws, and to regulate their domestic and social affairs in their own mode, subject only to the provisions of the Federal Constitution, with the privilege of admission into the Union whenever they have the requisite population for one Representative in Congress. *Provided always*, that none but those who are citizens of the United States, under the constitution and laws thereof, and who have a fixed residence in any such Territory, ought to participate in the formation of the constitution, or in the enactment of laws for said Territory or State.

8th. An enforcement of the principle that no State or Territory ought to admit others than citizens of the United States to the right of suffrage, or of holding political office.

9th. A change in the laws of naturalization, making a continued residence of twenty-one years, of all not hereinbefore provided for, an indispensable requisite for citizenship hereafter, and excluding all paupers, and persons convicted of crime, from landing upon our shores; but no interference with the vested rights of foreigners.

10th. Opposition to any union between Church and State: no interference with religious faith or worship, and no test-oaths for office.

11th. Free and thorough investigation into any and all alleged abuses of public functionaries, and a strict economy in public expenditures.

12th. The maintenance and enforcement of all laws constitutionally enacted, until said laws shall be repealed, or shall be declared null and void by competent judicial authority.

13th. Opposition to the reckless and unwise policy of the present administration in the general management of our national affairs, and more especially as shown in removing "Americans" (by designation) and conservatives in principle, from office, and placing foreigners and ultraists in their places: as shown in a truckling subserviency to the stronger, and an insolent and cowardly bravado toward the weaker powers: as shown in reöpening sectional agitation, by the repeal of the Missouri Compromise: as shown in granting to unnaturalized foreigners the right of suffrage in Kansas and Nebraska: as shown in its vacillating course on the Kansas and Nebraska question: as shown in the corruptions which pervade some of the departments of the government: as shown in disgracing meritorious naval officers through prejudice or caprice; and as shown in the blundering mismanagement of our foreign relations.

14th. Therefore, to remedy existing evils, and prevent the disastrous consequences otherwise resulting therefrom, we would build up the "American party" upon the principles hereinbefore stated.

15th. That each State Council shall have authority to amend their several constitutions, so as to abolish the several degrees, and institute a pledge of honor, instead of other obligations, for fellowship and admission into the party.

16th. A free and open discussion of all political principles embraced in our platform.

The HON. MR. WATKINS, a renegade from the American ranks, in East Tennessee, delivered a speech in Congress on the 6th of May, 1856; which speech we find reported in the *Washington Union* — a speech which betrays an utter ignorance of the point he undertook to discuss. It is due to *his betrayed constituents* that we should expose his ignorance, and the blundering fallacy of his attempts to justify his turning *Locofoco Cataline Judas Sag-Nicht*! He says, as reported by his political organ-grinder:

"But, sir, the platform recently adopted by the Philadelphia Convention cannot receive my approbation. I cannot support Mr. Fillmore, or any other distinguished Whig, upon that platform. The only solitary plank in the Philadelphia platform of June, 1855, was the twelfth section — that section which denied to Congress the right to interfere with slavery in the Territories, declaring the doctrine of non-intervention, and of popular sovereignty in the Territories. But, sir, that plank in the platform was stricken out by the convention recently held, and the sixth resolution of the platform then adopted substituted in its place. And what does that resolution endorse? Is there any non-intervention in the sixth resolution of the Philadelphia platform? Is there any denial of the right of Congress to interfere upon the subject of slavery in the sixth resolution of the Philadelphia platform? Certainly not."

In lieu of the *June* platform, we have this *February* platform. The June platform contained *no such denial to Congress*, as is here alleged by Mr. Watkins, of the right to interfere with slavery in the Territories! And it is marvellous, indeed, that a grave Member of Congress should undertake to discuss Platforms, which he had either never read, or the purport of which, if he had ever read them, he had either wholly forgotten, or lacked the sense to comprehend! The twelfth section of the June Platform says:

> "And expressly *pretermitting any expression of opinion* upon the power of Congress to establish or prohibit slavery in any Territory, it is the sense of this National Council, that Congress OUGHT NOT to legislate upon the subject of slavery within the Territories of the United States."

Thus, instead of *denying* to Congress the right to interfere with slavery in the Territories, as erroneously and recklessly charged by this new-born Democrat, all opinion on that subject was *"expressly pretermitted"* in the June Platform! Mr. Watkins was in such a hurry to join the Forney, Pierce, and Catholic Democracy, that he did not stop to examine even the Platform which most disgusted him! But this is not the worst blunder which he committed in that speech. He turned to the new Platform, and asked, with an air of triumph:

> "Is there any non-intervention in the sixth resolution of the (new) Philadelphia platform? Is there any denial of the right of Congress to interfere with the subject of slavery in the sixth resolution of the (new) Philadelphia platform?"

And he answers, *"Certainly not!"* The ignorant man, it would seem, only read as far as to the sixth section of the new Platform; and even *that* section contains a direct affirmative answer to his question; which, in order to place the American party in a false position, he answers, *"Certainly not!"*

Now, we ask such as may have noticed his *misrepresentations*, to read a *little further on*, at least to the end of the 7th section of this new Platform, and see where it leaves Mr. Watkins! Turn back to the 7th section, and it will be seen that this section, instead of *"pretermitting any opinion"* on the question, announces the doctrine that the citizens of the United States permanently residing in the Territories, have a *"right"* to frame their Constitution and laws, and to regulate their domestic affairs in their own mode, subject only to the provisions of the Federal Constitution!

The *New York Evening Post*, a Pierce and foreign Democratic organ, thus alludes to the action of the Convention which nominated FILLMORE and DONELSON:—

> "The 12th section of the June Platform, it is true, had been abrogated; BUT IT HAD BEEN REPLACED BY ANOTHER, MEANING PRECISELY THE SAME THING!"

The *Cincinnati Gazette*, an Abolition, Anti-American Foreign sheet, came out in opposition to the American nominees, in its issue of Feb. 29th, 1856, on account of the *Pro-slavery* character of the new Platform. The Gazette says:—

> "We are glad that the action of the Convention *proved so decided as to leave no doubt as to the character of the Platform.* THE LATTER IS CLEARLY AND DECIDEDLY PRO-SLAVERY AND NEBRASKA, *and in this respect corresponds precisely with the* PRINCIPLES OF THE PIERCE DEMOCRACY! *Fillmore*

and Donelson are therefore presented to the American people as candidates for the Presidency and Vice Presidency, ON A THOROUGH AND DECIDED NEBRASKA PRO-SLAVERY PLATFORM, and the citizens of Northern States are asked to vote for them!"

The *New York Tribune,* whose editor was a prominent member of the Pittsburgh Black Republican Convention, and who is violent in his opposition to FILLMORE and DONELSON, says:

"The object of the Know Nothings has dwindled down to this—TO DEFEAT THE REPUBLICAN PARTY! That is to say, this is the object of those who have managed the Philadelphia Convention, and nominated Mr. Fillmore. I have diligently inquired for a member who voted for *Banks* for Speaker, and now supports *Fillmore;* but up to this time—more than three days after the nomination—I have not heard of one. That sort must be scarce!"

The following is the OFFICIAL vote on the adoption of the new Platform by the National Council, which met four days previous to the Nominating Convention:

NEW HAMPSHIRE—*Nays*—Messrs. Colby and Emery.

MASSACHUSETTS—*Yeas*—Messrs. Ely, Weith, Brewster, Robinson, and Arnold. *Nays*—Messrs. Richmond, Wheelwright, Temple, Thurston, Sumner, Allen, Sawin, and Hawkes.

CONNECTICUT—*Nays*—Messrs. Sperry, Dunbar, Peck, Booth, Holley, and Perkins.

RHODE ISLAND—*Yeas*—Messrs. Chase and Knight. *Nays*—Messrs. Simons and Nightingale.

NEW YORK—*Yeas*—Messrs. Walker, Oakley, Morgan, Woodward, Reynolds, Chester, Owens, Sanders, Whiston, Nichols, Van Dusen, Westbrook, Parsons, Picket, Campbell, Lowell, Sammons, Oakes, Seymour, Squire, Cooper, Burr, Bennett, Marvine, Midler, Stephens, Johnson, Wetmore, Hammond, and S. Seymour. *Nay*—Mr. Barker.

DELAWARE—*Yeas*—Messrs. Clement and Smithers.

MARYLAND—*Yeas*—Messrs. Codet, Alexander, Winchester, Stephens, and Wilmot. *Nays*—Messrs. Purnell, Ricaud, Pinkney, and Kramer.

VIRGINIA—*Nays*—Messrs. Bolling, McHugh, Cochran, Boteler, Preston, and Maupin.

FLORIDA—*Yea*—Mr. Call.

NEW JERSEY—*Yeas*—Messrs. Deshler, Weeks, Lyon, and McClellan.

PENNSYLVANIA—*Yeas*—Messrs. Freeman, Nelclede, Gossler, Smith, Gillinham, Hammond, Wood, Gilford, Pyle, Farrand, and Williamson. *Nays*—Messrs. Johnson, Sewell, Jones, Parker, Heistand,

Kase, Kinkaid, Coffee, Carlisle, Crovode, Edie, Sewell, and Power.

LOUISIANA—*Yeas*—Messrs. Lathrop and Elam. *Nays*—Messrs. Harman and Hardy.

CALIFORNIA—*Yeas*—Messrs. Wood and Stanley.

ARKANSAS—*Yea*—Mr. Logan. *Nay*—Mr. Fowler.

TENNESSEE—*Yeas*—Messrs. Brownlow, Bankhead, Zollicoffer, Burton, Campbell, Donelson, Harris, Bilbo, and Beloat. *Nays*—Messrs. Nelson, Reedy, and Picket.

KENTUCKY—*Yeas*—Messrs. Stowers, Campbell, Raphael, Todd, Clay, Goodloe, and Bartlett. *Nays*—Messrs. Shanklin, Jones, Carpenter, Gist, and Underwood.

OHIO—*Yeas*—Messrs. White, Nash, Simpson, and Lippett. *Nays*—Messrs. Gabriel, Olds, Ford, Barker, Potter, Stanbaugh, Rodgers, Spooner, Hodges, Kyle, Lees, Swigart, Allison, Fishback, Thomas, Corwine, Chapman, Ayres, and Johnson.

INDIANA—*Yeas*—Messrs. Sheets and Phelps. *Nay*—Mr. Meredith.

MISSOURI—*Yeas*—Messrs. Edward, Fletcher, and Hockaday. *Nay*—Mr. Breckenridge.

MICHIGAN—*Yea*—Mr. Wood.

WISCONSIN—*Yeas*—Messrs. Lockwood, Cook, Chandler, and Gillies.

DISTRICT OF COLUMBIA—*Yeas*—Messrs. Ellis and Evans.

ILLINOIS—*Yeas*—Messrs. Danenhower and Allen. *Nays*—Messrs. Jennings and Gear.

IOWA—*Nays*—Messrs. Webster and Thorrington.

Yeas—108. *Nays*—77.

We will close this chapter by giving the delegates who seceded from the Nominating Convention, with the Address published by them on the occasion. That recession was a more inconsiderable affair than has been represented by the foreign party of this country. The author of this work was the Chairman of the large Committee on Credentials, and reported TWO HUNDRED AND SEVENTY-SEVEN delegates, which report was received without opposition, as to numbers. Of these, *forty-two* only seceded, viz.: 13 out of 28 from Ohio; *one* of two from New Hampshire; 6—all—from Connecticut; 2 out of 13 from Massachusetts; *one* out of 3 from Illinois; 7 out of 27 from Pennsylvania; *one* out of 4 from Rhode Island; 5—all—from Michigan; 5—all—from Wisconsin; *one*—all—from Iowa; 42 out of 277—not a *sixth*, and but little over a *seventh* of the whole!

ADDRESS.

The seceders or "bolters" made the following address, to which they appended their States and names. What they say of the *Louisiana* delegates, we have explained in another portion of this work:

"The undersigned, delegates to the nominating Convention now in session at Philadelphia, find themselves compelled to dissent from the principles avowed by that body; and holding opinions, as they do, that the restoration of the Missouri Compromise, as demanded by a majority of the whole people, is a redress of an undeniable wrong, and the execution of it, in spirit at least, indispensable to the repose of the country, they have regarded the refusal of that Convention to recognize the well-defined opinion of the country, and of the Americans of the free States, upon this question, as a denial of their rights and a rebuke to their sentiments; and they hold that the admission into the National Council and nominating Convention, of delegates from Louisiana, representing a Roman Catholic Constituency, absolved every true American from all obligations to sustain the action of either of the said bodies.

"They have therefore withdrawn from the nominating Convention, refusing to participate in the proposed nomination, and now address themselves to the Americans of the country, and especially of the States they represent, to justify and approve of their action; and to the end that a nomination conforming to the overruling sentiment of the country in the great issue may be regularly and auspiciously made, the undersigned propose to the Americans in all the States to assemble in their several State organizations, and elect delegates to a Convention to meet in the city of New York, on Thursday, the 12th day of June next, for the purpose of nominating candidates for President and Vice President of the United States."

Ohio—Thos. H. Ford, J. H. Baker, B. S. Kyle, W. H. C. Mitchell, E. T. Sturtevant, O. T. Fishback, Jacob Ebbert, Wm. B. Allison, H. C. Hodges, L. H. Olds, W. B. Chapman, Thos. McYees, Charles Nichols.

New Hampshire—Anthony Colby.

Connecticut—Lucius G. Peck, Jas. E. Dunham, Hezekiah Griswold, Austin Baldwin, Edmund Perkins, David Booth.

Massachusetts—Wild. S. Thurston, Z. R. Pangborn.

Illinois—Henry S. Jennings.

Pennsylvania—Wm. F. Johnston, S. C. Kase, R. M. Riddle, T. J. Coffey, John Williamson, J. Harrison, S. Ewell.

Rhode Island—E. J. Nightingale.

Michigan—S. T. Lyon, W. Fuller, W. S. Wood, P. P. Meddler, J. Hamilton.

Wisconsin—D. A. Gillis, John Lockwood, Robt. Chandler, G. Burdick, C. W. Cook.

Iowa—L. H. Webster.

THE ELECTION OF BANKS—THE SLAVERY QUESTION.

One of the issues in the Presidential contest now going on, is the *slavery question*. A. O. P. X. Y. Z. Nicholson, of the Washington Union, who canvassed this State in opposition to Scott, and shed his *crocodile* tears before every crowd he addressed, because so good a man as Fillmore, who had stood firm for the *rights of the South*, had been set aside by an ungrateful Convention at Baltimore, to give place to Scott, the favorite of *Seward*—this miserable hypocrite, we say, now comes out and says, "Fillmore's abolitionism will suit the North."

The Central Democratic Committee for East Tennessee, in a call for a District Convention at Clinton, in May last, through the *Knoxville Standard*, conclude said call in this language:

> "The time has again arrived when the national Democracy must rally to their country's call and preserve the Constitution as it is in its purity, and perpetuate the union of the States from the rain which the *Black Republican Party of the North*, aided by THEIR KNOW-NOTH-ING ALLIES OF THE SOUTH, would bring upon them. By order of the

> "CENTRAL COMMITTEE."

The *Sag-Nicht Convention* held at Somerville, on Thursday the 8th of May, and which selected D. M. Currin as their Electoral candidate, adopted the following resolution:

> "*Resolved*, That we have been appointed by the Democracy of this Electoral District to organize to fight, in the coming Presidential election, the BLACK REPUBLICANS AND KNOW-NOTHINGS. *Resolved*, That we *can* beat them, and we *will* do it. *Resolved*, That we will cordially receive the *co-operation of all Old-Line Whigs* who will assist us in carrying out these resolutions."

Now, the charge is here made that the Know-Nothings of the South are the allies of the Black Republicans of the North. This is the impression intended to be made, first by these *concealed calumniators* at Knoxville, and afterwards by the *open and avowed slanderers* of the same party at Somerville! With such *wholesale lying* as is displayed in both of these cases, we have but little patience: we only give their language, to show their recklessness in making such an issue. And although this Foreign party claim to be the guardians of Southern interests, we propose to show, before we conclude this chapter, that they are themselves the "allies of the Black

Republicans of the North," and are giving them more "aid and comfort" than all the other parties in the country!

FRANCIS P. BLAIR, former editor of Gen. Jackson's organ at Washington, was the President of the Black Republican Convention at Pittsburg, in February last! *John M. Niles*, Democratic Senator in Congress, was President of the Black Republican Convention held in Connecticut! In the Pittsburg Convention, over which Blair presided, PRESTON KING, ABIJAH MANN, DAVID WILMOT, and JACOB BRINKERHOFF, Old-Line Democrats, figured conspicuously.

For two long and cold winter months, the Democrats, both North and South, voted for *Richardson*, of Illinois, for Speaker, a violent *anti-slavery man*, whose speeches *against* slavery, and in *favor* of Abolitionism, were matters of record in the Congressional Globe, and were delivered on the floor of Congress so late as 1850! The *immortal 75* Democrats did not cease to vote for this man *Richardson*, until GEN. ZOLLICOFFER, of Tennessee, read his speeches upon him, in the presence of his friends!

On the 2d of February, SAMUEL A. SMITH, of Tennessee, a Democratic Representative in Congress, *renewed* his motion to adopt the PLURALITY RULE. His proposition, which it was evident would elect *Banks*, was carried by Black Republican votes, who went for it in a body. This would still not have elected *Banks*, but for the fact that the following *Democrats* voted for the odious plurality rule: *Clingman, Herbert, Hickman, Jewett, Kelley, Barclay, Bayard, Wells, Williams*, and SAMUEL A. SMITH! Mr. Clarke was the only American who voted for the odious rule!

MR. CARLILE, a national American, of Virginia, before the vote was taken upon this plurality rule, offered the following substitute for it:

> "*Resolved*, That the HON. WM. AIKEN, a Representative from the State of South Carolina, be, and he is hereby declared Speaker of the Thirty-Fourth Congress."

GOV. AIKEN is a sound Southern Democrat—never was any thing else—but COL. SMITH *objected*, and demanded the *previous question*, which cut off MR. CARLILE's resolution, and which was to prevent its adoption! The candidate of the Democratic party, at that time, MR. ORR, immediately *withdrew in favor of* GOV. AIKEN, upon the introduction of MR. CARLILE's resolution; and to *prevent Aiken's election*, SAMUEL A. SMITH cut off said resolution by a call of the previous question!

Banks was elected by *one* vote, and this could not be accomplished until SEVEN DEMOCRATS got *behind the bar*, and refused to vote at all! These were HICKMAN, PARKER, and BARCLAY, of Pennsylvania; CRAIG, of North Carolina; TAYLOR, of Louisiana; RICHARDSON, of Illinois; and SEWARD, of Georgia! Any *two* of these *Southern* Democrats could have made AIKEN Speaker, but they did not want him—they knew Banks to be a *Democrat*, if he were a Black Republican—and to elect him, they believed would give them the strength of that odious party in the coming contest.

We have before us the *Washington Union* of Sept. 27th, 1853, giving, editorially, a glowing account of the Massachusetts Democratic State Convention, reporting the speech of Nathaniel P. Banks, of Waltham, concluding that report in these words:

> "Mr. Banks emphatically and decidedly, on his own part, and on that of the *Democrats of Massachusetts*, disclaimed the truth of the rumors in certain newspapers that an arrangement had been entered into with another political party in the Commonwealth concerning the distribution of State offices. It was his and this Convention's and all true Democrats' desire, belief, and determination, that Henry W. Bishop should be elected governor of Massachusetts, and that the other Democratic State officers should also be elected. He was not afraid of defeat, and less afraid of *Whig success*, which, to judge by its recent effects, was simply equivalent to a defeat. [Applause.]"

It may be said, and doubtless will be, that *Banks* has allied himself with the Republicans. But Banks says he has *always been a Democrat*, and that he was *nominated as a Democrat in his district*. And certain it is, that he was elected Speaker by DEMOCRATS, under the *compulsion* of an odious plurality rule, and the *gag* of the previous question!

It will be said, and said truthfully too, that SIX AMERICANS FROM THE NORTH voted for MR. FULLER, of Pennsylvania. So they did; and in doing so, they voted for a sound national and conservative man. But did this justify *Southern* Democrats in *dodging* the question, and thereby electing a Black Republican Speaker? Gov. Aiken was the candidate of the *seven* Democrats—he was not the candidate of the *six* Americans! Democracy, moreover, had refused to vote for an American under any circumstances, and had, on the first day of the meeting of Congress, passed a resolution insulting the whole American party, in caucus! We would have seen them banished to the farthest verge of astronomical imagination, before we would have voted for any man that favored that insulting resolution!

In 1847, by a *unanimous vote*, both branches of the Legislature of New Hampshire adopted resolutions denunciatory of the institution of slavery, and approving of the Wilmot Proviso. These resolutions were reported to the House, by the Representative from Hillsboro, the native town of *Gen. Pierce*, and were in the *handwriting* of Pierce!

On the 2d of October, 1847, the Democratic Soft-Shells, who are now the supporters of Pierce's administration, and fill the offices he has to dispose of in New York, held a State Convention, and declared their *"uncompromising hostility to slavery"* in a string of resolutions they adopted and ordered to be published.

On the 16th of February, 1848, a Democratic State Convention for New York convened at Utica, to appoint Delegates to the National Convention to nominate candidates for President and Vice President, at which a string of anti-Southern resolutions were adopted, denouncing *"slavery or involuntary servitude,"* as repugnant to the genius of Republicanism.

On the 18th of July, 1848, the Democratic Soft-Shells held a mass-meeting in the park of New York, and, by way of making perfect their organization against General Cass, declared, by resolutions, their *"uncompromising hostility to slavery or involuntary servitude!"*

On the 13th of September, 1848, a Democratic mass-meeting convened at Buffalo, in New York, and, in a general Abolition jubilee, adopted resolutions condemning and denouncing the institution of slavery!

In 1852, while the contest was going on between Pierce and Scott, the *Washington Union* said, editorially:

> "THE FREE-SOIL DEMOCRATIC LEADERS OF THE NORTH, ARE A REGULAR PORTION OF THE DEMOCRATIC PARTY; AND GENERAL PIERCE, IF ELECTED, WILL MAKE NO DISTINCTION BETWEEN THEM AND THE REST OF THE DEMOCRACY IN THE DISTRIBUTION OF OFFICIAL PATRONAGE, AND IN THE SELECTION OF AGENTS FOR ADMINISTERING THE GOVERNMENT!"

The Black Republicans recently held a meeting in New York, at which *Benjamin F. Butler*, of "pious memory," and Van Buren Swartwout notoriety, presided! On his right hand sat, as Vice President of the meeting, *Moses H. Grinnell*, one of the Democratic "pipe-layers" of 1840, whom this Van Buren Attorney-General Butler made efforts to send to the State prison! Another Vice President, gravely looking on, and arranged in dignified grandeur upon the stand, was John W. Edmonds, ex-"blanket contractor" in a large swindle, and a practical spiritual-rapper! A third and last Vice President was the notorious *Dr. Townsend*, the sarsaparilla man, who has not yet wound up his controversy with a man of the same name, as to who is the greatest rascal in the way of manufacturing this medicine!

Among the other officers, secretaries, and prominent men in the meeting, was *C. A. Dana*, of the Tribune office, a *Fourierist*, who, at a public meeting on a former occasion, toasted "Horace Greeley, Charles Fourier, and Jesus Christ!" Prominent in the meeting was *C. A. Stetson*, of the Astor House, an *Amalgamationist*. Henry J. Raymond, the Abolition editor of the Times, and *Rudolph Garrigue*, a noisy German Abolitionist, looked and acted as though they believed the salvation of the Union depended upon the success of the Republicans! A fellow who made frequent motions, an Irishman by the name of *McMorrow*, had served an apprenticeship of twelve months in the State prison, for breaking open a store after night! The principal speaker, who spoke for two hours on the subject of slavery, was the notorious *Bingham*, an itinerant Abolitionist from Ohio. It was a queer medley of men, parties, principles, and characters—two-thirds of all the active partisans in the meeting having held offices in the ranks of Democracy! And still, that party boasts of its Northern wing being sound upon the slavery question.

And here is the resolution of the 8th of January *Democratic* Convention in Ohio, appointing delegates to the Cincinnati Pow-wow:

> "*Resolved*, That the people of Ohio now, as they have always done, look upon slavery as an evil, and unfavorable to the development of the spirit and practical benefits of free institutions; and that, entertaining these sentiments, they will at all times feel it to be their duty to use all power clearly given by the terms of the national compact, to prevent its increase, to mitigate, *and finally eradicate the evil*."

To show, just here, where Tennessee Democrats stand upon the infamous Wilmot Proviso question, we give the following extract from a recent number of the *Nashville Patriot*:

JAMES K. POLK,

who, in 1847, approved the Oregon bill, which contained this odious and unconstitutional clause: next in order is

CAVE JOHNSON,

now President of the Bank of Tennessee, who voted for the same bill which Mr. Polk sanctioned: next we have

AARON V. BROWN,

an aspirant before the Cincinnati Convention, who did likewise: then comes

JULIUS W. BLACKWELL,

a star whose light has been quenched in obscurity, but who voted with his colleagues for the Oregon bill in '47: next in the procession of Southern men "dangerous to the South" is

BARCLAY MARTIN,

President Pierce's U. S. Mail Agent, who cast a similar vote: following him we have

LUCIEN B. CHASE,

author of the History of the Polk Administration, at present a resident of New York city, but at the time he exhibited himself as "a dangerous man to the South," a representative in Congress from this State: he is succeeded by

FRED. P. STANTON,

for ten years a Democratic Congressman from the Memphis district: he voted for the Oregon bill, with the Wilmot Proviso annexed: behind him in the march is

ALVAN CULLOM,

a Democratic Congressman, who has squatted on the *other* side of one of his native mountains in the fourth district, and been quiescent for some years: he was one of the Tennessee "dangerous men:" he voted twice for the Wilmot Proviso: in the same category is

GEORGE W. JONES,

in the language of another, the "goose which cackles at the door of the Treasury vault:" notorious as a Southern supporter of the Squatter Sovereignty doctrine, with two votes on record in favor of the Wilmot Proviso. He may be reckoned as *very* "dangerous to the South:" last, but not least in this dread array of "dangerous men," is

ANDREW JOHNSON,

the present Governor of Tennessee, and Cincinnati aspirant: he voted *three* times for the Wilmot Proviso, and so doubtful are his doctrines on the slavery question, that many slaveholding members of his own party regard him as *extremely* "dangerous to the South."

By the way, in 1842, this same *Gov. Johnson* was a Senator in our State Legislature, and introduced the following *Abolition* resolutions, commonly called his *White Basis System*:

"*Resolved, by the General Assembly of the State of Tennessee*, That the basis to be observed in laying the State off into Congressional districts shall be the voting population, WITHOUT ANY REGARD TO THREE-FIFTHS OF THE NEGRO POPULATION.

"*Resolved*, That the 120,083 qualified voters shall be divided by eleven, and that each eleventh of the 120,083 of qualified voters shall be entitled to elect one member in the Congress of the United States, or so near as may be practicable without a division of counties."

The position of Gov. Johnson is this: he wishes the State entitled to her slave representation *as a State*, but *in her own borders* the representative districts are to be made according to her white population! In other words, he desires the State to retain her *ten* Congressmen, representing both her white and slave population, but wishes them appointed throughout the State without regard to the slave population: so that the county containing ten thousand white inhabitants, and double that number of slaves, should be entitled to no more representation than the county containing *ten* thousand white inhabitants and no slaves!

We heard Johnson last summer, in his debate with Gentry, in Campbell county, contend that the county of Campbell should have the same representation in Congress as the county of Shelby, which he stated had FIFTEEN THOUSAND NEGROES! He appealed to the prejudices and passions of the poor—inquired of the hard working-men of that county how they liked to see their wives and daughters *offset*, in enumerating the strength of the county, by the "*greasy negro wenches of Shelby, Davidson, Fayette, Sumner and Rutherford counties*." He made a real, stirring abolition appeal to the poor, and non-slaveholding portion of the crowd, which was in the proportion of *ten to one* of that county, to array them against the rich, and especially against the owners of large numbers of slaves. He told them that these Negro wenches belonged to the lordly slaveholders of Middle and West Tennessee, and that as our Constitution now is, these wenches were placed on an *equality* with the fair daughters and virtuous wives of laboring men. On this ground he advocated his infamous amendment to the Constitution, which would incorporate his "White Basis" scheme!

This is a rank Abolition measure, and fraught with more danger to the South than any thing proposed by the whole brood of Abolitionists, Free Soilers, and Black Republicans at the North. Already the South is weak enough, and not at all able to vote with the North in our National Legislature. The effect of this scheme is to deprive the South of one-third of her strength in Congress. Not only is this the effect, but it is the design of the mover. We hold that Johnson is a Free Soiler, and has been for years. It is stated by his Northern Democratic friends, that when he quit Congress, he came home to run for Governor—with a determination, if defeated, to remove to some of the Northwestern States, and take a new start! Had he been defeated by Maj. Henry in 1853, he would now be a Black Republican in one of the Free States, running for office! And yet the propagator of this infamous Abolition doctrine of a "White Basis" representation—this demagogue who arrays the poor against slaveholders, is the man for the ultra guardians of the slave interests of the South! A man who would not own negroes when he could, but loaned his money out at interest, and left his wife and daughters to do their own work—a man who is at heart and in his doctrines a rank Free Soiler—a man who has only remained in the South to *experiment* upon office-seeking! This is the man that Georgia, Alabama, Virginia, Mississippi, and Carolinas, rejoiced to see elected Governor of a Southern slave State!

It was seeing the position of Johnson on this question that induced the *"Democratic Herald"* in Ohio, in June, 1855, thus to notice our race for Governor:

> "TENNESSEE.—An animated contest is going on in this good old Democratic State for Governor, and the largest crowds flock to hear the candidates that ever attended political meetings since the Hero of New Orleans used to address the masses in person. The present incumbent, Andrew Johnson, is the Democratic candidate, and a *Mr. Gentry*, a *pro-slavery* renegade from the Federal Whig ranks, is the opposing candidate, brought out by a Know Nothing conclave. This man is on the stump abusing the Catholics, and denouncing them for their tyranny, while he openly advocates the *slavery doctrines of Southern Niggerdom!* On the other hand, his competitor, Gov. Johnson, well and favorably known to our leading Democrats of Ohio, HAS NO SYMPATHIES WITH SLAVERY, and is the advocate of such amendments to the Federal Constitution as will give all power to the people, and EFFECTUALLY PUT DOWN THE INSTITUTION OF SLAVERY!"

Now, this showing up of Democracy, on the Slavery question, may look *shabby* to many ultra Southern men, and it may induce them to charge that the Democratic party are *inconsistent*. We defend them against the charge of *inconsistency*, and maintain that what would be called *inconsistency* here, is nothing but *Democracy*. For instance, A. O. P. Q. X. Y. Z. Nicholson, the editor of the great official organ of Democracy at Washington, said, editorially, and "by authority," so late as 1855:

> "IT IS NO PART OF THE CREED OF A DEMOCRAT, AS SUCH, TO ADVOCATE OR OPPOSE THE EXTENSION OF SLAVERY. HE MAY DO THE ONE OR THE OTHER, IN THE EXERCISE OF HIS RIGHTS AS A CITIZEN, AND NOT OFFEND AGAINST HIS DEMOCRATIC FEALTY!"

Precisely so! A man may advocate the *abolition* of slavery where it exists; he may, as a Black Republican, arm himself with Sharpe's rifle, and go into Kansas, and shoot down pro-slavery men, and still be a consistent Democrat, if he vote for the party, and stand by the nominees of the party conventions! Hence, all the factions at home and from abroad—all religions—all the ends and odds of God's creation are now associated together, and are battling in the same unholy cause, in the name of *Democracy*!

And further to exhibit the inconsistency of this Democratic and Foreign party, it will be recollected that, in 1844, they nominated SILAS WRIGHT, of New York, for Vice-President, to run on the ticket with COL. POLK—a position he declined, because he would not agree to be *second best* on the ticket. In a letter to JAMES H. TITUS, ESQ., bearing date April 15, 1847, MR. WRIGHT says:

> "If the question had been propounded to me at any period of my public life, Shall the arms of the Union be employed to conquer, or the money of the Union be used to purchase Territory now constitutionally free, for the purpose of planting Slavery upon it, I should have answered, No! And this answer to this question is the Wilmot Proviso, as I understand it. *I am surprised that any one should suppose me capable of entertaining any other opinion, or giving any other answer as to such a proposition.*"

Now, if SILAS WRIGHT, one of the great "Northern lights" of Democracy, held these sentiments in 1847, what must they have been in 1844, when that party sought to elevate him to the second office within the gift of the nation? But we are just reminded of what is said in "the law and the prophets," that is to say, "*It is no part of the creed of a Democrat, AS SUCH, to advocate or oppose the extension of slavery!*" What a party!

TO REV. A. B. LONGSTREET,

PROFESSOR OF METHODISM, ROMANISM, AND LOCOFOCOISM.

From the Knoxville Whig for Sept. 22, 1855.

Reverend Sir:—I see a *pastoral address* of yours, to "Methodist Know-Nothing Preachers," going the rounds of the Locofoco Foreign Sag Nicht papers of the South, occupying from four to six columns, according to the dimensions of the papers copying. I have waded through your learned address, and find it to be one of more ponderous magnitude than the Report made to the British House of Commons, by Lord North, on a subject of far greater interest! And as I am one of the class of men you address, notwithstanding your great advantage over me in point of age and experience; and as no one has made a *formal* response to your *pious warnings*, it will not be deemed insolent in me to take you up.

My first acquaintance with you was in 1847, at an Annual Meeting of the Georgia Conference, held in Madison; and although the impressions made upon my mind by you, on that occasion, were any thing but favorable to you, as a man, still, I am capable, as I believe, of doing you justice. I supposed you then to be the rise of sixty years, certainly in your *dotage* and among the *vainest* old gentlemen I had ever met with. You obtained leave, as I understand, by your own seeking, to deliver a lecture to the Conference, upon the subject of *correctly reading and pronouncing the Scriptures*. I was in attendance, and listened to you with all the attention and impartiality I was capable of exercising. I thought it a little *presumptuous* for any one man to assume to teach more than one hundred able ministers how to read and pronounce the inspired writings; and the more so, when I knew that several of the number were presidents and professors in different male and female colleges, and that many others of them were graduates of the best literary institutions in the South. Still, my apology for you was, that you was a vain old gentleman, and that to listen to you, respectfully, was to obey the Divine teaching of one who has taught us to "bear the infirmities of the weak." Your *samples*, both of reading and pronunciation, were amusing and novel to me. And so far as I could gather the prevailing sentiment, it was, that to adopt your style would render the reading of the Scriptures perfectly ridiculous.

In your address to "Methodist Know-Nothing Preachers," I discover that you are still the man you were at Madison, in 1847: you have a great deal to say about *yourself,* and make free use of the personal pronoun I! *I* advise—*I* believe—*I* am satisfied—*I* will not agree—*I* warn and caution—*I* fear, or *I* apprehend, etc. To parse the different sentences in your partisan harangue syntactically, little else is necessary but to understand the *first person singular*, and to repeat the rule as often as it occurs: a peculiarity which characterizes every paragraph in your labored address. Beside, the frequent use of the pronouns *I, me, my, mine,* etc., too frequently occur to be worth estimating. And it will be seen, upon examination, that not merely the verbiage, but the sentiment, is thus egotistic throughout, exhibiting a degree of arrogance and self-importance, only to be met with in a *Clerical Locofoco,* used by bad men for ignoble purposes. To carry out the idea of your *vanity*, you say in the winding up of your address:

> "And now, brethren, have *I* or Mr. Wesley hit upon one good reason why you should not have joined the Know-Nothings? If either of *us* have, then *I* beseech you to come from among them. If *we* have not, there is yet another in reserve which, if it does not prevail will show — or prove to my satisfaction at least—that if *an angel from heaven* were to denounce your order, you would cleave to it still."

Any other man but yourself would, from considerations of *modesty*, have given JOHN WESLEY the preference, in this connection, and come in as *second best.* But no, you are *first in place,* and, in your own estimation, in *importance* likewise, as a religious teacher.

I have no doubt you consider yourself a much greater man than John Wesley ever was; and in proof of this, I need only cite what you have said in reference to Mr. Wesley's opposition to Romanism:

> "Even good old John Wesley caught the spirit of the times, and wrote that letter, from which it appears he thought if the Catholics got into power, they would abuse Protestants. What abuse they could have heaped on them, greater than they heaped on Catholics, short of cutting their throats, I cannot conceive."

The only superior you acknowledge is CARDINAL WISEMAN, a bigoted Roman Catholic, and you seem to knock under to him quite reluctantly, and not without informing the public that you have been a laborious student for forty years, and *"a profound thinker."* Here is your praise:

> "I have been a pretty severe student for near forty years, and a laborious, if not *profound thinker* for a long time; but when I compare myself in intellectual stature with that man, I shrink in my own estimation to the insignificance of a mite."

So much by way of noticing vanity. You are a literary and theological star of the first magnitude! You are an encyclopedia of the learning, science, patriotism, and religion of the country! Sir, if you possessed a little more *sheep-faced modesty,* and could exhibit a little less of *lion-headed impudence* than you do, you would be a much more useful, not to say successful minister of the New Testament!

Sir, you have taken the field in opposition to Know-Nothingism, *professedly* through your deep and abiding concern for Christianity, and the interests of Methodism. You say:

> "You cannot surely be so weak as to suppose you can crush Romanism by Know-Nothing agencies; but you have almost ruined Methodism by them already.
>
> "Now the ruler of this nation is spoken evil of by your party continually, and therefore, in the judgment of Wesley, I might stand up in the pulpit and defend him."

The truth is, you are influenced alone by partisan political feelings; and occupying a position in a Mississippi College, in the midst of Fire-eating Disunion Progressive Democracy, you desire to please them, rather than serve the interests of your country or Church. To take the stump, or the pulpit, in defence of *Frank Pierce* and his corrupt administration, would be a pleasant talk to you, who have been, all your life-time, an inveterate Locofoco in politics, and "a profound thinker" in favor of its iniquitous measures and principles. In your early political training, you have been swayed by interest and popular favor, and in most cases at the expense of truth, just as you now are, in your mad vindication of Romanism. A tool for others to work with, till you have found yourself in a condition to use such tools as you yourself have been, you are now a trimmer and weathercock, leading on men of less sense than yourself, to such distinction as interest and ambition may dictate!

Sir, you take the ground, throughout, that there is no danger of Catholics in this country, and that they do not seek to establish their religion. Here is a specimen of your logic:

> "Thank God no religious sect can tyrannize over another in this country, so long as they all respect the Federal Constitution. Until we see, then, the Catholics treating that instrument with disrespect, it is madness to entertain fears of them and worse than madness to form combinations against them."

Now, sir, the foregoing statement is untrue, and in making it you could not have been sincere. You are a man of too much sense, and of too much information, to believe what you are wickedly trying to palm upon others. Brownson's Quarterly Review, the most able, as well as the most authentic organ of Catholicism in the United States, employs the following language to the American people—mark it:

> "*Are your free institutions infallible?* Are they founded on *Divine right*? This you deny. Is not the proper question for you to discuss, then, *not* whether the Papacy be or be not compatible with republican government, but whether *it be or be not founded in Divine right*? If the Papacy be founded in Divine right, it is supreme over whatever is founded only in human right, and then your institutions should be made to harmonize with it: not it with your institutions!!! The real question, then, is not the compatibility or the incompatibility of the Catholic Church with *democratic institutions*, but, Is the *Catholic Church the Church of God*?
>
> "Settle this question first. But in point of fact, *democracy is a mis-*

chievous dream, wherever the Catholic Church does not predominate, to inspire the people with reverence, and to teach and accustom them to obedience to authority."

Here is still plainer language from the Roman Catholic Bishop of St. Louis:

"Heresy and unbelief are crimes; and in Christian countries, as in Italy and Spain, for instance, where all the people are Catholics, and where the Catholic religion is an essential part of the law of the land, they are punished as other crimes."

Here is what the *Boston Pilot* says, a Catholic paper of high standing:

"*No good government can exist* without religion, and there can be no religion without an *inquisition*, which is wisely designed for the promotion and protection of the *true faith*."

Here is the *Shepherd of the Valley*, published under the eye and with the approbation of the Bishop of St. Louis:

"The Church is, of necessity, intolerant. Heresy she endures when and where she *must*; but she hates it, and directs all her energies to its destruction. If Catholics ever gain an immense numerical majority, religious freedom in this country is *at an end*: so say our enemies —*so say we*."

And here is what the *Rambler* says, a devoted Catholic periodical, high in the confidence of the Bishops and Priests of that Church:

"You ask if he (the Pope) were lord in the land, and you were in the minority, if not in numbers, yet in power, what would he do to you? That, we say, would entirely depend on circumstances. If it would benefit the cause of Catholicism, he would tolerate you —if expedient, he would imprison you, banish you, fine you, probably he might even hang you; but, be assured of one thing, he would never tolerate you for the sake of the 'glorious principles' of civil and religious liberty."

I could give other quotations of this character, which have met your eye long since, but I forbear, as they would extend my letter beyond the limit I have prescribed for myself. These are the publications which, in part at least, have given rise to the Know-Nothing organization, so cordially hated by you.

You say there is no danger of injury to our institutions from the rapid strides of Romanism. Allow me to ask your attention to the following remarkable political prediction by the Duke of Richmond, late Governor-General of Canada, and a British noble, who declared himself hostile to the United States on all occasions. Speaking of our Government, this deadly enemy said:

"It will be destroyed; it ought not, it will not be permitted to exist." "The curse of the French revolution, and subsequent wars and commotions in Europe, are to be attributed to its example; and so long as it exists, no prince will be safe upon his throne; and the *sovereigns of Europe are aware of it*; and they have *determined upon its destruction, and have come to an understanding upon this subject, and have decided on the means to accomplish it;* and they will eventually succeed by SUBVER-SION *rather than conquest.*" "All the low and surplus population of the different nations of Europe will be carried into that country. It is and will be a receptacle for the bad and disaffected population of Europe, when they are not wanted for soldiers, or to supply the navies; *and the governments of Europe will favor such a course.* This will create a surplus and majority of low population, who are so very easily excited; and they will *bring with them their principles;* and in nine cases out of ten adhere to their ancient and former governments, laws, manners, customs, and religion; and will transmit them to their posterity; and in many cases propagate them among the natives. These men will become citizens, and, by the constitution and laws, will be invested with the right of suffrage." "Hence, *discord, dissension, anarchy and civil war will ensue;* and some popular individual will assume the government, and restore order, and the sovereigns of Europe, the emigrants, and many of the natives will sustain him." "The Church of Rome has a design upon that country; and it will in time be the established religion, and will aid in the destruction of that Republic." "I have *conversed with many of the sovereigns and princes of Europe, and they have unanimously expressed these opinions relative to the government of the United States, and their determination to subvert it.*"

But, sir, after eulogizing Catholics for their devotion to religious toleration in this country, you make two assertions, touching the Methodist Church, for which I wish to arraign you, and for which the authorities of said Church ought to arraign you, under that section of our Discipline which forbids *railing out against our Doctrines and Discipline.* You say:

"And if I were to take the stump against you, I would say to the honest yeomanry of the country. 'Good people, if you think your liberties will be *any safer in the hands of Methodists than Catholics, you are vastly mistaken.*'

"I would add, in humiliation but in candor, 'You have ten thousand times more to fear, just at this time, from Methodists, than Catholics; simply because the first are more numerous than the last, because the first are actually in the field for office, while the last are not.'"

If you have this opinion of the Methodist Church, you cannot be an honest man and remain within her jurisdiction. You ought to leave her communion forthwith, and go over to Rome; and in doing this, you would *not have far to go!* Occupying the position you do, and holding the sentiments you do, I would not send a child to any school or college over which you might preside. Nor do I think any Protestant parent or guardian ought to patronize any school under your care. Your influence, whatever you may possess, is against the Protestant faith, and in favor of Catholicism. In a word, you are a dangerous man in a Republican government.

Upon the subject of religious toleration by the Catholics, you seem to have fallen into the same error adopted by the Hon. Mr. Stephens, of Georgia—a man for whom you have great regard now, but who, in the days of *Clay Whiggery*, was a stench in your Locofoco nostrils! Mr. Stephens made the assertion, in a public speech in Augusta, that "the Catholic Colony of Maryland, under Lord Baltimore, was the first to *establish* the principle of free toleration in religious worship." The Colony of Maryland was a Catholic Colony, and the "Toleration Act" was written by Lord Baltimore himself. That Act is dated 21st April, 1649, when Lord Baltimore was in the zenith of his glory. Here is the language of that "Act" of religious toleration:

> "Denying the Holy *Trinity* is to be punished with *death*, and confiscation of land and goods to the Lord Proprietary, (Lord Baltimore himself!). Persons using any reproachful words concerning the Blessed Virgin Mary, or the Holy Apostles or Evangelists, to be fined £5, or in default of payment to be publicly whipped and *imprisoned, at the pleasure* of his Lordship, (Lord Baltimore himself!) or of his Lieutenant-General." *See Laws of Maryland, at large, by T. Bacon*, A. D. 1765. 16 and 17 *Cecilius's Lord Baltimore.*

God deliver us from such toleration! *Death* was the penalty for expressing certain religious opinions, not acceptable to Lord Baltimore and the Holy Catholic Church! Fines and *whipping at the post* was the penalty for speaking against the image-worship of the Catholic Church. But I need not pursue this subject further: the *onus propandi* is on your side.

Speaking of Mr. Wesley, you say:

> "If Wesley were alive, what would he think of your midnight plots, and open tirades against Papists? But a letter of his has been going the rounds of the newspapers, which the Know Nothings obviously think gives the sanction of that good man to their movement. Not so. Mr. Wesley was not the man to write as inconsistently as their version of this letter makes him write."

Why, sir, Mr. Wesley goes much further in his political opposition to Roman Catholics than the American party have ever proposed to go. The American party say only that they will not vote for Catholics, or put them in office, because their principles are antagonistic to the spirit of Republican institutions. Mr. Wesley lays down the comprehensive, but *true doctrine*, in this very letter, that *"no government not Roman Catholic ought to tolerate men of the Roman Catholic persuasion."* And to show how fully and clearly he sustains this position, I quote from his letter at length. You will find the letter in Vol. 5, page 817, of Wesley's Miscellaneous Works, dated January 12th, 1780. It was originally addressed to the Dublin Freeman's Journal. Here is what Mr. Wesley says, in the very letter you seek to *deny out of*:

> "I consider not whether the Romish religion is true or false: build nothing on one or the other supposition. Therefore, away with all your common-place declamation about intolerance and persecution for religion! Suppose every word of Pope Pius's creed to be true! Sup-

pose the Council of Trent to have been infallible; yet I insist upon it that no government not Roman Catholic ought to tolerate men of the Roman Catholic persuasion.

"I prove this by a plain argument—let him answer it that can— that no Roman Catholic does or can give security for his allegiance or peaceable behavior. I prove it thus: It is a Roman Catholic maxim, established not by private men, but by public council, that 'No faith is to be kept with heretics.' This has been openly avowed by the Council of Constance; but it has never been openly disclaimed. Whether private persons avow or disavow it, it is a fixed maxim of the Church of Rome. But as long as it is so, nothing can be more plain than that the members of that Church can give no reasonable security to any government for their allegiance and peaceable behavior. Therefore, they ought not to be tolerated by any government, Protestant, Mohammedan, or Pagan. You say, 'Nay, but they take an oath of allegiance.' True, five hundred oaths; but the maxim, 'No faith is to be kept with heretics,' sweeps them all away as a spider's web. So that still no governors that are not Roman Catholics can have any security of their allegiance.

"Again, those who acknowledge the spiritual power of the Pope can give no security of their allegiance to any government; but all Roman Catholics acknowledge this: therefore they can give no security for their allegiance. The power of granting pardons for all sins—past, present, and to come—is, and has been for many centuries, one branch of his spiritual power. But those who acknowledge him to have this spiritual power can give no security for their allegiance, since they believe the Pope can pardon rebellion, high treason, and all other sins whatever. The power of dispensing with any promise, oath, or vow, is another branch of the spiritual power of the Pope: all who acknowledge his spiritual power must acknowledge this. But whoever acknowledges the dispensing power of the Pope, can give no security for his allegiance to any government. Oaths and promises are none: they are as light as air—a dispensation makes them null and void. Nay, not only the Pope, but even a priest has power to pardon sins! This is an essential doctrine of the Church of Rome. But they that acknowledge this, cannot possibly give any security for their allegiance to any government. Oaths are no security at all; for the priest can pardon both perjury and high treason. Setting their religion aside, it is plain that, upon principles of reason, no government ought to tolerate men who cannot give any security to that government for their allegiance and peaceful behavior. But this, no Romanist can do; not only while he holds that 'no faith is to be kept with heretics,' but so long as he acknowledges either priestly absolution, or the spiritual power of the Pope.

"If any one pleases to answer this, and set his name, I shall probably reply. But the productions of anonymous writers I do not promise to take any notice of.

"I am, sir, your humble servant,
"JOHN WESLEY.

"CITY ROAD, January 12, 1780."

But, sir, you know as well as any living man that the history of the Church, from the days of the first Pope down to the iniquitous reign of Pius IX., sustains Mr. Wesley in his views on this subject, and justifies the steps taken by the American party. Notwithstanding the oft-repeated profession of Catholic liberality and Romish toleration, so triumphantly paraded by you, and other interested aspirants and unprincipled demagogues, the Catholic Church has invariably shown herself to be destitute of both, whenever she had the opportunity of using them. Sir, *intolerance* is an element of her faith, and *persecution* a specimen of her piety; and no man knows it better than you do. In taking upon herself the obligation of "true obedience to the Pope," the Catholic Church imposes upon herself a task that proves beyond all doubt she cannot, under any circumstances, remain faithful to that obligation, and yet maintain "allegiance" to such a government as ours!

Sir, I have no patience with a Protestant minister who stands forth as the apologist of Catholicism; nor have I any confidence in one who does it, provided he is a man of *intelligence,* as I admit you to be. The only excuse I can render for your strange and inconsistent conduct is, that you are in your dotage; that you are a violent old partisan; and that you are the tool of designing demagogues, infamous disunionists, and unmitigated repudiators. I shall not be at all surprised to hear that you have apostatized from the Methodist Church, and gone over to the Roman Catholics. I learn from the Little Rock Gazette, a Democratic paper, that but the other day, Gov. E. N. Carway, of Arkansas, a member of the Methodist Church, had actually apostatized from Methodism, and the Protestant faith, and united with the Roman Catholics. And what makes his defection from the faith of his fathers still more notorious, his organ is down upon the Protestant clergy in bitter and unrelenting denunciations! I believe that *you* are preparing to go over to the Roman Catholics; and to justify your change, when the time comes, you now assert, "in humiliation but in candor," you say, that the people "have *ten thousand times more* to fear from Methodists than from Catholics." If you believe this, you ought to leave the Methodist Church *instantly,* even without the formalities of a withdrawal or expulsion—even though you should be denied admittance into the Catholic Church! I deny that we have *"ten thousand times more to fear"* from the *Devil* than we have from the Catholics; and according to your argument, *the Methodists are worse than the Devil!* This, their most bitter revilers and enemies do not believe; and for obvious reasons. The Methodist Church has no St. Bartholomew's Day, with its rivers of blood staining her garments: she never indiscriminately slaughtered the Albigenses, or Waldenses, or Huguenots: she never established an infernal Inquisition: she never lit up the fires of Smithfield: never burned the Holy Bible, and prohibited, upon pain of eternal death, the printing and circulating of God's word; and last, but not least, she has not sought to keep the people in ignorance. Wherever Methodism has been planted, the people have become great and happy. If you please, wherever *Protestantism* has prevailed, the people have been prosperous and happy. But look to Old Spain, Italy, the German Confederacies, Sardinia, Naples, Austria, Belgium, Portugal, Bavaria, Baden, South America, and Mexico, where Romanism is the established religion, and the places of her influence are a hissing and a by-word in the eyes of the civilized world! Protestantism has done more for the world in the last hundred years than the Roman Catholic Church has for the *eighteen hundred years*!

Sir, the Puritans, of New England; the Hollanders, of New York; the Quakers, Lutherans, and German Reformed, of Pennsylvania; the Baptists, of Rhode Island; the Episcopalians and Presbyterians, of Virginia; the Lutherans and followers of Wesley and Whitefield, of Georgia; the Huguenots and Episcopalians, of the Carolinas; and the Seceders in several of the States, who were the religious pioneers of these States, were all Protestants and Know Nothings; and if they were living, they would be ashamed of you and your teachings. They selected this wilderness country as their home, in order that they might enjoy those religious privileges from which they had been debarred in the old world, by the very Church and people you are seeking to vindicate.

But you will say, as you have done in substance, that this is no longer the characteristic of Romanism. Why is it not? Has she ever changed for the better? When did she renounce her doctrines and practices? Never! Rome is the same tyrannical system now, where she has the power, that she ever has been, and for ever must be. Wo to this land of ours, if ever Rome gets the ascendancy here! Her creed is the same here and now, in this respect, that it has everywhere been, and must always be. It is her boast that she is always right, and knows no change. She practices her unholy inquisitorial and Jesuitical doctrines in this country, as far as she can and dare act them out. Her whole system is adverse to our republican institutions and she hesitates not to declare it. She has publicly burned our Bible in different States in this Union, and recently, in New York and Pennsylvania. Archbishop Hughes, the Head of the Catholic Church in this country, has taken an oath, administered by the Pope of Rome, of which this is a part:

> "Heretics, schismatics, and rebels to our said Lord (the Pope) or his aforesaid successors, I will, to my utmost power, *persecute and wage war with.*"

The Church of Rome declares all who are not its members to be heretics. It is painful, in view of all these things, to see an old Protestant minister, whose head has been withered by the frosts of seventy winters, openly in the field advocating a Church whose Bishops, Priests, and members are "drunken with the blood of saints."

There is but one remaining feature of your singular address to Know Nothing Methodist Preachers to be replied to, and I am through. You assail the new party on the score of its *secrecy*, and of its *concealment* of its acts from the public. Had this objection come from any one but a Methodist Preacher, and a known advocate of *Class-meetings being held with closed doors*, I would now dispose of it without occupying as much space as I shall do in my concluding remarks!

Notwithstanding all the *secrecy* in the new Order of Know Nothings has been set aside by the act of the National Council which created it; and notwithstanding our members tell all about their Councils, where and when they meet, and our orators read out and publish to the world our obligations, rules, and principles, it is still objected that ours is a secret Order, liable to be used for bad purposes; that we travel about with dark lanterns; that our proceedings are not restrained by the wholesome check of public opinion!

Now, this, the great objection to our Order, comes from men who belong to Lodges of Free Masons and Odd Fellows, and who have taken all the *binding* oaths attached to the different *degrees* of these respective Orders! The same objection is urged against the American party, by men who belong to the Order of Sons of Temperance, who have deemed a *rigid secret organization* necessary to combat successfully a *domestic* evil! It is urged in bitterness against the Order, by demagogues and partisans, who have acted for years with the *secret political conclaves* of their respective parties, who have held their meetings with *closed doors* — kept their *places* of meeting a profound secret — and when they have adjourned, they have enjoined *secrecy* upon all present! Last, but not least, this *secret feature* is urged against the American organization by the vile apologists for the Catholic Church, and its corrupt Priesthood and membership, in this country. These demagogues know that the Roman Catholic Church is a *secret society*, directed by a talented, designing, and villainous HIERARCHY — absolutely controlled by an *anti*-Republican Priesthood, to a degree which has never been exercised by any political party in the known world! The *Confessional* is a secret tribunal, before which every member of that Church is required to make known, not only *immoral* actions, but every thought and purpose of the heart, and upon pain of incurring the anathema of the Church, which is equivalent to a sentence of eternal damnation! The corrupt order of JESUITS, the infamous society of SAN FEDESTI, and the infinitely infernal society of IRISH RIBBON MEN — these are all oath-bound societies of the Catholic Church, connected directly with the horrid operations of the "*Holy Inquisition.*"

Now, I put the question to any man of reason and common sense, if Roman Catholics and their *patriotic Democratic* admirers and advocates, in this country, are not the last men on earth who should object to the *secret* doings of the order of Know Nothings, even if their secrecy were kept up? Every Roman Catholic in the known world is under the absolute control of a secret society, by considerations not only of a *temporal*, but of an ETERNAL WEIGHT!

But I am not done with these *Democratic* opposers of SECRECY. The Convention which formed the Constitution of the United States, sat in the old State House in Philadelphia, *with closed doors, from the 25th of May to the 17th of September*, wanting only eight days of four months. That body of men had a Doorkeeper and Sergeant-at-arms, both under oath, to keep their doors barred, and all their proceedings a secret. So says Mr. Jefferson's biography! And such men as Washington, Adams, Jefferson, Madison, Franklin, Harrison, Hancock, Hopkins, and others, composed that body! During the war of the Revolution, General Washington, Generals Lee, Wayne, Marion, and others, organized a *secret American Society*, with its branches extending from North to South, having their *passwords*, *signs*, and *grips*, and writing to each other in figures, and "an unknown tongue," as the Know Nothings have been doing, and all, too, with a view to oppose Foreign intrigues and oppressions! It is as well known as any political truth, that General WASHINGTON, at the time of his death, was the *President* of the Cincinnati Society, a secret political society, in which, we see it stated on unquestionable authority, no man was eligible to membership unless he was a *native American*. The *Columbian Order*, known as the *"Tammany Society,"* was a secret political society, and highly influential, and maintains its existence to this day, and without danger to the liberties of the country. Gen. SAM HOUSTON publishes to the world that himself and Gen. JACKSON were members of this Society. What say the *anti*-Americans to all these facts? Do they believe that Gen. Washington, or Jackson, would have united with any association or order not purely American? Would either have entered into any political league, when *secrecy* was enjoined, if he had not approved of the principle of secrecy in political associations? Never! From the characters of Washington and Jackson—the sacrifices they made for their country, united with their fervid patriotism, and their known preference for every thing *American*, I do not doubt for one moment, that if they were both now living, they would unite with the veritable Order of Know Nothings!

I believe the hand of God to be in this very movement, and as much in the *secrecy* of it, in the outset, as in any other feature. I regard the movement as one growing out of a great crisis in the affairs of our country, and a precursor of a sound, healthful, and vigorous nationality, and which will ultimately prevent the liberties of this country from being destroyed, by the machinations of such demagogues and factionists as now seek to *excuse* Romanism, and fellowship Foreign Pauperism. Secret societies are only dangerous to despots and tyrants, and history shows that these above all others have made war upon them. They have denounced and proscribed Masonry in every quarter of the globe, where they have had the power. The Pope, with the aid of his Cardinals, has crushed the ancient order of Free Masons in his dominions. There is not a Masonic Lodge in Italy. In our own country, not a single Catholic is to be found associated with the order of Free Masons; and why? Masonry is founded upon the Bible, and requires the reading of the Protestant Bible in all its Lodges, and this don't suit Romanism. We state these general and historical facts, without knowing any thing of our own knowledge of Masonry.

In the young and growing city of Knoxville, it is within our own knowledge, that many of the Irish Catholics attached themselves to the Order of the Sons of Temperance, with a view, as they said, of throwing around them the wholesome restraints of the Order. On the first visit of a priest to the city, commonly called "Father Brown," these Irish Catholics began to drop off one by one, until not one of them is now in the Order, and most of those who were, are daily seen drunk in our streets. Indeed, some of them in withdrawing had the candor to acknowledge that the priest required them to do so! And why? Because, in all the Divisions of the Sons of Temperance here, we have the Protestant Scriptures read, and have Protestant prayers offered up. This don't suit the Church of Rome!

I have the honor to be, very truly and frankly,

W. G. Brownlow.

TO THE RIGHT REVEREND
AARON V. BROWN, M. S.

Sir:—I have received by mail a pamphlet copy of your "Letter to the Bishops, Elders, and *other* Ministers, Itinerant and *Local*, of the Methodist Episcopal Church South," covering twenty-eight octavo pages. I thank you for a copy of your *Pastoral* address; and I am happy to be able to *infer* from its teachings that you have made a profession of religion, before taking upon yourself "Holy Orders." I suppose the *time* of your conversion, you date back to the memorable period when you "saw sights" on Mount Pisgah, and had conferred on you the degree of *Modern Seer*, and entered upon the duties of "High Priest" of Democracy! As I am one of the parties addressed, and the customs of the Church and the country require a response to so grave a document, I have felt it incumbent upon me to perform the task. I may style this the *Last* epistle of Aaron, the Priest, and illustrious Chief of Foreign Catholic Sag Nicht Locofocoism!

My first impulses were, upon reading your address, to call for your *credentials*, and to examine into your *authority* for assuming to dictate to the entire Ministry of the Southern portion of the Methodist Church. You must either enter the Ecclesiastical ring under the *imposition of the hands* of Bishop Soule or *Andy Johnson*. If Bishop Soule ordained you for the Ministry, and set you apart as the Lieutenant-General of the Methodist Episcopal Church South, the presumption is that he examined you on doctrinal points, and upon all questions affecting the government of the Church, as was his duty, and is our custom, and that he found you orthodox! It follows, as a matter of course, that you renounced your heresy you advocated in the Hartford Convention, held at Nashville, and that you obtained forgiveness for that and numerous other "sins of omission and commission"—aye, for the whole catalogue of your inward and outward iniquities, which so *eminently* disqualified you for the work of the Ministry! But if *Andy Johnson* ordained you for the work, of which there is no sort of doubt, the Church South, through me, protests against your authority, and utterly refuses to submit to your teachings. Our Church does not agree with Johnson on the "White Basis" issue, or the great question of slavery; and in proof of this, I cite to the fact of her separation from the North, in 1844, upon this very question. She has within her bounds of communion, rich men and poor, educated and uneducated, and is unwilling to unite with him in arraying the poor against the rich, or the unlearned against the learned. Nor does our Church believe that Jesus Christ was a Locofoco, as Johnson asserts in his Inaugural, and held that Christianity and Democracy, in converging lines, led to the foot of Jacob's Ladder, and thence to heaven, *via* Mount Pisgah, from whose lofty summit you first beheld the promised land!

It therefore follows, that, in presenting yourself as a spiritual leader in the Church, called to the work, as you have been, by *Andy Johnson*, your case is fully met by a quotation from Job:

"Now there was a day when the sons of God came to present themselves before the Lord, and *Satan* came also among them."

A second passage, from the Book of Jeremiah, meets your case, and leaves no doubt that the inspired Prophet had you in his eye:

"We have heard the pride of Moab, (he is exceedingly proud,) his loftiness, and his *arrogance*, and his pride, and his haughtiness of heart.

"I know his wrath, saith the Lord; but it shall not be so; his *lies* shall not so effect it."

To be candid with you, Gov. Brown, I regard your address, under all the circumstances, as a display of the most brazen-faced assurance and the most unmitigated impudence I ever met with in my life! I have known for years that you were capable of great presumption, but in this insolent and dictatorial address you surpass *yourself*—you positively out-Herod Herod! In the whole history of the country, and of parties, I venture the assertion, that a parallel piece of impudence, and downright bold-faced assurance, cannot be pointed to, as the act of any partisan. It is really past all belief, if I had not your production before me. But more of this hereafter.

Copies of your pamphlet were distributed through the aisles and seats of the Annual Conference room in Nashville, and have been sent all over the South, to members of other Conferences. Your *proof-sheet* was seen ten days before the meeting of the Middle Tennessee Conference, and your "work of faith and labor of love" was ready for distribution when the Conference first convened, but you held it back till the Conference was ready to adjourn, and to a period so late, that a reply, if one had been deemed necessary, could not be made. This was *cowardly*, and in keeping with your political tactics and code of morals. In saying that this was in keeping with your code of morals, I allude to the *Woodberry affair*.

I shall now take up your address, Governor, and wade through its twenty-eight pages of double-distilled Sag Nichtism, sublimated impudence, and concealed advocacy of *Romanism*, mixed up with contradictions, false assertions, and glaring absurdities, as it is, from beginning to end. In the opening paragraph, you predicate your right to instruct the "Bishops, Elders, and other Ministers" of the entire Church, South, upon the real or assumed fact, that you are "The son of a now sainted father, who for forty years ministered at your altars, the co-laborer of that noble band of Christian ministers, who, under Asbury and Coke, founded your Church in America!"

Alas, that any "sainted Father" should be represented by so degenerate a son—an irreligious son—not a member of any Church—but having the hardihood, in the face of those who know the facts, to disguise himself in the priestly robes of a "sainted Father"—like an ass in a lion's skin, to *bray out* against better men than himself, or, like a wolf in sheep's clothing, to *steal into the fold*, where that Father was accustomed to minister in holy things, and with soft and honeyed words, and hypocritical teachings, and Satan-like misrepresentations, seek whom he may devour! You tell the "Bishops, Elders, and other Ministers," that you really "approve" their "creed," and, what is still more soul-cheering, you have "witnessed their growth and progress for years, with the highest satisfaction." This is very *condescending* in the "son of a now sainted father!" It is quite flattering! But these "Bishops, Elders, and other Ministers," would receive all this with a greater degree of allowance, if they did not believe that your generous patronage, so lavishly bestowed upon them and their "creed," was prompted by a principle of which *selfishness* is the soul! They believe, and so express themselves in conversation, that your forced smile of approbation, your reluctant eulogy, have both been wrung from you, because you are a sycophantic partisan suitor for patronage, in the way of votes for your party. These Clergymen whom you address, think it a great pity that the "son of a now sainted father" should exhibit so much "satisfaction" at witnessing their prosperity, in *theory*, and manifest not one particle in *practice*. They think that you would be in your proper place, to be found among the *mourners*, instead of the *teachers* in their Church; and that it is high time, considering your age in life, and the extent of your iniquities, that you should be found upon your knees, in an altar full of fresh straw, at an old-fashioned Camp-Meeting, asking the pious to pray for you, and God, for the sake of the forty years labors of "a now sainted father," to have mercy upon you, and save your sinful old soul from that death that never dies.

Why, Sir, the Devil himself would blush to perpetrate such an act of arrogance as you have done, in thus volunteering your advice to the "Bishops, Elders, and other Ministers," of the Methodist Church. An old political party hack, who is not now, and never was, a member of any Church—an intriguing old sinner, who never even attends Church, and who, in this respect, shows that he neither fears God, respects the Christian Sabbath, nor "approves the creed" of any orthodox denomination, to be lecturing a numerous body of Clergymen, as to what they ought or ought not to do, it is the culmination of all that is called effrontery! The "Bishops, Elders, and other Ministers" of the Methodist Church, wish the *evidence* of your conversion to God, before they consent to obey you, as "having the rule over them." Your approval of their "creed," and the "satisfaction" with which you have witnessed their progress, is not sufficient to satisfy their doubting minds, as long as you continue to ride into Nashville on Sabbath, and retail political slang at the INN, or read Sag Nicht papers at the *Union Office*, to the neglect of the house of God, and the evil example set before young men, against the statute in such cases made and provided! We must, as Ministers, hear you relate your experience, in a regular class-meeting. Nay, more, knowing your *raising*, and your ability to "deceive, even the very elect," we must see you down upon your marrow-bones, surrounded by noisy and zealous officials, pounding you on the back, and exclaiming, as in the days of your "sainted father," *Pray on, Aaron*! We must hear you *groan*—we must see your sinful old bosom *heave*—we must witness the falling of *big tears*, as you publicly confess and manfully repent of your misdeeds—of the whole catalogue, of all the inward and outward iniquities of your past life—your sins of omission and commission, which God knows are more numerous than the hairs upon your old sinful head! I say we must see all this, and even more, before we can have faith in your teachings, as big as even a grain of mustard seed!

But you are the "son of a now sainted father"—you derive great "satisfaction" from the "growth and progress" of Methodism—you "approve" the Methodist "creed"—and hence, a glorious future awaits the Methodist Church: *provided* always, that her "Bishops, Elders, and other Ministers" hearken to and obey your teachings, a thing they are very certain not to do, in the matter under consideration. It is a melancholy fact, that many of the sons of Methodist, and other Ministers, are very wicked and unpromising men; and it is equally true, and certainly notorious, that where they turn out to be sinners, they are sinners above all offenders, dwelling either at Jerusalem or elsewhere! I have no hesitancy in pronouncing you as *hard a case*, in a moral point of view, as ever came before the Church, and the only appropriate reply her ecclesiastical dignitaries can make to your address, is to appoint a day of fasting and prayer to God, for your conversion, to be observed throughout her borders. I now, as the appointed organ of the Church, set apart the first day of January, 1856, and I pray you, as one desiring the salvation of your soul, to be in the spirit and in a proper frame of mind on that day! Humble yourself before God—tell him that you were in error in stealing the livery of Heaven to serve the Devil in! Tell him that you are an old worn-out political hack—that you have grown gray in the service of sin—that during the whole of a somewhat eventful life, your labors have been in the dirtiest pools of party politics—that you have been insincere and unscrupulous in all your teachings and acts—that you stand before the people of Tennessee publicly branded by *eight* respectable and reliable citizens of Wilson county, as a *falsifier* in the Know Nothing controversy of the past summer—and that you are sorry for having come forth steeped to the nose and chin in political profligacy, to lecture grave Clergymen upon subjects you ought to set at their feet and learn lessons about! Tell your God, what he doubtless knows, that though the "son of a now sainted father," you are as full of devils as ever Mary Magdalene was—that like the "Imps of Sin," in Milton, these "yelp all around" you—that this is no reflection upon a "now sainted father," whose seeming neglect of your early training grew out of his continual absence from home, as is the case with most Methodist Preachers,—aye, tell your God, that once out of this scrape, you will never be caught in another of the kind! You say,

> "From the foundation of our government, it has been a conceded and settled doctrine, that the various religious denominations should not, as such, intermeddle with the political contests of the day. No instance is now remembered where they have done so!"

This is a remarkable sentence, and partakes of the nature of your Wilson county assertions! The history of the Church, and of the world, contradicts every word of the foregoing, and demonstrates that the "settled doctrine" of the Catholic Church, has ever been, as it still is, to "intermeddle with the political contests of the day." I will trouble you with two instances in which "religious denominations, as such," have been guilty of what you deny. The Albany (N. Y.) State Register, a paper which usually does not say what it cannot maintain, states that ARCHBISHOP

HUGHES has issued a mandate, *commanding* all Catholics in the Albany District, in the exciting State election now coming off, to cast their votes for Mr. Crosby for the Senate. But Roman Catholics, you falsely tell us, never "intermeddle with the political contests of the day:" O no!

The other "instance now remembered," is the one in which you were a candidate for a seat in the Legislature of Tennessee, in the county of Giles: this was, according to my recollection, in 1831, or a quarter of a century ago. At that time, there was a small Manual Labor School in Giles, which had been incorporated by the Legislature, and at the head of which was a *Presbyterian*. The gentleman who ran against you, if not a member of the Presbyterian Church, "approved" their "creed," and "witnessed their growth and progress for years with the highest satisfaction." *You* charged upon the stump that the Presbyterians were seeking to establish their religion by law, to unite Church and State—appealed to the Methodist and Baptist to put them down by electing you, with a promise that you would check their march by counter-legislation—and you were elected upon this issue. At the same time, as the oldest inhabitants of Giles know, there were not fifty Presbyterians in the county! But "no instance is remembered" in which one sect has intermeddled with another—O no! You say:

> "In the mutations of parties in this country, a new one has lately arisen, to which, I apprehend, more of the Methodist ministers have attached themselves, at least in the State of Tennessee, than might have been expected. This party, known as the Know Nothings, is so *peculiar* in its organization, that it seems strange to me that any minister or professor of religion should be willing longer to continue in it."

Your apprehensions are well-founded, when you suppose that a very large proportion of the Methodist ministers in Tennessee are either members of this new party or sympathize with it. And, sir, more of the ministers of other denominations than you seem to be aware of, have either attached themselves to this party, "in the mutations of parties," or act with it, and endorse its aims and objects, than you have yet dreamed of! And "it seems strange" to these ministers, and thousands of the purest and best laymen in the Protestant ranks, "that any minister or professor of religion should be willing longer" to oppose the principles of this party, or array themselves under the black flag of Papal Rome, and of the pauper emigrants with whom she is flooding our land! But, sir, the object of your Address is, to persuade if you can, and if not, *to drive*, by motives of fear, the Clergy of the Methodist Church from their position on this great American and Protestant question. Alas, how little does the "son of a sainted father" understand the material he attempts to work upon! Methodist ministers are free men, the equals of other moral and upright men in heroic virtues, and far in advance of that of politicians in Tennessee who believe parties in religion, as in politics, are only "held together by the cohesive power of public plunder," and who assume to direct public opinion from a principle, of which *selfishness* is the Alpha and Omega, the beginning and the end! Sir, the violence, bitterness, and the very inflammatory tone, not to say language, of your Gallatin, Lebanon, and Columbia speeches, are enough, it seems to me, to *nauseate* every good and conservative citizen, and to disgust every "Bishop, Elder, and other Ministers, Itinerant and Local, of the Methodist Episcopal Church, South." Even in this Address, you insult these ministers on every page. I see not how any preacher, with a true Protestant and American heart in him, can read this address of yours through, without rising up from his seat and saying: "I have voted with this Anti-Protestant and Anti-American party for the last time."

In warning Methodist ministers to withdraw their sanction and approbation of Know Nothingism, you say:

> "I therefore call upon them this day to come out of these lodges, and never return to them: at all events, never return to them until all *secrecy*, all their bits of red paper, (indicating *blood*, even by the selection of color,) all their signs and signals, are utterly abolished and dispensed with. I call upon them to do this, and to do it forthwith—by their hopes of heaven—by their obedience to the word of God—by their allegiance to the Constitution and laws of their country—to come out from any party which has adopted a mode and plan of organization so fatal to the peace of society, and the progress of true religion."

What egotism! *You* call upon them! You make a freer use of the personal pronoun *I*, than even old Parson Longstreet, the Know Nothing slayer of Mississippi. To parse your different sentences syntactically, nothing else is necessary but to understand the first person singular, and to repeat the rule. Not only your verbiage but your sentiment is thus egotistic throughout!

Your appeal to the ministers to come out of this organization, on the ground of its *secrecy*, is a species of demagoguism, the more disgusting when it is considered that you are a *Free Mason*, and have, by all the arts and blandishment of your nature, sought to induce ministers to go into that organization. But, then, there is no violation of law or the Constitution in *Masonry*—"fatal to the peace of society and to the progress of true religion"—no, nothing! Understand me: I am not opposed to Masonry.

On this subject of the Romish creed, which you excuse, and even *advocate*, you admit that there are "*alleged* abuses," which have prompted the Protestant Churches to unite themselves with this new Order! Then you insultingly tell these Churches this tale:

> "But they ought to have remembered, that even a virtuous indignation can never justify *proscription and persecution*: these bring no remedy to the real or supposed evils, but are sure to increase and aggravate them. These errors in faith, and abominations in practice, if they really exist, were known to the Wesleys, and Cokes, and Asburys, who founded your Church: to the Lees, the Bruces, the Capers, the Logan Douglasses, the Summerfields, and the Bascoms, who subsequently extended and adorned it. But they never proposed to kindle, in this enlightened age of Christianity, the consuming fires of RELIGIOUS PERSECUTION."

Now, sir, every distinguished "founder" of the Methodist Church you have named, from WESLEY to BASCOM, has written and preached against the "errors in faith, and abominations in practice," of the Romish Church, and they each and all have taken this very ground upon the religious issues. I have heard *three* of these men preach, and I am familiar with the writings of the rest, and know whereof I speak.

You *intentionally* deceive and misrepresent the American party, when you charge that they seek to proscribe one class of our citizens — that they desire to interfere with the rights of conscience — and to say *how* men should worship God. Why don't you inform your readers that Archbishop Hughes, and other Catholic Bishops, were the first to introduce religion into political discussion in this country? This would not suit your purposes — it suits your objects, taste, and inclination better, to slander the American party by wholesale, and to charge upon its members the atrocities committed by your foreign and pauper allies. We only choose to vote against them, and to vote for American-born citizens and Protestants: which is as much our *right*, as it is the right of these foreign Catholics to vote against and proscribe American Protestants. For this, you and your villainous associates exhaust the whole vocabulary of Billingsgate upon the American party. What is their offence? Why, they simply place certain questions before persons desiring to act with them, which they think, at least, may affect the national welfare, and before the people of the Union, and ask their opinion of these questions at the ballot-box. The American party has always denied, and I again reiterate the denial, that we do, at all proscribe, or in any way interfere with, any class of our foreign citizens, save that we propose to send *convicts* from European prisons back to their own native and infamous dens, as fast as they land here — but these are not *citizens* of ours. I appeal to our Platform, and our Book of Constitutions, and I offer to any man a handsome reward — any man who will produce in either a statement containing the proscription you falsely charge against us. I now say, Gov. Brown, either do this, or cease your empty vaporing against the *proscriptive* features of our system, as you are pleased to style it. You declaim most lustily in favor of religious liberty for Catholics, which you know we do not propose as a party to interfere with; and this you plead for at the altar of Methodist "Bishops, Elders, and other Ministers," who know there is no religious liberty for Protestants where Catholics have the power to prevent it! You plead in the most plaintive tones for the rights of foreign Catholics to be sworn into good citizens in less than *one year* after they land here, but do not seem to remember the American Protestant wives and children, who have to subsist on charity during our severe winters, in consequence of their husbands and fathers being elbowed out of employment by the competition of foreign pauper laborers!

Sir, the American party, if in power, would put a stop to that proscription from office that has always characterized the party with which you act, and which has made the present Administration so very and so justly odious to the country. Proscription, indeed! Was there ever such *glaring* and *actual* proscription for the sake of religious and political creeds committed as by the present Administration? The infamous Sag Nicht party with which you act, and of which you are a leader and a High Priest, though the "son of a now sainted father," has applied the political guillotine to almost every man in office who has dared to differ with them in their high estimate of foreign paupers and Catholic vagabonds, in many instances turning out native-born Protestants, and filling their places with foreign Catholics. And yet, with a degree of effrontery that throws the Devil far into the shade, you turn round and charge the American party with proscription, and ask the "Bishops, Elders, and other Ministers," of the Methodist Church, "by their hopes of heaven—by their obedience to the word of God—and by their allegiance to the Constitution and laws of their country," to come out from a party so proscriptive! Why, sir, you out-Herod old Herod himself! Your teachings contrasted with your practice, would cause a crimsoned negative to settle on the cheeks of old Pilate! And still you are the "son of a now sainted father"—you "approve" the "creed" of Methodism, and have "witnessed its growth and prosperity for years, with the highest satisfaction!"

You quote from the Declaration of Independence, to show that toleration should be extended to Catholics and foreigners, and then insultingly add, as if you supposed no Methodist minister had ever perused the writings of Mr. Jefferson:

> "These are the words of Mr. Jefferson, but the immortal sentiment springs directly from the word of the living and true God. No: persecution at the stake, or by exclusion of Catholics from office, is not the weapon to be wielded by the Protestant Churches."

You know that the notes of warning given to his countrymen by the sage of Monticello, and the great APOSTLE of American Democracy, are in harmony with the doctrines of the Know Nothing party. But you choose to conceal this fact from the "Bishops, Elders, and other Ministers" of the Methodist Church, in the vain hope that their numerous pressing and official engagements will not allow them time to look up the documents. In Mr. Jefferson's Notes on Virginia, written in 1781, and published in 1794, pages 124-5, I find the following *Know Nothing doctrine*:

> "But are there no inconveniences to be thrown into the scale against the advantage expected from a multiplication of numbers by the importation of foreigners? It is for the happiness of those united in society to harmonize, as much as possible, in matters which they must of necessity transact together. Civil government being the sole object of forming societies, its administration must be conducted by common consent. Every species of government has specific principles. Ours, perhaps, are more peculiar than those of any other in the universe. It is a composition of the freest principles of the English constitution, with others derived from natural right and natural reason. To these nothing can be more opposed than the maxims of absolute monarchs. Yet *from such we are to expect the greatest number of immigrants*. They will bring with them the *principles of the government they leave, imbibed in early youth*: or, if able to throw them off, it will be in exchange for an *unbounded licentiousness, passing, as is usual, from one extreme to another. It would be a miracle were they to stop precisely at the point of temperate liberty.* These principles, with their language, they will transmit to their children. In proportion with their numbers, they

will share with us the legislation. They will infuse into it their spirit, warp and bias its directions, and render it a heterogeneous, incoherent, distracted mass. *I may appeal to experience during the present contest for a verification of these conjectures.* But if they be not certain in event, are they not possible? are they not probable? Is it not safer to wait with patience twenty-seven years and three months longer for the attainment of every degree of population desired or expected? May not our government be more homogeneous, more peaceable, more durable?"

Again, Mr. JEFFERSON, whilst our Minister to the Court of St. Cloud, addressed a letter to JOHN JAY, dated November 14, 1788, in which he uses this language:

"With respect to the *Consular* appointments, it is a duty on me to add some observations, which my situation here has enabled me to make. I think it was in the spring of 1784, that Congress (harassed by multiplied applications from foreigners, of whom nothing was known but on their information, or on that of others as unknown as themselves) came to the resolution that the interest of America would not permit the naming of any person, not a citizen, to the office of Consul, or Agent, or Commissary. *Native citizens, on several valuable accounts, are preferable to aliens, or citizens alien-born.* Native citizens possess our language, know our laws, customs and commerce, have general acquaintance in the United States, give better satisfaction, *and are more to be relied on in a point of fidelity.* To avail ourselves of our native citizens, it appears to me advisable to *declare, by standing law,* that no person but a native citizen shall be capable of the office of Consul. This was the rule of 1784, restraining the office of Consul to native citizens."

In 1797, Mr. JEFFERSON drafted a petition to the Legislature of Virginia, on behalf of the citizens of Amherst, Albemarle, Fluvana, and Gouchland Bounties, in which he uses the following language:

"Your petitioners further submit to the two Houses of Assembly, whether the safety of the citizens of this Commonwealth, in their persons, their property, their laws and government, does not require that the capacity to act in the important office of *Juror, Grand or Petty, civil or criminal,* should not be restrained in future to native citizens, or such as were citizens at the date of the Treaty of Peace which closed our revolutionary war; and whether ignorance of our laws, and natural partiality to the countries of their birth, are not reasonable causes for declaring this to be one of their rights incommunicable in future to adopted citizens." —*Jefferson's Writings, Vol. IX., page 453.*

Now, Sir, answer me in candor, are you not ashamed of having quoted Mr. JEFFERSON, and of having so basely misrepresented his position on this great American question? Did not Mr. JEFFERSON propose to carry his opposition to foreigners much farther than the American party now do?

But, you vile old demagogue, though "son of a now sainted father," I am determined you shall not escape the indignant powers of those "Bishops, Elders, and other Ministers," whom you have wickedly sought to deceive. It is known to you, and to the world, in what veneration all American Democrats hold the Virginia Resolutions of 1798 and '99, and the fame of Mr. MADISON, who was the ruling spirit of that session of the Legislature. That Legislature passed the following Resolution, which you may find by consulting Henning's Statutes at Large, Vol. 2, New Series, page 194:

> "That the General Assembly, nevertheless, concurring in opinion with the Legislature of Massachusetts that every Constitutional barrier should be opposed to the introduction of foreign influence into our National Councils, — *Resolved*, That the Constitution ought to be so amended that *no foreigner, who shall have acquired the right, under our Constitution and laws, at the time of making the amendment, shall hereafter be eligible to the office of Senator or Representative*, in Congress of the United States, nor to *any office in the Judiciary or Executive*. Agreed to by the Senate, Jan. 16, 1799."

I shall next consider two extracts from your Address, under one general head, relating to the *temporal* power of the Pope. You say:

> "But the genius of sophistry may fly to the rescue of Know-Nothingism, by pretending that it is not on account of *his religion* that the Catholic is to be excluded from office, but because he is subjected, not merely to the spiritual but the *temporal dominion* or jurisdiction of the Pope. No error has been wider spread than this."

Again:

> "A late distinguished Senator from Georgia, (Mr. Berrien,) in a recent address to the public, has copied a letter of Mr. Wesley, which may require a few observations. That letter was dated in January, 1780. All its conclusions were founded on the ASSUMED AND POPULAR OPINION of that day, that the Pope *did* claim a civil jurisdiction beyond his own dominions—that he *could* absolve the subjects of other governments from their oaths of allegiance, and *that there was* a principle in one of the tenets of that Church, that Catholics were justified in not keeping faith with heretics. Against these ASSUMED AND POPULAR OPINIONS, the Catholics of England in that day, as they now do in this country, were solemnly protesting."

This is a modest way of giving Mr. Wesley the *lie*, but it is nevertheless quite *direct*, and is the more surprising, as it comes from the "son of a now sainted father," who was a follower of Wesley, a "co-laborer of that noble band of Christian ministers" he was instrumental in starting out into the world—aye, the son of a "father who, for forty years, ministered at the altars" this same Wesley erected! In holding up John Wesley as the *vile calumniator* of the Catholic Church in England, it is well enough, Governor, to be modest about it, and cautious in the selection of your words, as you are addressing a class of men who believe in John Wesley, as a faithful man of God, and one incapable of misrepresenting the Catholics of England, the Pope of Rome, or any other sect or individual! John Wesley ministered at the sacred altars of religion for more than sixty years; he had with him the power of God, and the witness that he pleased Him; and the last words he uttered, with his hands clasped, and his eyes raised toward heaven, were these: "*The best of all is, God is with us!*" And yet the sons and grandsons in the gospel, of this venerated and sainted man of God, are insulted in Tennessee, by being told by an *impertinent old sinner*, and a *vile old party hack*, that he was A LIAR, while living, and the *slanderer of the Catholic Church*, now that he is no more! If Mr. Wesley "*assumed*" falsehoods in reference to the Romish Church in England, he either did it in *ignorance*, or with *a guilty knowledge* of the fact. He was a man of too much learning and information for his friends to get him out of such an indictment under a plea of ignorance. He is therefore, though dead, A WILFUL LIAR, according to "Ex-Gov. A. V. Brown," for the Governor goes on to argue the cause against him, and, on page 19 of his address, quotes *Catholic* authority to *prove* him a liar! Shame on the "son of a now sainted father," and on the *holy seer of Pisgah*! O! Aaron, thou priest of corrupt Democracy, you need not endeavor to gull "bishops, elders, and other ministers," with your *whining cant*, while you thus traduce their great spiritual head, who, under God, taught them the lessons of salvation!

Gov. Brown, go with me, as one of the admirers of John Wesley, to the humble dwellings of the miners of Cornwall, to the homely tents of the colliers of Kingswood and Newcastle, and to the equally humble workshops of the manufacturers of Yorkshire, in England, who are rejoicing in God their Saviour that a Wesley was ever born into the world, and ask them if they believe him capable of slandering the Catholics! Go with me among the backwoodsmen of North America, and examine them in their lone tents—go among the honest and virtuous settlers on our Western frontiers, amid the interminable forests of the far off West, whose thousands are brought into the fold of Christ, through the instrumentality of Wesleyan ministers, and ask them if they think the founder of their Church was *a wilful liar*!

Go with me to the rich pastures and luxuriant harvest-fields of your own native Middle Tennessee: enter the neat cottages and stately mansions of that glorious division of our State, and ask the intelligent and educated females, who are rejoicing in God, in hope of future and eternal life, through the prayers and sermons of Wesleyan ministers, as instruments in the hands of God, if they believe the founder of their Church was *a wicked calumniator*! Go to the islands of the sea, to the burning sands of Africa, and ask the benighted converts from heathenism, through the instrumentality of Wesleyan ministers, if they believe the venerable founder of their Church was a man of truth!

Enter the dwellings of the rich and fashionable planters of the South—ride around their sugar and cotton plantations, among the sable sons and daughters of Africa, and witness the blessed fruits of the pious life, Christian integrity, and triumphant death of John Wesley! Come over to East Tennessee, Governor, and enter the log-cabins of the virtuous, happy peasantry of the "hill country," and ask them whether they believe Mr. Wesley or your Catholic authorities, touching the temporal power of the Pope of Rome!

Alas! Gov. Brown, the Reformation dawned with LUTHER in Germany, but the sun of its glory rose with Methodism in England; the first streaks of *Protestant* light were seen on the horizon of the sixteenth century, but the meridian sun of the Reformation dawned in all his brightness on the Wesleys and Whitefield! But America has been the land of the glory and triumph of the doctrines of the man you labor to convict of the awful sin of lying!

But you deny that the Pope of Rome, in *temporal* matters, claims what Mr. Wesley attributed to him in the letter copied by Senator Berrien. You also deny that the Popes claim and have exercised the right to interfere with matters of government, and the right to absolve their followers in other countries, and under other governments, from their allegiance to such rulers and governments. I will proceed to vindicate Mr. Wesley, and, by the proof, saddle the lie on you! Whilst John was King of England, he had the "Magna Charta," the great charter securing, among other things, the right of trial by jury, wrung from him at the point of the bayonet. This great charter was annulled by Pope Innocent. Here is the proof:

> "While the king was employed in the siege of Rochester, he received the pleasing intelligence, that according to his request the charter had been annulled by the pontiff. Innocent, enumerating the grounds of his judgment, insists strongly on the violence employed by the barons. If they really felt themselves aggrieved, they ought, he observes, to have accepted the offer of redress by due course of law. They had preferred, however, to break the oath of fealty, which they had taken, and had appointed themselves judges to sit upon their lord. They knew, moreover, that John had enrolled himself among the crusaders; and yet they had not scrupled to violate the privileges which all Christian nations had granted to the champions of the cross. Lastly, England was become the fief of the holy see; and they could not be ignorant that if the king had the will, he had not at least the power, to give away the rights of the crown, without the consent of his feudal superior. He was therefore bound to annul the concessions which had been extorted from John, as having been obtained in contempt of the holy see, to the degradation of royalty, the disgrace of the nation, and to the impediment of the crusade. At the same time he wrote to the barons, re-stating his reasons, exhorting them to submit, requesting them to lay their claims before him in the council to be held at Rome; and promising that he would induce the king to consent to whatever might be deemed just or reasonable, to take care that all grievances should be abolished, that the crown should be content with its just rights, and the clergy and people should enjoy their ancient liberties." —*Lingard's History of England*, vol. ii., page 71.

Will it be said that this was not interfering with *temporal* matters? Will it be said that the right of trial by jury was a *spiritual* matter? Will it be said that the tyranny of King John, and his oppressions, of which the barons justly complained, were *spiritual* matters? No sensible advocate of Romanism will say this!

The next instance of an interference by the Pope in temporal affairs, to which I shall call your attention, Governor, is his excommunication of Elizabeth, Queen of England. She was immediately preceded on that throne by her sister Mary, who was a Catholic. For no other reason than that Elizabeth was a *Protestant,* and would not submit her rights and kingdom to the control of the Pope, Pius V. thundered forth at her devoted head the following anathema, from his throne at the Vatican, situated at the foot of one of the seven hills upon which Rome is built:

EXCOMMUNICATION AND DEPOSITION Of QUEEN ELIZA-BETH OF ENGLAND.

"Pius, etc., for a future memorial of the matter. He that reigneth on high, to whom is given all power in heaven and on earth, committed one Holy, Catholic and Apostolic Church, *out of which there is no salvation,* to one alone upon the earth, Peter the Prince of the Apostles, and to Peter's successor, the Bishop of Rome, to be governed in *fulness of power.* Him alone he made prince over all people, and all kingdoms, to pluck up, destroy, scatter, consume, plant and build, etc. But the number of the ungodly hath gotten such power, that there is now no place left in the whole world which they have not essayed to corrupt with their most wicked doctrines. Amongst others, Elizabeth, *the pretended Queen of England, a slave of wickedness,* lending thereunto her helping hand, with whom, as in a sanctuary, the most pernicious of all men have found a refuge; this very woman having seized upon the kingdom, and monstrously usurping the place of the supreme Head of the Church in all England, and the chief authority and jurisdiction thereof, hath again brought back the same kingdom to miserable destruction, which was then newly reduced to the faith, and to good order. For having by strong hand inhibited the true religion, which Mary, the lawful queen, of famous memory, had, by the help of this See, restored, after it had been formerly overthrown by King Henry VIII., a revolter therefrom, and following and embracing the errors of *heretics,* she hath removed the royal council, consisting of the English nobility, and filled it with obscure men, being heretics; hath oppressed the embracers of the Roman faith, hath placed impious preachers, ministers of iniquity, and abolished the sacrifice of the mass, prayers, fastings, distinction of meats, a single life, and the rites and ceremonies; hath commanded books to be read in the whole realm, containing manifest heresy, etc. She hath not only contemned the godly requests and admonitions of princes concerning her healing and conversion, but also bath not so much as permitted the Nuncios of the See to cross the seas into England, etc. We do, therefore, out of the fulness of our apostolic power, declare the aforesaid Elizabeth, being heretic, and a favorer of heretics, and her adherents in the matter aforesaid, to have incurred the sentence of anathema, and to be cut off from the unity of the body of Christ. And, moreover, we do declare her to be deprived of her pretended title to the kingdom aforesaid, and of all dominion, dignity, and privilege whatsoever; and also the nobility, subjects, and people of the said kingdom, and all others which have in any sort sworn unto her, to be for ever absolved from any such oath, and all manner of duty or dominion, allegiance and obedience; as we also do, by the authority of these presents, absolve them, and do deprive the same Elizabeth of her pretended title to the kingdom, and all other things aforesaid. And we do command and interdict all and every one of the noblemen, subjects, people, and others aforesaid, that they presume not to obey her, or her admonitions, mandates, and laws; and those who shall do the contrary, we do innodate with the like sentence of ANATHEMA.

"Given at St. Peter's at Rome, in the year 1569, and the fifth of our pontificate." — *Dowling's History of Romanism*, p. 564.

One more: Sixtus V. thunders his bull of excommunication at this same Queen of England — incites Philip of Catholic Spain to make war against her country — and graciously *gives* the British Isles to Philip! Here is the bull of Pope Sixtus:

"We, Sixtus the Fifth, the universal shepherd of the flock of Christ, the supreme chief, to whom the government of the whole world appertains, considering that the people of England and Ireland, after having been so long celebrated for their virtues, their religion, and their submission to our see, have become putrid members, infected, and capable of corrupting the whole Christian body, and on account of their subjection to the impious, tyrannical, and sanguinary government of Elizabeth, the bastard queen, and by the influence of her adherents, who equal her in wickedness; and who refuse, like her, to recognize the power of the Roman Church: regarding that Henry VIII. formerly, for motives of debauchery, commenced all these disorders by revolting against the submission which he owed to the Pope, the sole and true sovereign of England; considering that the usurper Elizabeth has followed the path of this infamous king, we declare that there exists but one mode of remedying these evils, of restoring peace, tranquillity, and union to Christendom, of re-establishing religion, and of leading back the people to obedience to us, which is, to depose from the throne that execrable Elizabeth, who falsely arrogates to herself the title of Queen of the British Isles. Being then inspired by the Holy Spirit for the general good of the Church, we renew, by the virtue of our apostolic power, the sentence pronounced by our predecessor, Pius the Fifth and Gregory the Thirteenth, against the modern Jezebel: we proclaim her deprived of her royal authority, of the rights, titles, or pretensions to which she may lay claim over the kingdoms of Ireland and England, affirming that she possesses them unlawfully and by usurpation. We relieve all her subjects from the oaths they may have taken to her, and we prohibit them from rendering any kind of service to this execrable woman; it is our will, that she be driven from door to door like one possessed of a devil, and that all human aid be refused her; we declare, moreover, that foreigners or Englishmen are permitted, as a meritorious work, to seize the person of Elizabeth and surrender her, living or dead, to the tribunals of the inquisition. We promise to those who shall accomplish this glorious mission, infinite recompenses, not only in the life eternal, but even in this world. Finally, we grant plenary indulgence to the faithful who shall willingly unite with the Catholic army which is going to combat the impious Elizabeth, under the orders of our dear son Philip the Second, to whom we give the British Isles in full sovereignty, as a recompense for the zeal he has always shown toward our see, and for the particular affection he has shown for the Catholics of the Low Country." — *De Cormenin's History of the Popes*, p. 262.

Here is what Macaulay, a reliable historian, says of the baneful effects of Romanism:

"From the time when the barbarians overran the Western Empire to the time of the revival of letters, the influence of the Church of Rome has been generally favorable to science, to civilization, and to good government. But, during the last three centuries, to stunt the growth of the human mind has been her chief object. Throughout Christendom, whatever advance has been made in knowledge, in freedom, in wealth, and in the arts of life, has been made in spite of her, and has everywhere been in inverse proportion to her power. The loveliest and most fertile provinces of Europe have, under her rule, been sunk into poverty, in political servitude, and in intellectual torpor, while Protestant countries, once proverbial for sterility and barbarism, have been turned, by skill and industry, into gardens, and can boast of a long list of heroes and statesmen, philosophers and poets. Whoever, knowing what Italy and Scotland naturally are, and what four hundred years ago they naturally were, shall now compare the country round Rome with the country round Edinburgh, will be able to form some judgment of the tendency of Papal domination. The descent of Spain, once the first among monarchies, to the lowest depths of degradation, the elevation of Holland, in spite of many natural disadvantages, to a position such as no commonwealth so small has ever reached, teach the same lesson. Whoever passes, in Germany, from a Roman Catholic to a Protestant principality, in Switzerland from a Roman Catholic to a Protestant canton, in Ireland from a Roman Catholic to a Protestant county, finds that he has passed from a lower to a higher grade of civilization. On the other side of the Atlantic the same law prevails. The Protestants of the United States have left far behind the Roman Catholics of Mexico, Peru, and Brazil. The Roman Catholics of Lower Canada remain inert, while the whole continent round them is in a ferment with Protestant activity and enterprise." — *Macaulay's History of England*, vol. i., p. 37.

I must be permitted to add, just here, that in 1848, when the people of France expelled Louis Philippe from the throne in Paris, and established a Republic, the present old drunken, goutified debauchee, Pope Pius IX., hurled at the French nation a fearful bull of excommunication, and denied them the right of revolution! Was this interfering in temporal matters? But no longer ago than the year 1854, this same old vagabond, Pope Pius, issued orders absolving his followers from all allegiance to the Sardinian Government, because that government chose to abolish the infamous monasteries, which had been so long supported at the expense of an oppressed people! Was this not interfering in temporal matters? I could multiply authorities, Governor, to an indefinite extent, sustaining Mr. Wesley's views, and falsifying all you say, but this would swell my reply beyond what I intended in the outset. Let me call your attention to Brownson's Review, for July, 1853, where you will find all this power, and even more, claimed for the Pope, over temporal sovereigns and their subjects, the world over! This *Review* is the acknowledged organ of *Archbishop Hughes*, the head and front of the Catholic Church in North America.

You state that our Declaration of Independence absolved from every possible obligation to the Pope in temporal matters. Your language is:

> "The moment it was read and proclaimed from old Independence
> Hall in Philadelphia, obedience in temporal matters, if it ever existed,
> ceased for ever, as to every native-born son in America."

You further add that the Constitution of the United States set aside all temporal power of the Pope in this country, and that if any doubts remain, the finishing touch is given by the following oath of naturalization, taken by our naturalized citizens:

> "I do solemnly swear that I will support the Constitution of the
> United States, and that I do *absolutely and entirely* renounce and abjure
> all allegiance and fidelity to any foreign prince, potentate, or state, or
> sovereignty *whatever*."

Sir, do you suppose that the "Bishops, Elders, and other Ministers," whom you have the impudence to address, are all fools? Do you suppose they are men of no reading or information? If they know any thing, they certainly know that the oath of naturalization they, the Catholics, take, weighs no more with them than a feather. A Catholic can evade the force of any oath, by a *mental reservation*. Here is what Sanchez says, the very highest Catholic authority, whose teaching, including this interpretation of oaths, has been endorsed by the Council of Trent:

> "It is lawful to use *ambiguous terms* to give the impression a dif-
> ferent sense from that which you understand yourself. A person may
> take an oath that he has not done such a thing, though in fact he has,
> by saying to himself it was not done on a certain day, or before he was
> born, or by concealing any other similar circumstances; which gives
> another meaning to it. This is extremely convenient, and always very
> just, when necessary to your health, honor, or prosperity."

In addition to this, let me tell you, if you never before knew the fact, that Judge Gaston, a distinguished Jurist, and a gentleman of excellent character, though a rigid Roman Catholic, of North Carolina, was appointed to a seat upon the Supreme Bench of that State. The Constitution of that State, unlike those of almost all other States, requires every Judge to take an oath, among other things, that HE

BELIEVES IN THE TRUTH OF THE PROTESTANT RELIGION. Mr. Gaston asked time to think over the matter—he repaired to the Archbishop at Baltimore, doubtless obtained a dispensation—wrote back to Raleigh from there, that he would take the oath—returned, and in due time solemnly swore that *he believed in the truth of the Protestant Religion.* He died in Raleigh, one of the Judges of the Supreme Court—but lived and died a Roman Catholic!

During the past month, in this city, W. G. McAdoo, the Attorney General for this Judicial Circuit, had some Irish Catholics brought before the Grand Jury, to testify in cases of unlawful gaming and the retailing of ardent spirits. The Clerk swore them on a common English Testament, and they returned to the Jury room, and testified that they knew of no cases! The Attorney for the Commonwealth then procured the *Catholic Douay Bible*, with a large *Cross* upon its outside, swore them upon this—sent them in, and they *disgorged*, telling of various cases, and enabling the Jury to find bills against even some of their own folks! An oath, then, is nothing with strict Roman Catholics, who believe their Priests can absolve them from the obligations of any and all oaths. For notwithstanding your denial of the fact, it is notoriously true, that the members of the Catholic Church believe their Priesthood to exercise, by Divine right, the power to fix and determine their eternal destiny. Nay, every Roman Catholic in the known world is under the absolute control of the Catholic Priesthood, by considerations not only of a temporal, but an eternal weight. This is what gives their Priesthood such power and influence in elections; an influence they are using in every State, against the American party. And it is this faculty of concentration, this political influence, this power of the Priesthood to control the Catholic community, and cause a vast multitude of ignorant foreigners to vote as a *unit*, and thus control the will of the American people, that has engendered this opposition to the Catholic Church. It is this aggressive policy and corrupting tendency of the Romish Church; this organized and concentrated political power of a distinct class of men; foreign by birth; inferior in intelligence and virtue to the American people, and not their religion and form of worship, objectionable as these are known to be, which have called forth the opposition of the American party to the Catholic Church.

But, sir, you occupy several pages in copying and commenting upon the several oaths administered to the members of the American party—oaths which, as you tell us, are revolting in their character, and lead to the indiscriminate proscription of all foreigners. I meet all your conjectures and wild speculations in reference to these several oaths and obligations, by saying, just here, that I have taken them all, and that they express my sentiments and feelings to the very letter; and I am willing, for the remainder of my days, to go before an acting Justice of the Peace, for the county of Knox, and have all three of these oaths administered every Monday morning, upon the "Holy Bible and Cross."

You have failed, in your zeal to advocate Romanism and oppose the American party, to tell the "Bishops, Elders, and other Ministers," whom you address, that we resort to our oaths and obligations to combat successfully the most powerful oath-bound organization the world ever knew. The oath of every *Roman Catholic Bishop* and *Archbishop* binds him to absolute and unquestioned obedience, not only to the present Pope but to his successors, "canonically coming in," and to "oppose and persecute" all who do not submit to his authority! The oath of every *Priest* binds him to the Church of Rome "as the chief head and matron above all pretended Churches throughout the whole earth," and to "further her interests more than his own earthly good." The oath of the *Jesuit* binds him to the Pope, as "Christ's Vicar-General," by "all the saints and hosts of heaven," and to "denounce and disown any allegiance as due to Protestants, or obedience to any of their inferior magistrates or officers." The oath of the *San Fedisti*, a secret Order established by the Papal government in 1821, binds them to sustain "the Papal altar and throne, and to exterminate heretics, without pity for the cries of children, or of men and women." The oath of the *Irish Ribbon Men*, an Order established by the Papal government, and introduced into this country by *Bedini*, the Pope's Nuncio, but a few years ago, binds him "to extirpate all heretics, and all the Protestants, and to walk in their blood to the knees." Is it not time to take the alarm, Governor, and to combine to resist all these secret oath-bound associations, which now threaten us with the loss of all that freemen and Protestant Christians hold dear on earth?

It is a matter of utter astonishment to find a great political party in this country, most of whom are native-born Protestants, taking sides with a foreign Church, whose designs against this country, according to the avowals of the Duke of Richmond, lately Governor-General of Canada, are of the most wicked and fearful character! Speaking of this government, the Duke said in a public address, on our northern border:

> "It will be destroyed: it ought not, and will not be permitted to exist. The curse of the French revolution, and subsequent wars and commotions in Europe, are to be attributed to its example; and so long as it exists, no prince will be safe upon his throne; and *the sovereigns of Europe are aware of it*, and they have *determined upon its destruction, and have come to an understanding upon this subject, and have decided on the means to accomplish it*; and they will eventually succeed, by SUBVERSION *rather than conquest*. All the low and surplus population of the different nations of Europe will be carried into that country. It is and will be a receptacle for the bad and disaffected population of Europe, when they are not wanted for soldiers, or to supply the navies; *and the governments of Europe will favor such a course*. This will create a surplus and majority of low population, who are so very easily excited; and they will bring with them their principles, and in nine cases out of ten adhere to their ancient and former governments, laws, manners, customs, and religion, and will transmit them to their posterity; and in many cases propagate them among the natives. These men will become citizens, and by the Constitution and laws will be invested with the right of suffrage. Hence, discord, dissension, anarchy, and civil war will ensue; and some popular individual will assume the government, and restore order, and the sovereigns of Europe, the emigrants, and many of the natives, will sustain him. The Church of Rome has a design upon that country; and it will in time be the established reli-

gion, and will aid in the destruction of that Republic. *I have conversed with many of the sovereigns and princes of Europe; and they have unanimously expressed these opinions relative to the government of the United States, and their determination to subvert it.*"

The monarchs of Europe, says the Duke of Richmond, will aid in sending us a surplus of "low, excitable, bad, and disaffected men," who will bring with them their principles, and will adhere to their foreign notions of government, laws, manners, customs, and religion—and that religion Catholic; and yet *you*, the "son of a now sainted father," of Protestant raising, have the brazen effrontery to call upon the "Bishops, Elders, and other Ministers" of an American Protestant Church to aid you, your corrupt party, and the monarchs of Europe, in destroying both our government and Church!

Sir, it is passing strange that Protestant Christians and their children should be found side by side with you, Bishop Hughes, Gov. Johnson, and the thousands of bad men who are seeking to build up a Roman Hierarchy in this free country of ours! What do you promise the country and yourselves, if Romanism proves successful in this contest? The history of the past informs us that Rome has slain 1,000,000 of Albigenses and Waldenses; 1,500,000 Jews, in Spain; 3,000,000 Moors, in Spain. France will never forget St. Bartholomew's Night, when 100,000 souls perished in Paris alone! The blood of Protestants has fertilized the soil of England, Germany, and Ireland. I mean by this, that enough of Protestant blood has been shed to *enrich* all the poor lands of England, Germany, and Ireland, if it were properly distributed. In all, the authentic records of the Romish Church show, (and of this she makes her boast,) that she has put to death SIXTY-EIGHT MILLIONS of human beings, for no other offence than that of being *Protestants* in their religious faith! Average each person slain at four gallons of blood, and medical writers say a healthy person yields more, and it makes TWO HUNDRED AND SEVENTY-TWO MILLIONS OF GALLONS!—enough to overflow the banks of the Mississippi, and destroy all the cotton and sugar plantations in Mississippi and Louisiana!

But you argue, in your blasphemous publication, that this is no longer a characteristic of the Romish Hierarchy. Why is it not? Has she ever changed for the better? When did she ever renounce these doctrines and practices? Never, no, never! Hers is the same tyrannical system now—where she has the power—that it always has been, and always must be, in the very nature of things! It is her boast, and the boast of her standard authors, that she is always right, and knows no change! And wo to this land of ours, if ever Rome gets the ascendancy here! Her whole system is adverse to our Republican institutions, and she hesitates not to declare it! *Brownson* says in his Review:

> "Let us dare to assert the truth in the face of the *lying world*, and, instead of pleading for our Church at the bar of the State, *summon the State itself to plead at the bar of the Church, its divinely constituted judge.*"

No wonder, sir, that the American people are aroused! Such bold and startling avowals are calculated to arouse and unite the somewhat divided bands of Protestant Christians; to wake up a host of Luthers, Calvins, Cranmers, and Wesleys;

to bind together "the heretics condemned in a mass." The very latest thing I have seen is the "Pastoral Letter" of the Bishops of the Province of St. Louis, just issued. That document explicitly says:

> "We maintain the superiority of the *spiritual* over the *temporal* order. We maintain that the temporal ruler is *bound* to conform his enactments to the Divine law. We maintain that the Church is the supreme judge of all questions concerning faith and morals; and that in the determination of such question, the *Roman Pontiff, Vicar of Jesus Christ*, constitutes a tribunal from which there is no appeal; and to whose award all the children of the Church must yield obedience."

Now, sir, after this authoritative and official announcement, I don't want to see any more of your wire-drawn distinctions between spiritual and temporal allegiance to the Pope. These Bishops say that both are alike binding. Nor do I want to see any more of your malignant efforts to fix the *lie* upon Mr. Wesley, for affirming in Europe, during the past century, what the Bishops of the United States have announced, in a Pastoral Address, in the present day!

Pope Pius IX. has, by a special act, made the Virgin Mary the special patron of these United States; but the Protestants of this country have also made a decree, and that decree is, that Jesus Christ, and not the Virgin Mary, shall be the patron of these United States.

And I am happy to have it in my power to inform you, notwithstanding the influence of your Address, that the "Bishops, Elders, and other Ministers" of the Methodist Church, both North and South, are ready to make a common, determined, prayerful effort to save our native land from the threatened slavery of submission to the decisions of the Council of Trent, and the equally corrupt conventions of Progressive Democracy!

Assuming what is notoriously *false*—that the Know Nothings are in favor of all measures fatal to the South, and destructive to the Constitution—you ask on page 25 of your *infinitely infernal* Address:

> "What if a proposition be pending to repeal the Fugitive Slave Law—the Kansas and Nebraska law—the rejection of a State asking admission into the Union, because its constitution may tolerate slavery?"

You know, sir, that the 12th Plank in the Philadelphia Platform of the American party is a safer guaranty upon this slavery question, and the perpetuity of existing laws, than is to be found anywhere in the creeds of political parties. Here it is in full:

> "The American party having arisen upon the ruins, and in spite of the opposition of the Whig and Democratic parties, can not be held in any manner responsible for the obnoxious acts or violated pledges of either; and the systematic agitation of the slavery question by those parties having elevated sectional hostility into a positive element of political power, and brought our institutions into peril, it has there-

fore become the imperative duty of the American party to interpose, for the purpose of giving peace to the country, and perpetuity to the Union. And as experience has shown it impossible to reconcile opinions so extreme as those which separate the disputants, and as there can be no dishonor in submitting to the laws, the National Council has deemed it the best guaranty of common justice and of future peace, to abide by and maintain the existing laws upon the subject of slavery, as a final and conclusive settlement of that subject in spirit and in substance.

"And regarding it the highest duty to avow their opinions upon a subject so important, in distinct and unequivocal terms, it is hereby declared as the sense of this National Council, that Congress possesses no power, under the Constitution, to legislate upon the subject of slavery in the States where it does or may exist, or to exclude any State from admission into the Union, because its Constitution does or does not recognize the institution of slavery as a part of its social system; and expressly pretermitting any expression of opinion upon the power of Congress to establish or prohibit slavery in any Territory, it is the sense of the National Council that Congress ought not to legislate upon the subject of slavery within the Territories of the United States, and that any interference by Congress with slavery as it exists in the District of Columbia, would be a violation of the spirit and intention of the compact by which the State of Maryland ceded the District to the United States, and a breach of the national faith."

In the "wild hunt" for territory by the progressive Democracy, and their efforts to settle our Western lands with foreigners who are to a man Free Soilers and Abolitionists, the South has more to fear than from all other considerations. What is Gov. Johnson's iniquitous Homestead Bill, but a bid for foreigners? He proposes to give to the heads of families one hundred and sixty acres of land, thus *hiring* all the convicts and paupers of Europe to come and settle in our Western States and Territories! Sir, but let your progressive, sublimated, double-distilled, converging-lines, Johnsonian Democracy bring into this Union one million of Spanish Papists—black, brown, sorrel, and tawny—under the guise of acquiring Cuba for the South: let them bring eight hundred thousand French and English Papists, under the name of acquiring Canada for the North: let them bring two millions of Mexican Papists—brown, tawny, red and black, being a mixture of all colors and all nations—under the specious pretence of "extending the area of freedom"—let all this be done—and your party, made up of native traitors, and foreign vagabonds, and Catholic paupers, are aiming at it—let it be done, I say, and farewell to liberty, and all that is sacred in this country! With five millions of Papists in our midst—four millions and a half being of foreign birth, and four millions speaking a foreign language—all taught from infancy to hate and detest Protestantism as a crime—an American party would become an absolute political necessity. Well do the Free Soil papers comprehend this matter. Hear the infamous but influential *Chicago Tribune,* one of your Douglass organs—one of your foreign Catholic organs. I quote from the paper itself:

> "It is now a well-attested fact, that Atchison is a member of the Superior Order of the Spangled Banner, or Know Nothings, and that his infernal villainy in Kansas has been carried on under the protection and patronage of the lodges in Western Missouri. This is a matter that all men in the North should understand, that Northern voters may be exceedingly cautious how they give countenance or support to an Order that, in any of its phases or localities, is capable of producing such results. It is further said, that the members of that Kansas Legislature, now outraging all sense of right and justice by their devilish enactments, are the chosen men of the affiliated Know Nothings in Missouri and Kansas, who back then up in whatever thing they do. Atchison and his gang are the friends of the Order, and through it and Southern Know Nothing support they are sure that their efforts to establish a despotism in the Territory, if necessary, at the point of the bayonet, will be successful. These facts account for many things heretofore inexplicable, and they develop the true reason of the hostility of the border-ruffians to the foreign immigration that would, under other circumstances, people that vast and fertile country west of the Missouri."

Thus it appears that a host of *lousy* foreigners, fresh from the emigrant ships, in which they are brought over to this country as *ballast*—having the right to vote conferred upon them by an infamous *progressive* Democratic feature in the Kansas Bill, were expected to get the control of affairs in Kansas. It further appears, however, that Senator Atchison and his pro-slavery associates supposed that, though fresh from their farms, and crossing the line of their State into the new Territory, they too had the right to vote without being *naturalized* in Kansas. Hence, in the estimation of this Sag Nicht organ at Chicago, a great outrage is committed upon Germany, Ireland, and Italy!

Sir, you need not lay the flattering unction to your soul, that you can drive the clergy generally from the noble stand they have taken upon this great question. Nor need you suppose, for one moment, that the American party are conquered, though defeated in several States in the recent elections. The party will remain true to its ends. Though it fail to command office, it cannot fail to exercise large power. Office is not always strength; but sometimes, nay, frequently, as in the case of the present Administration, weakness, as time will prove! The aim of the American party is, by fair party means, to correct a great social evil and political wrong; and if they cannot do that, to mitigate the evil and the wrong; if they cannot do that, to prevent its *further increase*; and if neither can be done, why, then I confess to you, the party will have failed. But, sir, if such a failure take place, rest assured that the "Bishops, Elders, and other Ministers" of the Methodist Church, South, will not help to bring about such a failure! We can afford to let such minions of party as you are, rave and rant, and publish their expositions, and issue their warnings to Churches: they will all serve to swell our ranks. All true American hearts, not chained to the car of party, or bound down by the cords of plunder, think alike upon the great questions that have called the American party into existence. Little do we regard the slanders of the pensioners of party. Let their speeches and publications teem with wholesale slanders of our creed: the political jockeyism of these thimble-riggers, as in your own case, is too apparent!

From Maine to the shores of the Pacific the country is convulsed with intense excitement upon this subject. Shall Americans govern themselves, or shall Foreigners, unacquainted with our laws, and brought up under monarchical governments, rule? Shall those who are temporally and spiritually subject to a foreign prince be our legislators, post-masters, foreign ministers, and military leaders, and change our laws as they are directed by the Pope of Rome? Such results the American party have set out to prevent. The present excitement will not cease; true Americans and Protestants will labor and pray until our distracted country shall be redeemed from the influence of civil and ecclesiastical tyranny.

Now, Governor, I have noticed all your charges, arguments, and appeals, but one, and that is the allegation that Methodist clerical Know Nothings are *conspirators*. Your argument is—and I wish to represent you correctly—"The offence of conspiracy is not confined to the prejudicing of a particular individual; it may be to injure public trade, to affect public health, or to *violate public policy.*"

You cite Blackstone's Commentary, and other English Law Books, to satisfy the Clergy as to the *law of conspiracy.* This done, you overwhelm them with this sage and logical conclusion:

> "The gist of the offence of conspiracy consists in a confederacy to do an *unlawful act,* and the offence is complete when the confederacy is made."

I will concede, for the sake of the argument, that this is sound law, and that yours is a logical deduction. Nay, I will concede more—I grant that it is an unlawful act for native Americans, and Protestant Christians, whether ministers or laymen, to resolve, or swear, as we Know Nothings have all done, that we will not vote for Catholics and Foreigners for public offices! I take the ground you do, that a man's vote is not his own, and that it is only to be disposed of by the leaders of the party with which he may act!

And now, if you and I, both great men, and *Doctors of Law,* are correct in laying down the law, and the *privilege of voters in this free country,* what an infamous body of conspirators the Democrats are, and have always been! For a quarter of a century, they have conspired to keep the Whigs out of office—have succeeded in doing so most of that time—and have kept thousands of them who are poor from becoming rich! More recently, they have conspired with Abolitionists, Free Soilers, Fourierites, Spiritualists, Roman Catholics, Irish, French, and German paupers, and all manner of European convicts, to keep the American party out of office, and have succeeded in Virginia, North Carolina, Georgia, Alabama, Pennsylvania, Ohio, Illinois, Texas, and other States—thereby depriving the Americans of "lots" of money and honors, both of which they need, and both of which are their *birthrights!*

The "Bishops, Elders, and other Ministers," whom you address, in opposition to the great sin of *conspiracy*, would more cheerfully unite with you to enforce law and order, and to prosecute offenders, but for the fact that the *Abolition wing of your party* once conspired against them, to deprive their wives, children, widows, and orphans, of their lawful portion of the great Book Concern in New York, and they were compelled to punish the conspirators, at great expense, however, in the District and Supreme Courts of the United States!

But, Sir, upon the subject of *oaths*, you are eloquent, apt in your quotations of Scripture, and evince great learning in the legal profession! You charge that "Know Nothingism is both unchristian and unlawful, because of its *oaths*, which have no Scripture warrant for their administration!" One of your quotations from the Bible is this: "Swear not at all: neither by heaven, for it is God's throne: nor by the earth, for it is his footstool." Your mind has undergone a great change upon the subject of *oaths* and *hard swearing*, since the 21st of June, 1845, when you delivered your celebrated "Mount Pisgah" speech at Athens. You then advised the people of the State to administer "horrible oaths," and to swear by the "*heavens*," aye, "God's throne." But then you were a Know Nothing. Here is what you say in your *revised* copy of that memorable speech:

> "Go up with me in imagination and stand for awhile on some lofty summit of the Rocky Mountains. Let us take one ravishing view of this broad land of liberty. Turn your face toward the Gulf of Mexico: what do you behold? Instead of one lone star faintly shining in the far distant south, a whole galaxy of stars of the first magnitude are bursting on your vision and shining with a bright and glorious effulgence. Now turn with me to the west—the mighty west—where the setting sun dips her disk in the western ocean. Look away down through the misty distance to the shores of the Pacific, with all its bays, and harbors, and rivers. Cast your eyes as far as the Russian Possessions, in latitude fifty-four degrees and forty minutes. What a new world lies before you! How many magnificent States to be the future homes of the sons and daughters of freedom! But you have not gazed on half this glorious country. Turn now your face to the east, where the morning sun first shines on this land of liberty. Away yonder, you see the immortal old thirteen, who achieved our independence; nearer to us lie the twelve or fifteen States of the great valley of the Mississippi, stretching and reposing like so many giants in their slumbers. O! now I see your heart is full—it can take in no more. Who now feels like he was a party man, or a southern man, or a northern man? Who does not feel that he is an American, and thankful to Heaven that his lot was cast in such a goodly land? When did mental vision ever rest on such a scene? Moses, when standing on the top of Mount Pisgah, looking over on the promised land, gazed not on a scene half so lovely. O! let us this day *vow* that whatever else we may do, by whatever name we may be called, we will never surrender one square acre of this goodly heritage to the DICTATION of any king or potentate on earth. SWEAR IT! SWEAR IT! my countrymen, and let HEAVEN RECORD THE VOW FOR EVER!"

In conclusion, Governor, suffer a few words of advice, and I will bring this letter, already too long, to a close. You are advanced in years, nay, you have grown gray in the service of sin, and political intrigues; and at most you have not long to live. Cease your political aspirations, and turn your attention to future and eternal things! You have been a member of our State Legislature; subsequently, a member of Congress; and more recently the Governor of our State; honors and stations, to say the least of it, equal to your merits and talents!

As a true "son of a now sainted father," from whom you have been separated for many years, so demean yourself in future, that you may not be separated, world without end! Humble yourself before God; confess your numerous sins; and instead of lecturing God's ministers upon the subject of party politics, ask them, with tears in your eyes, to pray for you! Exercise a living faith in Christ, who came down from heaven, and made upon the cross a full, perfect, and sufficient sacrifice, oblation, and satisfaction, for the sins of the whole world. Thus obtaining forgiveness, cease your Sunday discussions on political subjects; attend at the house of God, and set an example to other ungodly Sag Nichts, and lead a new and different life!

Very respectfully, your obedient servant,

W. G. BROWNLOW,
A Local Methodist Minister.

GOVERNOR JOHNSON
AND EDITOR EASTMAN.

On the 9th of October, 1855, and while the Legislature was in session at Nashville, we delivered a speech to an immense crowd on the Public Square; which, after certain preliminary remarks, we will give to the public, just as it was spoken. The reason why the call was made on us to deliver the speech was, that we had, the previous weeks, delivered the same, in *substance*, at Shelbyville and Clarksville, and the American party at Nashville hearing of it, and approving what was said, desired us to repeat it; and, to be candid, we desired to repeat it there and then!

Mr. Wise, of Virginia, gained great notoriety, in the spring of 1855, by his abuse and blackguardism, heaped upon the American party. He was successful; and Johnson, of Tennessee, whose ambition was to gain a more infamous notoriety, profiting by the example of Wise, plunged into the lowest depths of Billingsgate, and piled his vulgar epithets upon the party *indiscriminately*. Wise, then, like all inventors and originators, has had numerous *imitators*, and among the most successful of these are Johnson, of Tennessee; Stephens, of Georgia; and Clingman, of North Carolina. But as an adept in low Billingsgate slang, coarse blackguardism, and as a slanderer and maligner of better men than himself, Johnson has excelled his patron, Wise, and left far in the shades of the distant caverns of abuse, both Stephens and Clingman!

To prepare the public mind for the degree of severity we used in reference to the Governor of the State, we will introduce as many as *five* different extracts from his speeches, in his late canvass for Governor, at Murfreesboro' and Manchester; as reported by his partisan organ, the *Nashville Union*, and his *pliant tool*, its Abolition editor, *E. G. Eastman*:

"THE DEVIL, HIS SATANIC MAJESTY, THE PRINCE OF DARKNESS, WHO PRESIDES OVER THE SECRET CONCLAVE HELD IN PANDEMONIUM, MAKES WAR UPON ALL BRANCHES OF CHRIST'S CHURCH. THE KNOW NOTHINGS ADVOCATE AND DEFEND NONE, BUT MAKE WAR UPON ONE OF THE CHURCHES, AND THUS FAR BECOME THE ALLIES OF THE PRINCE OF DARKNESS."—[Speech of ANDREW JOHNSON, at Murfreesboro'.

"A DENOMINATION LIKE THIS, TO SET UP AS THE GUARDIANS OF THE RELIGION AND MORALS OF THE COUNTRY! A DENOMINATION BOUND TOGETHER BY SECRET AND TERRIBLE OATHS: THE FIRST OF WHICH, ON THE VERY INITIATION, FIXES AND REQUIRES THEM TO CARRY A LIE IN THEIR MOUTHS."—[Speech of ANDREW JOHNSON, at Murfreesboro'.

"SHOW ME THE DIMENSIONS OF A KNOW NOTHING, AND I WILL SHOW YOU A HUGE REPTILE, UPON WHOSE NECK THE FOOT OF EVERY HONEST MAN OUGHT TO BE PLACED."—[Speech of ANDREW JOHNSON, at Manchester.

"THEY ARE LIKE THE HYENA, AND COME FROM THEIR LAIR AFTER MIDNIGHT TO PREY UPON HUMAN CARCASSES."—[Speech of ANDREW JOHNSON, at Manchester.

"I WOULD AS SOON BE FOUND IN THE CLAN OF JOHN A. MURRELL AS IN A KNOW NOTHING COUNCIL."—[Speech of ANDREW JOHNSON, at Manchester.

The *blackguard* and *calumniator* using this language, was elected by a majority of two thousand votes: that majority being cast by *Foreigners and illegal voters;* and consequently, his competitor, COL. GENTRY—than whom there is not a more talented, patriotic, and honorable gentleman in Tennessee—was fairly and justly elected. This, then, is the language used by the Governor of Tennessee, *towards a majority of the legal voters of the State!* Under these circumstances, we made the speech that follows, to an immense crowd on the Square: the correspondence preceding which, will explain itself:

NASHVILLE, Oct. 10th, 1855

W. G. BROWNLOW, ESQ.:

Dear Sir:—The undersigned, having heard your speech on the Square, last night, respectfully request that you embody the substance of the same, and publish it in the Knoxville Whig. The desire to see it in print is very general; and those who heard it approved its severity, without it were such as were bitter against the American party.

Your friends,
Charles G. Smith,
John Morrison,
F. M. Burton,
Robt. S. Northcutt,
Saml. Davis.

NASHVILLE, Oct. 13th, 1855.

MESSRS. SMITH, MORRISON, AND OTHERS:

Gentlemen:—Your note requesting me to publish the substance of my remarks on the Square, last Tuesday night, has been received, and I would have replied sooner, but for my absence at Shelbyville. I have now made the same speech at Clarksville, Nashville, and Shelbyville; and my only regrets are, that my engagements prevent me from delivering the same speech at every point in this State, where Gov. Johnson held me up as the "High Priest of the Order," and argued therefrom the *want of respectability* for the Order. In addition to your request, I have had verbal applications from many gentlemen to publish my remarks—gentlemen who have been mild and moderate throughout their political course. I shall, therefore, comply with your request and theirs, at my earliest convenience.

I hold that no man's position in life should shield him from the rebukes he may merit by his bad conduct; and as for the present Governor of Tennessee, his wholesale abuse of the American party, towards whose members, without a single exception, he has indulged in language which ought not to be tolerated within the precincts of Billingsgate, no epithet is too low, too degrading, or disgraceful, to pay him back in.

Respectfully, &c.,
W. G. BROWNLOW.

Fellow-Citizens:—The occasion which has called you together to-night, is the special appointment of our young friend, Mr. Crowe, to whose eloquence we have all listened with pleasure. I have made no appointment to speak here; nor have I prompted the loud and long calls made upon me, this evening, by this large Nashville audience. I shall speak to you; but not upon the *issues* of the late canvass, nor upon those of the approaching canvass of 1856. I will discuss *Andrew Johnson* and *E. G. Eastman*; and if they are in the assembly, I hope they will come forward and take seats on this stand, that I may have the pleasure of looking them full in the face, as I denounce them in unmeasured terms: which is my purpose to-night, let the consequences be what they may!

On a memorable night in August, after it was understood that *Andrew Johnson* was reëlected to the office of Governor, a procession was formed in Knoxville, composed of the worst materials in that young and growing city—such as drunken, red-mouthed Irishmen, lousy Germans, and insolent negroes, with three or four men of respectable pretensions thrown in, to exercise a controlling influence over these bad materials. This riotous mob halted in front of my dwelling, in East Knoxville, and *groaned* and *sang* for my especial benefit: all which was natural enough—as they had triumphed over me in the election of a Governor. I took no offence at their rejoicing over the election of Gov. Johnson, as I told them; and for the reason, that I knew them to be of that class of men who would *actually need the exercise of the pardoning power*, at the hands of the present Governor, to release them from the penitentiary, before his present term of service would expire!

From my humble dwelling, this *beautiful* procession marched to the Coleman House, on Gay street, yelling like devils, and insulting the inmates of every house they passed. "Huzza for *Andy McJohnson*!" exclaimed one. "Three cheers for *Andy O'Johnson*!" exclaimed another. While, to cap the climax—"Well done, my *Johnsing* and the *White Bastard*," (meaning *Basis*,) exclaimed a drunken negro! Halting in front of the Coleman House, the Governor elect mounted a goods box, and under feelings of great excitement, hatred, and malice, delivered a speech abusive of the whole American party, excepting none, in coarse, bitter language, in a style peculiarly his own—adapted alone to the foul precincts of Billingsgate—rounding his periods with a diabolical and infernal *grin*, alone suited to a display of oratory by a land pirate!

I reported this slanderous speech—not in as offensive style—as it was delivered; for his *looks* and *grins* no man can report on paper. I also wrote the substance of what he said to Major Donelson, in a letter, of which I shall have something more to say before I leave this stand. Just here, I will repeat what the Governor did say, and what I reported him to have said in my paper. I wish this large audience to hear me distinctly, and to recollect the points I make; for I shall wind up on the Governor and his miserable tool, *Eastman*, with a degree of severity you have not been accustomed to, but which shall be warranted by the facts in each case.

Gov. Johnson said this new party of self-styled Americans professed to have organized with a view to purify and reform the old political parties. A beautiful set, said he, to reform! The Order of Know Nothings was composed of the worst men in the Whig and Democratic parties. As a *sample* of these men, he pointed out *Andrew J. Donelson*, by name—exclaiming as often as twice, *Who is Andrew J. Donelson?* He is a soured, office-seeking, disappointed politician, who has been kicked out of the Democratic party. To illustrate his views more fully, he told the crowd to imagine a large gang of *counterfeiters* out there! and an equally large gang of *horse-thieves* out yonder! Take from these two companies the worst men in their ranks, form a third party of these, and you have a representation of this Know Nothing party. This was a beautiful party to propose reform, or to speak of other parties being corrupt! He was interrupted repeatedly; and I think I may safely say, among hands, they gave him the d——d lie fifty times! James M. Davis, a respectable mechanic, asked him if he would say that to Major Donelson's face? He replied, that he heard the hissing of an adder, or a goose, and went through with certain stereotyped phrases you have all heard from his lips. This call upon him by Mr. Davis was not named in my newspaper report, nor in my letter to Major Donelson. Indeed, I did not anticipate a denial of his abuse.

Now, fellow-citizens, it was in this connection, as well as in the most offensive language, that Gov. Johnson introduced the name of Andrew J. Donelson, repeating it more than once, emphasizing upon it, and repeating it with scorn and bitterness. This is the report, *in substance*, I made of his speech through my paper, and in a letter I addressed to Major Donelson. And to the truth of my report, there are one hundred respectable gentlemen in Knoxville who will make oath upon the Holy Bible. There are now a half-dozen respectable gentlemen in this crowd who were in the street at Knoxville on that occasion, and heard every word the Governor said, and will sustain me in my account of it. Among these I will name Messrs. White and Armstrong, members of the House, Senator Rogers, Col. James C. Luttrell, and Mr. Fleming, the editor of the Knoxville Register.

Well, gentlemen—and I am proud to have an opportunity of vindicating myself before so large a Nashville audience as this is—I say Major Donelson came to Nashville, after receiving intelligence of the abuse of the Governor, and was seen walking these streets with a *large and homely stick* in his hand, looking *grum*, as any gentleman would do under the circumstances. The friends of Gov. Johnson seeing what would likely be the result of this affair, asked for, and very properly obtained that letter, with a view to laying it before their slanderous and abusive

Executive officer, that he might *lie out of what he said* about an honorable and brave man; and thereby avoid the disgrace of a cudgelling! Did he lie out of the scrape? He did: aye, he *ingloriously lied out* of what he had said—leaving Major Donelson no ground for any difficulty with him: although the Major had a right to suppose that any man base enough to make such charges, would have no hesitancy in lying out of his disreputable and cowardly abuse. I therefore pronounce your Governor, here upon his own dunghill, an UNMITIGATED LIAR AND CALUMNIATOR, and a VILLAINOUS COWARD, wanting the *nerve* to stand up to his abuse of better men than himself!

But it will be said that the Governor *proves* me a liar, by a citizen of Nashville, who was present at Knoxville and heard his speech. That is so, but I prove both him and his witness liars, by a multitude of witnesses who were also present, and who are gentlemen of the first standing. But who is it that testifies that I have lied? It is *E. G. Eastman*, the editor of the Sag Nicht organ in this city. And who is *E. G. Eastman*? He is a dirty, lying, and unscrupulous Abolitionist, from Massachusetts, who once conducted an Abolitionist paper either in that State, or the State of New Hampshire. He was brought out to this State to lie for the unscrupulous leaders of his party. He is paid for *telling* and *writing* falsehoods, and would, if the interests of his party required it, and a consideration were paid him in hand, *swear lies* as readily as he would write them down for publication. He is a poor devil, as void of truth and honor as he has shown himself to be of courage and resentment. He edits a low, dirty, scurrilous sheet; and, like his master, Gov. Johnson, never could elevate himself above the level of a common blackguard. No epithet is too low, too degrading, or disgraceful to be applied to the members of the American party, by either of these Billingsgate graduates. Decent men shun coming in contact with either of them, as they would avoid a night-cart, or other vehicle of filth. As some fish thrive only in dirty water, so the Nashville Union and American would not exist a week out of the atmosphere of slang and vituperation. A fit organ, this, for all who arrange themselves under the dark piratical flag of Andrew Johnson and his progressive Democracy. I am the more specific in reference to *Eastman*, because I understand he is in this assembly!

But, fellow-citizens, I am not yet through with this Knoxville speech of the Governor. Maj. Donelson visited Knoxville, one month after this slanderous speech was made against him; he visited there upon the invitation of the American party, to address a Mass Meeting. I waited upon Maj. Donelson, upon his arrival, and found him at the house of Doct. Curry. I told the Major that I was tired of having questions of veracity between me and Governors and Ex-Governors of Tennessee, and that I desired that others should state to him what had been said by the Governor. Accordingly, different gentlemen, citizens of character, informed him that they were in the crowd and heard Johnson, and that he did say all that was attributed to him, both in the letter he had received from me, and in the two Knoxville papers. Consequently, when Maj. Donelson made his speech next day, he denounced the Governor as a miserable calumniator, and refuted his villainous charges, in a manner becoming the occasion, and with a frankness which carried with it a conviction of its truth, and gave satisfaction to his numerous friends.

And now, gentlemen, I take occasion to state, that there is no longer an adjourned question of veracity between me and Johnson and Eastman. The issue is between Johnson and Eastman, on the one hand, and various respectable gentlemen of Knoxville, on the other hand. Either the Governor and his man Friday have basely lied, or a number of the citizens of Knoxville and vicinity, have testified to what is false. I assert, once more, that the Governor and his dirty Editor have lied out of the villainous abuse the former heaped upon better men than himself. And if their friends are willing to see them remain under the charge, the American party are satisfied with the settlement of the question.

Fellow-citizens, while I am on the stand, I will notice some other points personal to myself. And before I enter upon these, I will call your attention to the wholesale abuse of the Governor, of some thirty-five or forty thousand voters in Tennessee. In his Murfreesboro' speech, he asserted that *"the Devil, his Satanic Majesty, presides over all the secret conclaves"* held by the Know Nothings, and that *"they are the allies of the Prince of Darkness."* I quote from his printed speeches from memory, but it will be found that I quote correctly. In that same speech, he asserts that all Know Nothings are *"bound by terrible oaths to fix and carry a lie in their mouths!"* In his Manchester speech, I believe it was, he called all members of the new party *"Hyenas,"* and *"huge reptiles, upon whose neck the feet of all honest men ought to be placed."* And in this same speech he says he "WOULD AS SOON BE FOUND IN A CLAN OF JOHN A. MURRELL'S MEN, AS IN A KNOW NOTHING COUNCIL!"

What an imputation upon nearly one half of the legal voters of Tennessee! He has used the most odious terms his *limited* knowledge of the English language would enable him to employ, to deride, defame, insult, and blackguard every man who has joined the new party, or dares to act with them in politics. In the plenitude of his bitter and supercilious arrogance, Andrew Johnson has indulged in language against the entire American party, which would not be tolerated within the precincts of Billingsgate, or the lowest fish-market in London. And from Johnson to Shelby counties, during the entire summer, this low-flung and ill-bred scoundrel, pursued this same strain of vulgar and disgusting abuse. And whether speaking of the most enlightened statesman, the purest patriot, or the most pious clergyman, he pursued the same strain of abuse. With him, a vile demagogue, whose daily employment is to administer to the very worst appetites of mankind, no virtue, no honor, no truth, exists anywhere, but in the breasts of such as are either corrupt enough or fool enough to follow him, and a few malignant falsifiers who worship at his shrine. He is a wretched and vile caterer to the morbid foreign and Catholic appetite of this country. "It is a dirty bird that fouls its own nest," says the proverb; and it applies to this man Johnson with as much force as to the dirtiest of the feathered tribe.

> "Where is the wretch, so lost, so dead,
> Who never to himself hath said,
> This is my *own*, MY NATIVE LAND!"

He now disgraces the Executive Chair of this gallant State. Most of God's creatures, human and brute, have an attachment to "HOME, SWEET HOME;" but here is a contemptible and selfish demagogue who discards all such feelings, and would transfer his country and home to strangers and outlaws, to European paupers and criminals, if he could thereby receive a temporary election, or receive a pocket-full of money. For such a wretch I have no sympathy, and no feelings but those of scorn and contempt, and hence it is that I speak of him in such terms.

On every stump in Tennessee, he held me up as "the High Priest of the Order," representing Col. Gentry as *my* candidate. Since I came to Middle Tennessee, I have been informed that he pointed to the fancied fact that I was the head of the Order, as an evidence of *its utter want of respectability*. Turning up his nose, and grinning significantly, he would inquire, *Who is William G. Brownlow?*

Now, gentlemen, since he makes this issue of *respectability* with me, I will accept it. Since he throws down the glove, I will take it up, and I will show you that he is the last man on God's green earth to call in question the respectability of other men, or their families! It would be both cruel and unbecoming in me to speak of what the dishonest and villainous relatives of Gov. Johnson have done, if he conducted himself prudently, and did not abuse others with such great profusion. I am not aware of any relative of mine ever having been hung, sent to the penitentiary, or being placed in the stocks. I have no doubt that persons related to me, directly or remotely, have deserved such a fate long since. There is not a man in this vast assembly who can say, and tell the truth, that he has no mean kin. Can Gov. Johnson say so? Rather, can he say he has any other kind? He is a member of a numerous family of Johnsons, in North Carolina, who are generally THIEVES and LIARS; and though he is the best one of the family I have ever met with, I unhesitatingly affirm, to-night, that there are better men than Andrew Johnson in our Penitentiary! His relatives in the Old North State, have stood in the Stocks for crimes they have committed. And his *own born cousin*, Madison Johnson, was hung in Raleigh, for murder and robbery! I told him of this years ago, in Jonesboro', and he denied it, and put me to the trouble of procuring the testimony of Gov. John M. Morehead to prove it! The Governor was petitioned to pardon Madison Johnson, and declined, as he knew he suffered justly. This explains why this *scape-gallows* has been so bitter against Whig and Know Nothing Governors. They have been so unfeeling, as to suffer his dear relatives to *pull hemp without foothold*, when a jury of twelve honest men have said that they deserved death! Is he not one of the last men living to talk about a want of respectability on the part of any one? Certainly he is!

Well, gentlemen, Johnson is again the Governor of Tennessee; but if he could be mortified, he would have the mortification to know that he is the Governor with a majority of the *legal native votes of the State* cast in opposition to him. We all committed one capital blunder in the late canvass, and that alone defeated Gentry, and elected Johnson. We copied from the Book of Pardons a list of FORTY-SEVEN names of culprits pardoned out of our State Prison by Johnson—some for negro-stealing, some for counterfeiting, house-breaking, rape, and other *Democratic* measures—more pardons than all his "illustrious predecessors" ever granted. In copying this list, we said to the voters of the State that Johnson had spoken his honest sentiments when he said he preferred being among a clan of Murrell men, to being found in a Know Nothing Council; and in the same breath we assured them that if Gentry was elected, he would let all such rascals stay in prison as long as the courts of the country decreed they should. And while thousands of honorable, high-minded men voted for Johnson, under the lash of party, or because they were blinded by his glaring demerits, it is not to be disguised that all the *petit larceny* and *Penitentiary men* in the State voted for him. There never was a time in Tennessee when there were not five thousand voters who either *had been stealing*, or *intended to steal!* These would naturally look to where they would find a friend, in the event of their being overtaken by justice. In the person of Andrew Johnson, they felt assured of "a friend indeed, because a friend in *need.*" He had publicly told them that he preferred the company of Murrell men to the society of the most respectable lawyers, doctors, preachers, farmers, and mechanics in the State, who met in certain councils. The fact of his turning so many Murrell men out of the State Prison, and of his having been *raised up in such society*, left no doubt of the sincerity of his profession!

In conclusion, fellow-citizens, if Gov. Johnson cannot lawfully canvass the State a *third* time for the office he now fills, I hope the Legislature will legalize such a race by a special act, and I propose to be the candidate against him. I will show the people of the State in his presence, from the same stand, who are Murrell men, and who are not able to look honest men in the face!

If I have said any thing to-night offensive to your Governor, or any of his friends or understrappers in this city, they know where to find me. When I am not on the streets, I can be found at No. 43, on the lower floor of Sam Scott's City Hotel, opposite the ladies' parlor. I shall remain here for the next ten days only, and whatever punishment any one may wish to inflict upon me, it must be done in that time. I say this, not because I seek a difficulty, but because I don't intend it shall be said that I made this speech and took to flight!

I thank you, gentlemen, for the patience with which you have heard me in a matter personal to myself, and I hope you are prepared to acquit me of lying in the Donelson case, although Gov. Johnson and Editor Eastman bear testimony against me. I thank you, and now bid you good night!

We beg leave to add, that in March, 1842, Andrew Johnson laid hold of us in a speech in Blountville, when we were in Jonesborough, distant twenty miles. He held up a picture or drawing of us, and accompanied it with many abusive remarks. In turn, we held him up in the Whig of the 29th of the same month, and gave his *pedigree* in full, and with it a *representation of his cousin Madison Johnson, under the gallows* in Raleigh!

The first Monday in April following, Johnson spoke in Jonesborough, and denied *most solemnly that he ever had a relative by the name of Madison Johnson—denied that a man of that name had ever been hung in Raleigh—and asserted that the man hung there in 1841 was by the name of Scott—a nephew, he said, of General Winfield Scott!* This bold denial, made in the presence of a large and anxious crowd, overwhelmed us *for the time being*, as Johnson was raised in the vicinity of Raleigh, and had learned his trade there. He was supposed to know, and for the moment we were branded with falsehood. To aid him in his war upon us, the *"Jonesborough Sentinel,"*

Johnson's organ, came out upon us, and noticed his denial of our charge and his speech, in an article of which the following is an extract:

"Brownlow said, some time back, that Col. Johnson had a cousin hung in North Carolina. The Colonel developed the fact the day he used up or skinned Brownlow alive in Jonesborough, *that instead of its being his cousin, it was the nephew of Gen. Winfield Scott*, now a *quasi* Coon candidate for the Presidency. Brownlow *is so silent!*"

After this, the Sentinel noticed us again, and this notice drew out WESTON R. GALES, the then editor of the Raleigh Register, in the following:

EDITORIAL COMPLIMENTS.

"We find the following editorial in the 'Jonesboro' (Tenn.) Sentinel,' a Locofoco print, in relation to the editor of the 'Jonesboro Whig:'

"BROWNLOW made an awkward attempt last week to caricature a person who was hung some years ago in North Carolina, whom he termed the cousin of Col. JOHNSON. But it turns out to have been the nephew of Gen. WINFIELD SCOTT, a distinguished Coon leader. Poor BROWNLOW!—it ought to be his time next. Wonder how many hen-roosts he robbed last summer?"

"We have nothing to do with whose time it is to be hung next, nor with the number of hen-roosts robbed, nor by whom robbed, but we will take occasion to correct the 'Sentinel' as to the person hung here 'some years ago.'

"In the spring of 1841, a man named MADISON JOHNSON was hung in this place for the murder of HENRY BEASLEY, but we were not aware that he was any relation of Col. JOHNSON, if it be meant thereby Col. R. M. JOHNSON, of Kentucky. He was, however, connected with A. JOHNSON, the candidate for Congress in the Jonesboro' District, MADISON and he being first cousins.

"The last man hung in this place by the name of SCOTT, was MASON SCOTT, in 1820, and if the 'Sentinel' means to reflect upon the Whig party by saying he was a nephew of Gen. WINFIELD SCOTT, a 'distinguished Coon leader,' we are willing for him to indulge in such misstatements.

"IF THE 'SENTINEL' HAD TAKEN THE TROUBLE TO CONSULT MR. A. JOHNSON ON THE SUBJECT, HE WOULD HAVE SATISFIED HIM OF THE FACTS, AS HE WAS IN THIS CITY ABOUT THE TIME MADISON WAS EXECUTED."

It will be seen, that while Johnson was uttering his *solemn but false denial* at Jonesborough, he *knew he was lying*, for he was in Raleigh *"about the time Madison was executed!"*

But we told our friends to hold on, to have patience, and to give us time, and we would make good our charge. Accordingly, in the same issue in which we brought out this extract from the Raleigh Register, we published the following letter from Gov. MOREHEAD, in answer to one we had written him:

RALEIGH, 24th April, 1843.
[EXECUTIVE OFFICE.]

"DEAR SIR—I have the honor to acknowledge the receipt of yours of the 14th inst., requesting me to inform you what was the name of the man hung in Raleigh in the spring of 1841.

"His name was MADISON JOHNSON. His case was taken to the Supreme Court, and you will find it reported, December Term, 1840, vol. 1st, page 354, Iredell's Reports.

"He was hung for the murder of Henry Beasley. A strong effort was made to procure a pardon for him; but believing his case a clear murder, I refused to grant it.

"The only man named Scott that was ever convicted of murder at this place, was Mason Scott, in 1820.

"You will find his case reported in the reports of the Supreme Court, January Term, 1820, 1st Stark's Reports, page 24.

"I am not aware that any other man named Scott was ever convicted of a capital offence in this county.

"I have the honor to be
"Your most ob't serv't,
"J. M. MOREHEAD."

"Rev. W. G. BROWNLOW."

In conclusion, after this letter appeared, and Johnson was elected, he sent an appointment to Raleigh, for a speech—attended there, and blackguarded and vilified "Morehead and Brownlow" for two hours. He made the *letter* of Morehead the pretext for his abuse, but the real cause was the Governor's refusal to *pardon his cousin.* Johnson was there to procure his pardon, and brought every appliance to bear within his power, but the North Carolina Governor was inflexible in the discharge of his sworn duty! We do not make the point against Johnson that he has *mean kin,* only so far as it may *offset* his abuse of others, for who of us are without mean kinsfolks? But our point is, his *deliberate lying* before a Jonesboro' audience!

GOVERNOR JOHNSON'S THANKSGIVING DAY.

From the Knoxville Whig of Dec. 1, 1855.

As the sixth of the present month has been set apart by our Governor, to be observed as a day of prayer and thanksgiving to Almighty God for his numerous and unmerited mercies conferred upon the people of our State and nation; and as it is desirable that the different sects shall act in concert on the occasion, and at least pray "with the understanding," that is to say, *appropriately*, we have been at the trouble to prepare a form of prayer for the occasion. This we do in no irreverend spirit, but in all candor and sincerity, after this wise:

ALMIGHTY and everlasting God, in whom we live, and move, and have our being: we, thy needy creatures, render thee our humble praises, for thy preservation of us from the beginning of our lives to this day of public thanksgiving, and especially for having delivered us from all the dangers and afflictions of the year about to close. By thy knowledge, most gracious God, the depths were broken up during the past seed-time and harvest, and the rains descended: while by night the clouds distilled the gentle dew, filling our barns with plenty: thus crowning the year with thy goodness, in the increase of the ground, and the gathering in of the fruits thereof. And we beseech thee, O most merciful Father, give us a just sense of this great mercy: such as may appear in our lives, by an humble, holy, and obedient walking before thee all our days!

To thy watchful providence, O most merciful God, we are indebted for all our mercies, and not any works or merit of ours; for many of us entered into the scramble to elevate to the Executive Chair of the State the present incumbent, with a perfect knowledge that he had abused thy Son, JESUS CHRIST, our Lord, on the floor of our State Senate, as a swindler, advocating unlawful interest: we knew that he had voted in Congress against offering prayers to thee: we knew that he had opposed the temperance cause, which is the cause of God and of all mankind: we knew that he had vilified the Protestant religion, and slandered the Protestant clergy, defending and eulogizing the corruptions of the Roman Catholic Church, throughout the length and breadth of our State; yet such was the force of party ties, O most mighty God, that we went into the support of our INFIDEL GOVERNOR blind, and, by our zeal in his behalf, gave the lie to our professions of piety, rendered ourselves hateful in the eyes of all honest and consistent men, meriting a degree of punishment we have never received! We do most heartily repent, O merciful God, for these shameful sins: we humble ourselves in lowest depths of humility, and ask forgiveness of a God whom we have justly provoked to anger, and the forgiveness of our insulted brethren, whom we have wickedly blackguarded, to the great injury of the cause of Christ!

O most merciful God, who art of purer eyes than to behold iniquity, turn not a deaf ear to our supplications on this day, because the day has been set apart by a Governor who really does not subscribe to the Christian religion; does not attend Divine service; who swears profanely; and has insulted Heaven and outraged the feelings of all pious Christians, by teaching the blasphemous sentiment that Christianity is of no higher or holier origin than his Democracy! Have mercy, our Father and God, upon that portion of this congregation who have endeavored to find peace to their souls by travelling along the "converging lines" of a spurious Democracy, in search of the foot of "Jacob's Ladder," and give them repentance and better minds! And do thou, O God of pity, show all such, that instead of ascending to heaven on an imaginary "Ladder," they are chained fast to the Locomotive of Hell, with the Devil for their Chief Engineer, the Pope of Rome as Conductor, and an ungodly Governor as Breakman; and that, at more than railroad speed, they are driving on to where they are to be eternally punished by Him whom thou hast appointed the Judge of quick and dead, thy Son JESUS CHRIST, our Lord. Amen!

THE FOREIGN SPIRIT ILLUSTRATED.

From the Knoxville Whig of May 24, 1856.

The following correspondence will explain itself, whilst it will serve to show the spirit which governs this Bogus Foreign Catholic Democracy:

RICHMOND, April 21, 1856.

REV. AND DEAR SIR:—It cannot be unkind in me, though personally unknown to you, to address you on a subject in which our peace as citizens is alike concerned. I see in the Fincastle Democrat of 18th inst. what purports to be a review of an article of yours in the Knoxville Whig of 5th inst., in which I suppose, from the remarks contained in the Democrat, I have been very, *very* severely handled by you, for an offence I never committed. You will allow me to say, sir, that I have no recollection of ever writing or speaking a disrespectful word of you in all my life, but, on the contrary, have frequently spoken approvingly of much you have written. Such being the fact, you will not be surprised to learn how deeply I regret that the purest innocence on my part has failed to be a protection against personal abuse. That you have been misled by some person, is to my mind very plain, and if, through the influence of another, you have inflicted a wound upon one that never harmed you, nor ever designed to harm you, is it not within the range of a generous nature—of an honest man—to repair the injury by at once giving up to the injured party the name of the deceiver, or publish him to the world as authority for the assault, and let him assume its responsibilities?

In a change of circumstances, I should feel bound, by the honor of a man, to do that much, and in my present relation to the case I ask nothing more. It is perhaps due to you to be informed, that I have not seen your article, nor do I know a word it contains, and it is due to myself to say that I knew nothing of the article in the Democrat assailing you, till I saw it in print some hundred of miles from home, where I have not yet arrived after an absence of nearly two months. On the subject of dues, I may add that it is due to the public that the name of the deceiver be given them. I of course suppose him to be a man of great personal courage, ready to assume all his own responsibilities. In conclusion, permit me to say, that any effort on your part to aid in concealing the hand that uses the dagger in the dark, will detract largely from the estimate I have placed upon your character, as a man without hesitation or fear, when the claims of justice are presented. My address is Fincastle, Botetourt Co., Va., and I am very respectfully,

S. D. HOPKINS.

Knoxville, May 21st, 1856.

Rev. S. D. Hopkins:

Sir—Through the weakness, mismanagement, and culpable remissness of the contemptible Jesuit now at the head of the Post Office Department, and his numerous lackeys—all of whom you sustain in their politics—a letter written by you one month ago was received a few days since, while I was absent at a Know Nothing Convention, aiding my political brethren in placing before the people of this Congressional District an electoral candidate, to aid in the great Christian and patriotic work of overthrowing the corrupt, profligate, unprincipled, Foreign Catholic Bogus Democratic party, of which *you* are a member, and in the service of which you are an editor! But my delay in replying to your letter shall be atoned for in the *length* and *plainness* of my reply.

It is true, sir, that I published an editorial in my paper, of some severity against you; but the article was in *reply* to a low, cowardly, and abusive editorial against me in the "Fincastle Democrat," of which you are the editor. And "you will allow me to say, sir," that at the time this attack was made upon me in *your* paper, I never had said a word about you or your paper in my life, either "good, bad, or indifferent;" and "if through the influence of another you have inflicted a wound upon one that never harmed you, is it not within the range of a generous nature—of an honest man"—to repair the injury by taking back the article, and apologizing through the same medium for the injury? If, however, you believe you have not "been misled by some person," and have done me no more than justice in that abusive article, hold on to it. Having made oath that the horse is *fifteen feet high*, allow of no correction!

In all frankness, you must permit me to say, that I believe you expected to find in the office on your return to Fincastle, a letter from me demanding your authority for admitting into your paper such an article against me, who, as you very well knew, up to that hour had never said one word, publicly or privately, against you or your paper. I think you concluded to *take the start of me*, and thus to *forestall* me, by writing from Richmond some twenty-four hours before you would arrive at home!

In your paper of the 18th of April, issued only three days before this letter was written at Richmond, an editorial of half a column appears, in which *your* paper styles me a "notorious blackguard"—a "bullying blackguard"—an "unwanted and lying man"—who "is mean enough to lie, cheat, or even steal"—a man "wearing the garb of righteousness to serve the Devil in;" and in the same article, the case of a Locofoco editor, who was involved in a shooting scrape on account of his attack upon a lady, is actually attributed to me! Although you are a Reverend Methodist Preacher, and a grave and dignified Steam Doctor, conducting one of the organs of the Foreign and Anti-American party in Virginia, you must pardon me for saying, as I now do, that in calling upon me for my authority for what I had said in reply to the unmitigated abuse of *your* paper, you have proven to my mind, that if you do not possess the cool and collected impudence of the *Devil*, you are at least possessed of the lion-headed impudence of an unprincipled Sag Nicht partisan, hired to do the dirty work of an equally unprincipled and dirty organization!

But it is due to the history of this controversy that I should say, this second attack upon me sets forth that you are from home, and that "the *Junior* is responsible for the article." This might be credited, if, on your return home, you had protested against such abuse, but it seems from your silence to have met with your heart's approval, and gave "general satisfaction," at least to *you*! It is true that you were absent at the time of both these publications, but it does not follow, as a matter of course, that you were not the veritable author, and that they did not find their way to the "Democrat" office at the same time and in the same way that your "Baltimore Correspondence" got there. The "Junior," as he styles himself, claims the fraternity; and were it not that he is too well known in Fincastle for any sane man to believe that *he* wrote the articles, he might have the credit (if credit there be attached to it) of so low, malicious, and lying articles. But he is known in Fincastle to be a brainless man, and to be incapable of writing a paragraph on any subject. He is known to have no use of language, and to be incapable of applying epithets to any one. So that, if *you* did not write these articles, they were manufactured at "Irish Corner," in Fincastle, your "Junior" not being able to do it, for the reason that he is wholly incapable. My opinion is, that the articles were manufactured by the "Great Mogul" of the Anti-American party in your town, and if he will only avow himself the author, I will make some disclosures upon him that will make him wish himself back in "Swate Ireland," where he "lives, and moves, and has his being;" no disclosures are necessary—his books, and his person, damn him to everlasting infamy. He has the filthiest-looking mouth, and the most offensive breath, of any man in the Valley of Virginia. No man who knows him will meet him square on the pavement, or place himself in a position, if it can be avoided, of meeting a breeze from that great reservoir of all nastiness, his mouth! It is really a wonder how any human being can LIVE, and emit all the time a stream of such overwhelming and uninterrupted STENCH! You must permit me to christen this man as the But-Cut of Original Sin, and the Upper-crust of all Nastiness!

It may not set well upon your stomach, that being a "Minister of the Gospel, and having the care of souls," I should seem not to place implicit confidence in your denial of any participation in this unprovoked war upon me. I will be candid with you, and though it is possible for me to be mistaken in my views, still, if I am, I am honestly deceived. I have no confidence in the moral honesty and Christian integrity of any Protestant Preacher, of any denomination, in this country, who openly arrays himself against the American party, and takes the side of the Catholics, Foreigners, and self-styled Democrats associated with them. Nor will I hear one such preach or pray, if I know him to be such, and can get out of his hearing. The growing light and improvements of this age forbid that an intelligent and pious man and minister should identify himself with that party. And the fiery genius, corrupting tendencies, and uncompromising intolerance of that party, are rapidly driving good and true men out of the party.

There never was a time since the division of parties in this country, when I had so little confidence in what is called the Democratic party as at present; and as at present organized and constituted, I believe it to be the most corrupt organization. It is made up of the odds and ends of all factions and parties on the continent, and is one of the most anomalous combinations of fanaticism, idolatry, prostitution, crime, and absurdities conceivable! The *isms* composing the party of which you are a member, are: Abolitionism; Free-soilism; Agrarianism; Fourieritism; Millerism; Radicalism; Woman's Rightsism; Mobism; Mormonism; Spiritualism; Locofocoism; Higher-Lawism; Foreign Pauperism; Anti-Americanism; Roman Catholicism; Deism, and modern Sag Nichtism! All this tide of fanaticism and error, originating North of Mason and Dixon's Line, went for Pierce in the last Presidential contest: they are with that party now, against the American party; and it is bad company in which to find a Protestant minister! Yet, miserable Protestants hesitate not to commend these enemies of the natural rights of man, and of the Christian religion, as being just as good Christians as their neighbors!

> "Oh! judgment, thou hast fled to brutish beasts;
> And men have not their reason!"

But, Doctor, why were you at Baltimore? Why, sir, during the past year, you and other conscientious Methodists took it into your heads to arraign a young man who was travelling your circuit, Mr. Hall, and, for the Church's good, to have him expelled, whose great sin was that he was a *Know-Nothing*, or sympathized with the Order! The authorities of the Church, after a patient hearing of the whole case, pro and con, acquitted the young man. You followed him up to the Annual Conference, as the representative of and attorney for Sag Nichtism. The Conference acquitted the young preacher again, and sent him to an enlightened circuit in Maryland. This so offended you, and your patriotic, not to say *pious* associates, that, for the Church's good, they resigned their stewardship in the Church, and were so offended at the course of the Presiding Elder, *Rev. M. Goheen*, than whom there is not a more modest, unassuming, conservative Christian gentleman in the Valley of Virginia, that, at a recent Quarterly Meeting there, they refused to attend church, or to hear him preach. This is just the spirit that actuates your party, everywhere.

You demand of me the name or names of such person or persons as have given me information in reference to you. Reconsider this demand, if you please, and ask yourself if, under all the circumstances, it is not a cool piece of impudence. I have published nothing about you upon the authority of others, but upon my own authority and responsibility. You *suspect* some of your neighbors for writing to me, and hence you make this demand. It is true, I have friends in Fincastle, and some of these write to me, and when I publish any thing about you, or any one of your associates, and give these friends of mine as authority, I will give you their names, if called upon to do so; or I will assume the responsibility myself. What I have said in reply to the wicked, slanderous, and cowardly assault upon me, in the dirty paper controlled by you, I have said upon my own responsibilities, as a man, and as a member of the same Church to which you belong; and whether my "peace as a citizen" is preserved or destroyed, I am not the man to be intimidated or driven from my position. My failure to give you the names of any citizens of your vicinity, who may have written me private letters, relating to your war upon young Hall, the Circuit Preacher, "will detract largely from the estimate you have placed upon my character." This I am sorry to hear, as I do not wish to fall below the "estimate" placed upon my character in the two issues of your paper, now before me! This would be reaching "a lower deep," as the poet classically styles it!

Now, sir, I have a letter from a town in Virginia, not far distant from Fincastle, written by a gentleman of as "great personal courage" as you or myself, who states, that a gentleman who was present at the trial of Rev. Mr. Hall, heard you make the assertion, on that occasion, that you alone were responsible for all the editorials that appeared in the "Democrat," and that the "Junior" partner was not! If you think proper to make an issue with this gentleman, you can have his name!

I am, Dr. Hopkins, your humble servant,

W. G. Brownlow,
Editor of the Knoxville Whig.

TO STEPHEN TRIBBLE.

From the Knoxville Whig.

Villainous Sir:—Letters from my friends in the West inform me that you are making a full team in the service of the Devil, Locofocoism, and crime, in portions of Missouri and Kentucky! You have recently held forth in Charleston, a pleasant post-village, the capital of Mississippi county, Missouri, about six miles southwest of the "Father of Waters!" In that town you undertook to inform the good people, the Circuit Judge being present, *who I am*, and to demonstrate that I am not entitled to credit in any thing I say! You claimed to have once lived in East Tennessee—to know the people and the country—and to have known William T. Senter and James Y. Crawford, two other Methodist preachers, whose *pedigrees* you pretend to give!

Mr. Senter was an able man—a moral and upright man—and a Whig Representative in Congress, from the District you represented *in the jail of Sullivan county*, for a long time previous to your being *branded in the hand and on the cheeks*, for MANSLAUGHTER, the particulars of which I will remind you of before I close this familiar letter! Mr. Senter could have gone to Congress longer, but voluntarily retired. Mr. Crawford was a brother-in-law to Mr. Senter, and was a preacher of respectable talents, and in good standing in his Church. They are both in their graves, beyond the reach of your malice, where the sound of your infamous voice, and the words of your lying tongue, can never penetrate their ears! But I am still above ground, daily kicking, and making war upon the Locofoco Paupers and Foreign Catholics, as well as Native Traitors, with whom you are associated, and with whom you act in politics. I acknowledge myself to be game for you to hunt down!

You are now a *Campbellite preacher* as well as a *Sag Nicht Missionary*; and the garb of religion you wear, gives a degree of weight to your falsehoods and slanders, among strangers, that they otherwise would not have. The idea of *"Stev Tribble,"* who ingloriously fled from this country for crimes he could not meet in open court, being a preacher, and itinerating through the West, "in search of the lost sheep of the house of Israel," is so ridiculous, as scarcely to be believed at all, although there is no doubt but what he has been regularly installed in Kentucky, and now has the "care of souls."

Why, you unmitigated old villain, your whole career, from your "youth up," has been one of crime and revolting blackguardism. While a boy and a young man, where Hoss's school was taught in Washington county, your vulgar conversation, immoral practices, indecent habits, and blackguardism, disgusted the entire neighborhood, and rendered you so odious that no decent family would board you! All the waters of the far-famed *Jordan*, in the palmiest days of that bold stream, were not sufficient to wash your sins away! If the Lord Bishop of London were to *immerse* you as often as "seventy times seven," in the waters of "bold Jordan," and in the name of the holy Trinity, you would still remain what you were when you fled from this country to avoid the extreme penalty of the law—one of the greatest scoundrels for whom Christ died!

Yourself and half-brother *Havron* were confined in Blountville Jail, for the murder of *William Humphreys*, a promising young man, whom you brutally assaulted and murdered in open daylight in the streets of Kingsport, in Sullivan county, and without provocation! *You* were tried and convicted of *manslaughter*, and branded in the *hand* and on the *cheek*. After being branded, you *bit the letters out of your hand*, and *clawed them out of your face*, but the *scars* are to be seen in both. Indeed, I have been written to, to know why these scars are on your face! I take this method of answering those inquiries; and publishing them in my "Whig," which has a circulation of 5,000, and our "Campaigner," which circulates 7,000 copies, I shall be able to introduce you to as many persons as may have heard you preach my funeral.

While in the Blountville Jail, with your half-brother, Havron, whose blow killed Humphreys, after you had weakened him, you caught hold of the jailor, Montgomery Irvin, and held him in a scuffle, when he entered the room with your dinner, until Havron made his escape. Havron would have pulled hemp, had he not escaped; and had our penitentiary system existed at that time, you would have been sentenced for life! But you would not have remained there longer than the past summer, as we have a Governor who pardons out all such men, and has more sympathies for them than any other Executive Officer in the nation. You have a half-brother who is a Sag Nicht member of our Legislature, and a great friend and supporter of our Governor and his foreign associates, and he could have turned you out and procured for you an office if you had remained. But then you followed the teachings of "the spirit" of Sag Nichtism, in leaving between two days, and emigrating to Kentucky, as many precious souls would never have "heard the word," or had their sin washed away, but for you!

In an unmentionable and disgraceful enterprise, you became possessed of a *broken leg*, and were mean enough to abscond without paying the bill of your physician, Dr. Patton, whose unremitting attention saved you from your grave, and from the clutches of the Devil, sooner than the old fellow was prepared for your reception! If you had the honor of a first class thief, you would pay this medical bill out of the proceeds of the first public collection you take up, either in Missouri or Kentucky. And if you suffer it to go unpaid until your infinitely infernal career is wound up, the Day of Judgment will disclose the manner of your breaking your leg! If I were you, I would sooner pay this bill now, than to be asked in the great day how my leg was broken!

Disgraced as you are, unprincipled and villainous, you have gone into Kentucky, taken upon yourself "holy orders," and married a wife, imposing most shamefully upon the family into which you married. The woman you have thus imposed upon, would be justifiable now, in the eyes of both God and man, in forsaking you and applying for a divorce. And no court or jury would refuse her application, when made acquainted with your character.

It is a remarkable fact—one that I desire to call, not so much to your notice, as to the notice of the public generally—that while all the members of this Foreign Democratic party are by no means villains, destitute of principle; yet, all the assassins, cut-throats, thieves, and hypocrites in the country have crowded into the ranks of that party! Fawned upon, fostered and pampered by the villainous leaders, demagogues, and tricksters of the party, who need the services of all such scavengers, you are encouraged to act with them. These leaders, who are really no better than you are, *generously* admit you to a fellowship, and *courteously* acknowledge all such abandoned rascals to be their equals! Such men, to a great extent, now constitute the free-democracy of the country—they desecrate the ballot-box—disgust decent men wherever they come in contact with them—blaspheme the name of God—and swear that they will either rule or ruin the country!

But, Sir, it was said of a certain man in the Scriptures, that he was a "sinner above all the sinners that dwell in Jerusalem." So it may in perfect truth be said of you, that you are a scoundrel above all the scoundrels in the hateful ranks of Sag Nichtism. You deserve, for your depraved course of life, a greater punishment than you have received or are likely to receive in this life. The guilt of foul calumny, of the most black and odious kind, attaches to every sentence uttered by your lying tongue. Guilt, the offspring of fiend-like malice, shamefully false, deeply corrupt, and badly matured: perfidy, dishonesty, and rank poison—hot incense of murder, theft, inhuman spoliation, and deep, dark forebodings of damnation have been rooted and grounded in your heart, for lo! these many years! Dark despair, endless death, inexpressible misery, manifold, and worse than death, follow in the ghastly train of your crimes, and riot in your corrupt bosom, as with infernal drunkenness of delight! The record of your deep depravity, of your utter want of principle, and of your ten thousand villainous exploits, is *stereotyped* upon the burning sands of eternity, and stamped on the imperishable walls of the *rotunda* of the Devil's Hell, to which you are driving at railroad speed! In upper East Tennessee, where you are known, it would disgrace an *Algerine Bandit* to sit and hear you pretend to preach! *You* pretend to preach Christ and him crucified, and *immerse* persons in the name of the Trinity! Shrouded in the *sackcloth and ashes* of disgrace, enclosed in a *vault* filled to the brim with *buried and putrefied venality*, and steeped to the very nose and chin in crime, how dare you attempt to preach!

I repeat, you vile slanderer of the living and the dead, that, in justice to the cause of God and of civilization, I will keep spread the unfurled banner of your infamy on every breeze, and cause it to float in the atmosphere of every State in this Union, until your very *name* becomes a mockery and a by-word! And I call upon the people of Kentucky and Missouri to ring the loud knell of your infamy, from steep to steep, and from valley to valley, until their swelling sounds are heard in startling echoes, mingling with the rush of the criminal's torrent, and the mighty cataract's earthquake-voice!

W. G. Brownlow,
Editor of the Knoxville Whig.

June 7th, 1856.

AN EXPOSE OF ROMAN CATHOLICISM.

The following articles, setting forth the DESIGNS and TENDENCY of Romanism in the United States, appeared in the "KNOXVILLE WHIG" of May and June, 1856, and will speak for themselves. The writer has opposed the Papal Hierarchy for twenty years; and in a series of articles, now filed in a number of the "JONESBOROUGH WHIG," published *sixteen years ago,* he *predicted* that the very state of things we are now realizing would come upon us as soon as the year 1860, and that the party calling itself by the revered name of *Democrat,* would identify itself with political Romanism!

THE CATHOLIC QUESTION.—NO. I.

The American Party and the Religious Test—The Louisiana Delegation and the Gallican Catholics—The vote of the Philadelphia Convention to admit the Louisiana Delegates—The American Councils in Louisiana—Catholics proper cannot be true citizens of a Republic.

It is sometimes said by the Anties, that the American party, at their late Philadelphia Convention, dismissed the Catholic Question from their platform, and that they admitted into their Council a Catholic Delegation from Louisiana. We were in that Convention, from the hour of its opening until its final close, and we deny both statements. The fifth and tenth sections of the platform adopted at Philadelphia, and for which we voted, are in the following words, and they express all our platform says upon that subject:

5th. No person should be selected for political station, (whether of native or foreign birth,) who recognizes any allegiance or obligation of any description to any foreign prince, potentate, or power, or who refuses to recognize the Federal and State Constitutions (each within its sphere) as paramount to all other laws, as rules of political action.

10th. Opposition to any union between Church and State; no interference with religious faith or worship, and no tests oaths for office.

The American party was against political Romanism—against all who acknowledge any allegiance to a foreign Prince, Potentate, or Power; or who acknowledge any authority on earth, higher and more binding than the Constitutions of our States, and General Government. And those who are familiar with the temporal assumptions of Popery, and the political intrigues of the Order of Jesuits, can have no other feelings than those of disgust, upon hearing the Locofoco demagogues of the country cry out against the American party for their opposition to the poor Catholics! Against Popes confined to *Rome*, we make no war; but against Popes usurping civil and spiritual authority, in America, we protest most solemnly, and intend to make war, unrelenting and unceasing war!

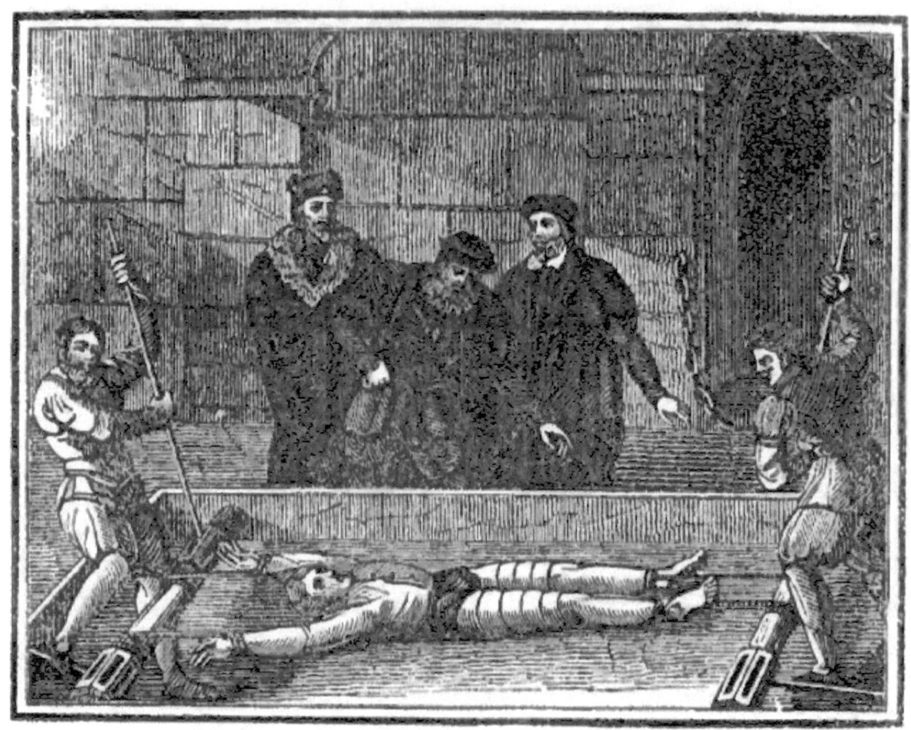

CATHOLIC PERSECUTION.
ROMAN CRUELTIES OF THE INQUISITION—THE RACK.

The Louisiana Delegation, five in number, were *two* Methodist—*one* Old School Presbyterian—one Episcopalian—and the other, Mr. Eustes, a member of Congress, not a member of any Church. Those gentlemen presented their credentials for admission, and they were objected to, because Roman Catholics were admitted into the Order by the Louisiana State Council. A warm debate ensued, on a motion to admit the Delegation, on their credentials, which finally prevailed, by yeas 67, nays 50, many of the members having left for their lodgings, because of the lateness of the hour, and of their fatigue. *We* were in favor of their admission, and so was Mr. Nelson, of East Tennessee, and we both claim to be *ultra* Protestant, if the reader please.

The "Catholicism" of Louisiana, we wish it borne in mind—that is the Gallican wing of the Church—is a very different species of "Catholicism" from that of our Irish and German Hierarchy taught in this country, under the training of Archbishop Hughes and Monseigneur Bedini, the Pope's villainous Nuncio. The French Gallican Church has so little respect for the Pope of Rome, that when the

King of Sardinia was in Paris, less than twelve months ago, though he was under the interdict of a Papal Bull of excommunication from Pius IX., the Gallican Archbishops of Pius, and other Priests associated with them, visited him regularly, and tendered him unbounded courtesies and honors. The Gallican wing of the Catholic Church of France is liberal, as well as hostile to the insulting claims and pretensions of the Pope. But it is diluted still more with liberality, and with opposition to these claims of the Pope, among the French Creoles of Louisiana. Most of them, though Roman Catholics by name, from being educated in the forms of the Roman Church, have just about as much respect for Rome, and confidence in the Pope, as we have, and God knows that is very little. They denounce Papal Bulls, interdicts, and Nuncios. They throw off all temporal and spiritual allegiance to the Pope—the civil authorities of the United States with them are supreme—they are American born—and hence, our platform does not exclude them, and consequently they were admitted at Philadelphia, or, which is the same, their representatives.

In 1652, under Louis XIV., the Gallican clergy met in Paris, and adopted the following point: "That the Pope has no power, of *Divine right*, to interfere with the temporal affairs of independent States." Thus, the Catholics of Louisiana rejecting the doctrine of the temporal power of the Pope, are not proscribed by the American party. They constitute a sound portion of the American party.

Mr. Lathrop, a Presbyterian Elder, and a Delegate from Louisiana, read to the Convention from the ritual of the subordinate organizations of the American party of Louisiana, and showed that, while it admitted those to membership who professed the Roman Catholic religion, IT REQUIRED OF THEM THE DENIAL OF ALLEGIANCE TO ANY TEMPORAL AUTHORITY NOT COGNIZABLE IN THE STATE AND UNITED STATES CONSTITUTIONS; and from each secured a pledge, UPON OATH, that they would not divulge the secrets of the Order! He defended the Louisiana Catholics, as being true Americans, recognizing no civil or spiritual power in their Priests, and resisting every attempt, whether by a Bishop or Priest, to interfere with the institutions of our country. He cited cases which had occurred in Louisiana, of controversies between the Clergy and Laity, for the control of Church property, and the decisions of courts over which Gallican Catholic Judges presided, in favor of titles and control vesting in Trustees, the Laity. He showed that the native Catholics of Louisiana were the friends of common schools, and the advocates of popular education. He proclaimed aloud that the native Catholics of his State recognized no persons as proper depositaries of office, who acknowledged an allegiance to any person, civil or ecclesiastical, superior to that of the laws and Constitution of our country. He proclaimed that the Nuncios of the Pope of Rome hated these Louisiana Catholics, with a more perfect hatred than they did the "apostle heretics" called Protestants! This speech was received with unbounded applause, the question was called, and, as we have before stated, it was sanctioned, very properly too, by a vote of 67 to 50!

The American party not only advocate religious toleration, but religious liberty, which is a very different thing. Toleration is not the word in our vocabulary—it does not express enough, because it implies the right to *permit* or *prohibit*. We contend for LIBERTY, the meaning of which is, that men are not responsible *to each other, to Popes, Bishops, or Priests*, for their religious opinions or practices, and that consequently religion is not a subject of toleration.

The Catholics, proper, have taken an oath of allegiance to the Pope of Rome, a "foreign prince, potentate, and power," and their obligations to him are higher, more sacred, and more binding, than any obligations they can take upon them to support the laws and Constitution of this country. These are the men that we refuse to vote for, or put in office. They are not and cannot be true Americans. The oaths of the priests bind them to war upon all Protestant sects, and upon all Republican powers of Government. These oaths bind them to the foot of the Papal Throne; and with these oaths upon their souls, they cannot be true citizens of this Republic without perjury. And if guilty of perjury, the State prison should be their residence.

In our next, we shall consider this subject more at length, in connection with the oath of allegiance to our country, and the Catholic evasion of that oath.

THE CATHOLIC QUESTION—No. 2.

Ambiguous terms in swearing—The case of Judge Gaston—Temporal
power of the Pope—Catholic authorities in Europe—The spirit of
the Catholic press in America!

We are told by the Democratic sympathizers with the Catholics, that all Catholic emigrants to this country take an oath of allegiance to the United States upon becoming naturalized. Yes, they do, and the oath after it is taken, has no more weight with them, than has a regular-built Know Nothing speech.

Here is a paragraph from SANCHEZ, the highest authority in the Catholic Church, Pope Pius only excepted. This writer, "by authority," shows how this oath of allegiance is evaded by a mental reservation:

> "It is lawful to use ambiguous terms to give the impression a different sense from that which you understand yourself. A person may take an oath that he has not done such a thing, though in fact he has, by saying to himself it was not done on a certain day, or before he was born, or by any other similar circumstances, which gives another meaning to it. This is extremely convenient, and always very just, when necessary to your health, honor or prosperity."

Here, then, we have it from the highest Catholic authority, that Catholics are absolved from all allegiance to this government, because they take the oath of allegiance without committing perjury, by the holy process of a mental reservation—the use of "ambiguous terms," setting forth one thing while they swear another! We have no doubt that Chief Justice TANEY, a devoted Catholic of Baltimore, and now at the head of the Supreme Court of the United States, took his oath of office requiring him to support the Constitution, with this same mental reservation. We have no doubt that those Catholic Judges upon the Federal Bench in several States in the Union, and those Catholic Attorney Generals, appointed to office by Mr. Pierce, so understood their oaths of office, and of allegiance! And the practice of

Post-Master General Campbell, a bigoted Catholic, and a member of the order of Jesuits, proves that he so understood his oath to support the Constitution. As true Catholics, they are bound to swear with this mental reservation, because they could not owe allegiance to a government of "heretics," such as they believe ours to be. As Catholics, they are bound to overthrow our Constitution, and aid in the destruction of our government.

CATHOLIC PERSECUTION.
BURNING OF BRADFORD, RIDLEY, LATIMER, PHILPOT, AND OTHERS; AND THE HOLY BIBLE!

It is a matter of history that when the Legislature of North Carolina elected Judge GASTON to the Supreme Bench in that State, he hesitated as to whether he would take the oath or not. And why? He was, although an able man, and in all the private relations of life a most excellent man, a decided and devoted Roman Catholic. This is not all. The oath of a Judge in that State, which is not common in other States, requires the man taking it to avow his belief in the Protestant religion. Judge Gaston asked for a few days to consider—he went instantly to Baltimore, as was believed, to consult the Catholic Bishop, who then resided there—obtained a dispensation, as was supposed—wrote back that he would accept the office—returned, was qualified, and to the day of his death was on the Bench! This affair illustrates Romanism. And what Rome was, she is, and always will be. Can Rome change? Can the Ethiopian change his skin, or the leopard his spots?

Here is what Philopater, an approved Catholic authority of the first grade, says, touching the principle in controversy:

> "All theologians and ecclesiastical lawyers affirm that every Christian government, as soon as it openly abandons the *Romish faith*, is instantly degraded from all power and dignity: all the subjects are absolved from the oath of fidelity and obedience which they have taken, and they may and ought, if they have the power, to drive such government from every Christian State, as an apostate, heretic, and deserter from Jesus Christ. This certain and indubitable decision of all the most learned men is perfectly conformed to the most apostolic doctrines."

Our Locofoco advocates of Romanism deny that the Pope lays claim to the supremacy charged by the American party. On this point, we desire that the Catholics may speak for themselves. One of their standard writers, FARRARIS, in his Ecclesiastical Dictionary, a work endorsed by their Council of Bishops and Cardinals, under the article headed "Pope," uses this emphatic and expressive language:

> "The Pope is of such dignity and highness, that he is not simply man, but, as it were, God, and the vicar of God. Hence the Pope is such supreme and sovereign dignity, that, properly speaking, he is not merely constituted in dignity, but is rather placed on the very summit of dignities. Hence, also, the Pope is rather father of fathers, and he alone can use this name, because he only can be called father of fathers: since he possesses the primacy over all, is truly greater than all, and the greatest of all. He is called most holy, because he is presumed to be such. On account of the excellency of his supreme dignity, he is called bishop of bishops, ordinary of ordinaries, universal bishop of the Church, bishop of diocesan, of the whole world, divine monarch, supreme emperor, and king of kings."

PETER DENS, of Maynooth College notoriety, whose "Theology" is the highest Catholic authority known this side of the Vatican at Rome, gives entire the Bull of Pope Sixtus V. against the King of Navarre and the Prince of Conde, whom he styles the *sons of wrath*. In this Bull, issued in the year 1585, he says:

> "The authority given to Saint Peter and his successors, by the immense power of the eternal King, *excels all the power of earthly kings and princes*. It passeth uncontrollable sentence upon them all. And if it find any of them resisting God's obedience, it takes more severe vengeance on them, casting them down from their thrones, however powerful they may be, and tumbling them down to the lowest parts of the earth, as the ministers of aspiring Lucifer."

Here is what *Daniel O'Connell* said so late as 1843, and he was a true Catholic and a true exponent of this faith:

"You should do all in your power to carry out the intentions of His Holiness the Pope. Where you have the electoral franchise, give your votes to none but those who will assist you in so holy a struggle.

"I declare my most unequivocal submission to the Head of the Church, and to the hierarchy in its different orders. If the Bishop makes a declaration on this bill, I never would be heard speaking against it, but would submit at once unequivocally to that decision. They have only to decide, and I close my mouth: they have only to determine, and I obey. I wish it to be understood that *such is the duty of all Catholics."* — *Daniel O'Connell,* 1843.

Here comes one of the Pope's organs in France:

"A heretic, examined and convicted by the Church, used to be delivered over to the secular power and punished with death. Nothing has ever appeared to us more necessary. More than one hundred thousand persons perished in consequence of the heresy of Wickliffe; a still greater number for that of John Huss; and it would not be possible to calculate the bloodshed caused by Luther; and it is not yet over." — *Paris Univers.*

"As for myself, what I regret, I frankly own, is that they did not burn John Huss sooner, and that they did not likewise burn Luther; this happened because there was not found some prince sufficiently politic to stir up a crusade against Protestants." — *Paris Univers.*

But here is the Pope himself arguing with the authorities already quoted:

"The absurd or erroneous doctrines or ravings in defence of liberty of conscience, is a most pestilential error—a pest, of all others, most to be dreaded in a State." — *Encyclical Letter of Pope Pius IX., Aug.* 15, 1852.

Now, let us hear their organs in our own country:

"Heresy and unbelief are crimes, and in Christian countries, like Italy and Spain for instance, where all the people are Catholics, and where the Christian religion is an essential part of the law of the land, they are punished as other crimes." — *R. C. Archbishop of St. Louis.*

"For our own part, we take this opportunity of expressing our hearty delight at the suppression of the Protestant chapel at Rome. This may be thought intolerant, but when, we would ask, *did we ever profess to be tolerant of Protestantism,* or favor the doctrine that Protestantism *ought to be tolerated?* On the contrary, we hate Protestantism—we detest it with our whole heart and soul, and we pray that our aversion to it may never decrease. We hold it meet that in the Eternal City no worship repugnant to *God* should be tolerated, and we are sincerely glad that the enemies of truth are no longer allowed to meet together in the capital of the Christian world." — *Pittsburg Catholic Visitor,* 1848.

"No good government can exist without religion; and there can be no religion without an *Inquisition*, which is wisely designed for the promotion and protection of the true faith." —*Boston Pilot*.

"You ask, if he (the Pope) were lord in the land, and you were in a minority, if not in numbers, yet in power, what would he do to you? That, we say, would entirely depend on circumstances. If it would *benefit the cause of Catholicism*, he would tolerate you—if expedient, he would imprison you—banish you—possibly, *hang you*—but be assured of one thing, he would never tolerate you for the sake of the *'glorious principles' of civil and religious liberty*." —*Rambler*.

"Protestantism of every form has not and never can have any rights where Catholicity is triumphant." —*Brownson's Quarterly Review*.

"Let us dare to assert the truth in the face of the lying world, and, instead of pleading for our Church at the bar of the State, *summon the State itself to plead at the bar of the Church, its divinely constituted judge*." —*Ibid*.

"I never think of publishing any thing in regard to the Church without submitting my articles to the Bishop for inspection, approval, and endorsement." —*Ibid*.

In view of the foregoing, and other facts and arguments which we will hereafter present, we cannot be mistaken in our views of Roman Catholicism. We cannot tamely surrender our dearest rights as Protestants, without a struggle. We cannot cry peace, peace, when there is no peace!

"Protestantism, of every kind, Catholicity inserts in her catalogue of moral sins; she endures it when and where she must; but she hates it, and directs all her energies to effect its destruction." —*St. Louis Shepherd of the Valley*.

"Religious liberty, in the sense of a liberty possessed by every man to choose his religion, is one of the most wretched delusions ever foisted on this age by the father of deceit." —*The Rambler*, 1853.

"The Church is of necessity intolerant. Heresy she endures when and where she must, but she hates it, and directs all her energies to its destruction. If Catholics ever gain an immense numerical majority in this country, religious freedom is at an end. So say our enemies. So say we." —*Shepherd of the Valley*.

"The liberty of heresy and unbelief is not a right.... All the rights the sects have, or can have, are derived from the State, and rest on expediency. As they have, in their character of sects hostile to the true religion, no rights under the law of nature or the law of God, they are neither wronged nor deprived of liberty, if the State refuses to grant them any rights at all." —*Brownson's Review, Oct., 1853*, p. 456.

"The sorriest sight to us is a Catholic throwing up his cap, and shouting, 'All hail, Democracy!'" —*Ibid, October, 1852, pp. 554-8.*

"We think the 'masses' were never less happy, less respectable, and less respected, than they have been since the reformation, and particularly within the last fifty or one hundred years, since Lord Brougham caught the mania of teaching them to read and communicate the disease to a large proportion of the English nation; of which, in spite of all our talk, we are often the servile imitators." —*Shepherd of the Valley, Oct. 22, 1853.*

THE CATHOLIC QUESTION—No. 3.

The Catholic Church supreme over all authorities—Meddling in Political Contests—Brownson's Review and the Boston Pilot reflecting the sentiments of that Church—Protestants advocating Romanism—The Nashville Union in 1835.

The Anti-American, Foreign-loving, Catholic admirers of the Locofoco school of politics, everywhere seek to frighten native Protestant citizens with the bugbear cry of religious proscription. But let Americans and Protestants watch with increased vigilance both the Roman and Locofoco Jesuits around them. To call the damnable and accursed system of political intrigue practised for past centuries by the Roman Church by the term *Religion*, is a solemn mockery of the hallowed word. Religion teaches love and obedience to God, and the legally constituted authorities of the country. Romanism teaches fear of and obedience to a crowned potentate called the Pope, and opposition to all Protestant governments, as worthy to be cast down to hell! The one tends to free and ennoble the soul: the other to enslave and debauch every faculty of man's nature which likens him to the Almighty! The one is republican: the other is barbaric, and at war with every principle of free government!

The American party does oppose and denounce Romanism *as a political system at war* with American institutions; and we here ask candid men to weigh the evidence we shall adduce to sustain this charge. We shall quote none other than Roman Catholic authority—the organs of Romanism—so as out of their own mouths to condemn them. Brownson's Review is the accredited organ of Romanism in the United States. He ostentatiously parades the names of the Archbishops and Bishops on the cover of his Review, to give it the stamp of authority, and asserts in the work:

"I NEVER THINK OF PUBLISHING ANY THING IN REGARD TO THE CHURCH WITHOUT SUBMITTING MY ARTICLES TO THE BISHOP FOR INSPECTION, APPROVAL, AND ENDORSEMENT."

Let us then look to his pages for an exposition of the doctrines of his Church. In the January number for 1853, he says:

"For every Catholic at least, the Church is the supreme judge of the extent and limits of her power. She can be judged by no one; and this of itself implies her absolute supremacy, and that the temporal order must receive its laws from her."

The uniform practice of the Church of Rome has been, and still is, to assert her power—not in *words*, but in *deeds*—to GIVE OR TAKE AWAY CROWNS—to depose ungodly rulers, and to absolve their subjects from their "horrible" OATHS OF ALLEGIANCE!

CATHOLIC PERSECUTION.
HORRIBLE CRUELTIES INFLICTED BY THE CATHOLICS ON THE PROTESTANTS IN IRELAND, IN 1641.

Again, in the July number for 1853, Brownson says:

"The Church is supreme, and you have no power except what you hold in subordination to her, either in spirituals or in temporals.... You no more have political than ecclesiastical independence. The Church alone, under God, is independent, and she defines both your powers and hers."

"They have heard it said from their youth up that the Church has nothing to do with politics; that she has received no mission in regard to the political order."

"In opposing the nonjuring bishops and priests, they believed they were only asserting their national rights as men, or as the State, and were merely resisting the unwarrantable assumption of the spiritual power. If they had been distinctly taught that the political authority is always subordinate to the spiritual, and had grown up in the doctrine that the nation is not competent to define, in relation to the ecclesiastical power, its own rights—that the Church defines both its powers and her own, and that though the nation may be, and ought to be, independent in relation to other nations, it has, and can have, no independence in the face of the Church, the kingdom of God on earth: they would have seen at a glance that support of the civil authority against the spiritual, no matter in what manner, was the renunciation of their faith as Catholics, and the actual or virtual assertion of the supremacy of the temporal power."

In the same number, page 301, he says:

"She (the Church) has the right to judge who has, or has not, according to the law of God, the right to reign: whether the prince has, by his infidelity, his misdeeds, his tyranny and oppression, forfeited his trust, and lost his right to the allegiance of his subjects; and therefore whether they are still held to their allegiance, or are released from it by the law of God. If she have the right to judge, she has the right to pronounce judgment, and order its execution: therefore to pronounce sentence of deposition upon the prince who has forfeited his right to reign, and to declare his subjects absolved from their allegiance to him, and free to elect themselves a new sovereign."

We might multiply authorities of this kind on this point, to an almost indefinite extent, from the debate between Bishop Hughes and Mr. Breckenridge, and the controversy between Hughes and Erastus Brooks, but it is wholly unnecessary.

As early as 1844, the Catholics took their stand as a body in the arena of political strife; and the illustrious CLAY and the virtuous FRELINGHUYSEN were the victims of their particular hostility. Mr. Frelinghuysen was the President of the Board of Foreign Missions, and this was made the *excuse* for the bitter animosity of the Catholic press, and of the clergy and membership of the Catholic sect, against Mr. Clay. Brownson, in his July number for 1844, in the very heat of the contest, thus assailed Mr. Clay:

"He is ambitious, but short-sighted. He is abashed by no inconsistency, disturbed by no contradiction, and can defend, with a firm countenance, without the least misgiving, what everybody but himself sees to be a political fallacy or logical absurdity.... He is no more disturbed by being convinced of moral insensibility, than intellectual absurdity.... A man of rare abilities, but apparently void of both moral and intellectual conscience.... He is, therefore, a man whom no power under that of the Almighty can restrain; he must needs be the most dangerous man to be placed at the head of affairs it is possible to conceive."

The Boston Pilot, another Catholic organ, published under the eye of the Bishop, discloses *the same plot*, in its issue for the 31st of October, 1844, only six days before the election! Here is what this organ said:

> "We say to all men in the United States, entitled to be natural-
> ized, become citizens while you can—let nothing delay you for an
> hour—let no hindrance, short of mortal disease, banish you from the
> ballot-box. To those who are citizens, we say, vote your principles,
> whatever they may be—never desert them—do not be wheedled or
> terrified—but vote quietly, and unobtrusively. Leave to others the
> noisy warfare of words. Let your opinions be proved by your deliber-
> ate and determined action. We recommend you to no party; we con-
> demn no candidate but one, and he is Theodore Frelinghuysen. We
> have nothing to say to him as a Whig—we have nothing to say to Mr.
> Clay or any other Whig, as such—but to the President of the Ameri-
> can Board of Foreign Missions, the friend and patron of the Kirks and
> Cones, we have much to say. We hate his intolerance—we dislike his
> associates—and shudder at the blackness and bitterness of that school
> of sectarians to which he belongs, and amongst whom he is regarded
> as an authority."

Protestants! do you hear that? Old Line Whigs! do you hear that? If so, do
you think that Americans are warring upon civil and religious liberty, when they
take an oath that they will rebuke such infamous sentiments? These appeals of
Brownson, Hughes, and the Pilot, had the effect to defeat the Clay ticket in New
York, and that State lost him his election. The Catholics were all at the polls, and
voted for Polk and Dallas. On the 9th of November, 1844, Frelinghuysen wrote to
Mr. Clay as follows:

> "More than 3,000, it is confidently said, have been naturalized in
> this city (New York) alone since the first of October. It is an alarming
> fact that this foreign vote has decided the great questions of American
> policy, and contracted a nation's gratitude."

And after they achieved the victory of 1844, Brownson came out with this
avowal:

> "Heretofore we have taken our politics from one or another of the
> parties which divide the country, and have suffered the enemies of
> our religion to impose their political doctrine upon us; but it is time
> for us to begin to teach the country itself those moral and political
> doctrines which flow from the teachings of our own Church. We are
> at home here, wherever we may have been born; this is our country,
> and as it is to become THOROUGHLY CATHOLIC, we have a deeper
> interest in public affairs than any other of our citizens. The sects are
> only for a day; the Church for ever."

When Gen. Cass made his speech in the Senate, in 1852, in favor of free worship and the rights of conscience for Americans abroad, reflecting on the Catholics
by name, Brownson came out in his October number, and said:

> "We are glad to see Gen. Cass laid on the shelf, for we can never
> support a man who turns radical in his old age."

In the same number, Brownson continues:

> "The sorriest sight to us is a Catholic throwing up his cap and shouting, 'All hail, Democracy!'"

This too at the very time he was supporting the Democratic party in the Presidential contest! He would sooner have heard the cry, "All hail, Catholicism!" and he was only using Democracy as an instrument to advance his primary wish!

We offer no comments on the foregoing extracts, of our own, but leave every reader to judge for himself. The price of liberty is eternal vigilance. We apply the remark to religious as well as civil liberty. All we ask of the people is to be vigilant. Do not support men at the ballot-box who are in league with these enemies of our Republic, and of the Protestant religion!

Behold the enemy is at our gates! A foreign priest has been lecturing here in Knoxville, within the last ten days, avowing sentiments similar to these, and claiming that this country would ultimately become a Catholic country! The crisis is approaching! Rouse up, Americans, and hasten to your country's salvation! Not a moment is to be lost! GOD AND OUR COUNTRY, must be the watchword of every Christian and patriot, of every political party in the land. America expects us all to do our duty!

And is there no cause for alarm?

Eighteen months ago, a Protestant minister, Baptist, Methodist, or Presbyterian, might expose Romanism, and warn his congregation against its corrupting influences, for hours at a time—come down out of his pulpit, and his congregation would, without distinction of party, say, "Well done, good and faithful servant!"

But let him now dare *allude* to Romanism—he offends one-half of his congregation—he is *preaching* politics—they will hear him no more; or forsooth, which is more common, they will withhold his support and starve him out! Are not these signs alarming?

But here in Tennessee, *Protestant* Tennessee, on the 15th of May, 1855, the *Nashville Daily Union*, the organ of the self-styled Democratic party, came out at the Capital of the State with this daring broadside against the Protestant clergy and their religion:

> "A Church that can boast of an existence of thirteen centuries— passing through all the various vicissitudes of her eventful career unscathed, can certainly show, with all her atrocious barbarity, many bright spots which may be placed in favorable contrast with the Protestant Church, with its thousand and one wrangling sects. Men are beginning to see through the transparent gauze that veils this Know-Nothing movement. They are beginning to ask 'What has Protestantism done for the world? What has she done to alleviate and elevate the down-trodden? Is the race any better off for having accepted her faith? THESE REVEREND HYPOCRITES—these scribes and pharisees, are treading on a terrible volcano. They will find their treasonable schemes and infernal plotting against the liberties of man

tried and condemned by the pure light of God's own truth and love, which shines and throbs in every pulsation of humanity's heart. If Protestantism prove recreant to her high trust, she will have to pass the ordeal of enlightened public opinion and be consigned to her merited obscurity.

"Popery, with all its crimes against God and man, adapts itself to the times and to the circumstances, and thus saves itself from being absorbed in the mass of conflicting elements."

THE CATHOLIC QUESTION—No. 4.

A Catholic Priest the Minister from the Rivas-Walker Government— Nicaragua, Texas, and Gen. Jackson—Bishop Hughes and Orestes Brownson—Buchanan bidding for the Catholic vote—A. H. Stephens, of Georgia—Lord Baltimore and Religious Toleration.

Three months ago, PARKER H. FRENCH arrived in Washington, as the Representative of the Walker Government of Nicaragua—an American-born citizen and a Protestant—but the Government declined to recognize him, upon the ground that Walker's Government was not established even *de facto*. Since then, our Government has recognized Walker's Government, and endorsed his war upon Costa Rica, although the former objection of our Government lies with as much force against such recognition now as it did three months ago. That the approach of the Cincinnati Convention, and the importance of conciliating the "Young American" wing, and the Filibustering division of the Democratic party, had great influence in producing this recognition, there can be no sort of doubt. But a still more palpable reason why this Government gave its sanction to the Rivas-Walker Government is, that PADRE VIJIL, the second Minister sent here, is a ROMAN CATHOLIC PRIEST, and a shrewd Spaniard—better understands the influences that prevail at Washington. When we remember that a Roman Catholic, and a member of the Order of Jesuits, is a member of Pierce's Cabinet, the Postmaster-General—and when we remember that Democracy now, without the Catholic-Foreign vote, is almost a nullity in the United States, we have a clear solution of this preference given the Spanish priest, PADRE VIJIL, over the American citizen, but a few weeks afterwards! As a sign of the times, the fact is one worthy of note. It shows, at least, that when Protestantism cannot prevail with the Administration of Pierce, Roman Catholicism can; and that hence, when we proclaim the power of the Pope, even in America, we but utter demonstrable facts. Romanism is even carrying Democracy from all its old wayside land-marks. In December, 1836, GEN. JACKSON sent a special message to the Senate of the United States, in relation to a proposition to recognize the new Government of Texas, and he gave reasons *against* it, which are exactly applicable to this Rivas-Walker affair:

"Upon the issue," he says, "of this threatened invasion by Mexico, the independence of Texas may be considered as suspended; and were there nothing peculiar in the relative situation of the United States and Texas, our acknowledgments of its independence at such a crisis could scarcely be considered as consistent *with that prudent reserve with which we have heretofore held ourselves bound to treat all similar questions."*

The existing Government of Nicaragua is in a far more critical condition now than that of Texas was in 1836, when Gen. Jackson went on to say:

"It becomes us to beware of a too early movement, as it might subject us, however unjustly, to the imputation of seeking to establish the claim of our neighbors to a territory, with a view to its subsequent acquisition by ourselves. Prudence, therefore, seems to dictate that we should still stand aloof, and maintain our present attitude, if not until Mexico itself, or one of the great foreign powers, shall recognize the independence of the new Government, at least until the lapse of time or the course of events shall have proved, beyond cavil or dispute, the ability of the people of that country to maintain their separate sovereignty, and to uphold the Government constituted by them. Neither of the contending parties can justly complain of this course. By pursuing it, we are but carrying out the long-established policy of our Government—a policy which has secured to us respect and influence abroad, and inspired confidence at home."

But Romanism is rapidly leading Democracy to the Devil! Archbishop Hughes—the head and front of the Papal Hierarchy in this country—has openly declared the grand aim and object of the Catholic Church is "TO MAKE ROME THE DISTRICT OF COLUMBIA FOR THE WHOLE WORLD!" This same Archbishop is now engaged in raising an immense fund, for the avowed purpose of ESTABLISHING A COLLEGE IN ROME, for the education of a high order of Priests and Jesuits for the United States; the Roman Pontiff deeming the education of Priests defective if obtained in this land of liberty! This same Archbishop Hughes has now actively enlisted for the Presidential contest, for 1856, in order, to use his own language, "TO BREAK THE SPINAL CORD OF THE AMERICAN PARTY." The Irish Catholic vote is to be fused with the Black Republicans in the North, to prevent the success of the Fillmore ticket, and the Irish and German Catholic vote is to be cast for Democracy in the South and North-West—the Archbishop stipulating for special legislation for Rome, and for promoting this mammoth college!

ORESTES BROWNSON, a leading Catholic authority, and the editor of Archbishop Hughes's organ—one of the most zealous as well as able advocates of Romanism in America—declares: "THE POPE IS MY INTERPRETER OF THE CONSTITUTION OF THE UNITED STATES!" The Supreme Court at Washington is subordinate to the Vatican, situated at the foot of one of the seven hills upon which Rome is built! Through the influence of the *Jesuit* who is a member of Pierce's cabinet, the Papal Nuncio, who was sent from Rome two years ago, clothed with *foreign* authority, was received by our government at Washington, and sent around the lakes to the North-West at government expense; and allowed to adjudicate upon a secular question AFFECTING TERRITORIAL JURISDICTION in the great State of New York!

Mr. Buchanan, one of the several candidates before the Cincinnati Convention for the Presidential nomination, said, in a public speech in Baltimore, just before the meeting of that Convention, *by way of bidding for the Catholic vote*:

> "In the age of religious bigotry and intolerance, Lord Baltimore was the first legislator who proclaimed the sacred rights of conscience, and established for the government of his colony the principle, not merely of toleration, but perfect religious freedom and equality among all sects of Christians."

Lord Baltimore was a Catholic; and with a view to enlist the same influence, Hon. Alexander H. Stephens, of Georgia, sent forth a published speech last summer, from which we make the following extract:

> "The Catholic colony of Maryland, organized under the auspices of Lord Baltimore, was the first to establish the principle of free toleration in religious worship on this continent.

> "The Colony of Maryland afforded protection to *all* persecuted sects."

Now, in order to judge of Mr. Buchanan's *"perfect religious freedom and equality,"* and Mr. Stephens's *"principle of free toleration,"* let us examine an Act passed April 21, 1649, when Lord Baltimore was in the zenith of his power:

> "Denying the Holy *Trinity* is to be punished with *death*, and confiscation of land and goods to the Lord Proprietary (Lord Baltimore himself!) Persons using any reproachful words concerning the Blessed Virgin Mary, or the Holy Apostles or Evangelists, to be fined £5, or in default of payment to be publicly whipped and *imprisoned, at the pleasure of* his Lordship, (Lord Baltimore himself!) or of his Lieutenant-General." *See Laws of Maryland at large, by T. Bacon, A. D. 1765. 16 and 17 Cecilius's Lord Baltimore.*

S. F. Streeter, Esq., of Baltimore, is the author of a work entitled *"Maryland two hundred years ago."* In this work, at page 26, Mr. Streeter says:

> "The policy of Lord Baltimore, in regard to religious matters in his colony, has, in some particulars at least, been misapprehended and therefore misstated. The assertion has long passed uncontradicted, that toleration was promised to the colonists in the first conditions of plantation; that the rights of conscience were recognized in a law passed by the first assembly held in the colony; and that the principal officers from the year 1636 or '37, bound themselves by on oath not to molest on account of his religion any one professing to believe in Jesus Christ. I can find *no authority* for *any* of these statements. Lord Baltimore's first and earlier conditions of plantation breathe not a word on the subject of religion: no act recognizing the principle of toleration was passed in the first or in any following assembly, until fifteen years after the first settlement, at which time (1649) a Protestant had been appointed Governor, and a majority of the Burgesses were of the same faith; and when, *for the first time*, a clause involving a promise not to molest any person professing to believe in Jesus Christ, the words

> "and particularly a Roman Catholic," were inserted by the direction of Lord Baltimore in the official oath."

McMahon, the tried friend of Lord Baltimore, speaking on this same subject, says:

> "The proprietary dominion (Lord B.'s) had never known that hour, (when there was opportunity to persecute.) The Protestant religion was the established religion of the mother country, and any effort on the part of the Proprietary (Lord B.) to oppress its followers would have *drawn down destruction on his government*. The *great body* of the colonists were themselves Protestants, and, by their *number* and their participation in the government, they were fully equal to their own protection, and *too powerful* for the Proprietaries in the event of an open collision."

Thus it will be seen that in Maryland, as everywhere else, in all past ages, so far as toleration is concerned, it was granted *to* Catholics—never *by* them.

THE CATHOLIC QUESTION—No. 5.

Popish aims at supremacy—Avowals by distinguished Catholics—
The order of Jesuits—Startling disclosures and authentic references!—The strength of Romanism in the United States!

The Romish hierarchy aims at supremacy in the Church and the State. It is nothing more nor less than a great *political* system, arrogating to itself the right to sway the spiritual and temporal concerns of men—a right it claims to have derived from God, and that therefore the Romish Church is above all, and may rule all. Hence the conspiracy against our government emanating from the Vatican, and planned by the Pope, his Cardinals and Bishops, in the late grand council at Rome! They there and then resolved on affecting the objects of the *Leopold Foundation*, established in Vienna, May 13, 1829, to support Catholic missionaries in the United States. Every member of this Society—and its branches are numerous, being scattered over the whole earth—agrees to offer prayers daily to *St. Leopold*, and every week to contribute as much as a *crucifix*. The valley of the Mississippi has been surveyed and mapped by the Jesuits, under the directions of the Vatican, and Popish Cardinals in Europe are boasting of the certainty of their subjecting this land of freedom at no distant day to papal supremacy! Rev. Dr. JAMES, an eminent clergyman of England, says:

> "The Church of Rome has determined to compensate herself for her losses in the old world, by her conquest in the new."

Hence, too, a Papal editor in Europe conducting a Catholic organ, and advising vigorous measures for the extension of Papal power, says:

> "We must make haste—the moments are precious—America may become the centre of civilization."

The Rev. Dr. Reze, of Detroit, a priest of distinction, who is now in custody at Rome, a few years since, writing from Michigan to his master, the Pope, says:

> "We shall see the truth triumph—the temple of idols over-thrown—the seat of falsehood brought to silence—and all the United States embraced in the same faith of that Catholic Church, wherein dwell truth and temporal happiness."

A Catholic priest in Indiana told a Protestant minister, an able Methodist clergyman, in a controversy, "The time will come when Catholics will make Protestants wade knee-deep in blood in the valley of the Mississippi!"

Bishop England, one of their master-spirits in this country, in a letter to the Pope written from Charleston, and which was so good that his Holiness caused it to be published, said:

> "Within thirty years, the Protestant heresy will come to an end. If we can secure the West and South, we will take care of New England."

This same dignitary said to his brethren at Vienna in that memorable letter, by way of advice and encouragement:

> "All that is necessary is money and priests, to subjugate the mock liberties of America."

The Jesuits profess to be a more devoted branch of the Pope's army than any other order. The Abbe De Pradt, formerly Roman Archbishop at Malines, calls them "the Pope's zealous militia:" another correctly calls them "the Pope's body-guard, organized for the express purpose of defending the Papal See, and under-taking a spiritual crusade against heretics." Pius VII., in his Bull of August 7, 1814, reëstablishing the order, which Clement XIV. had suppressed, says: "We would be guilty of a great crime," if, amid the dangers threatening the Papal interests, and "if, placed in the barque of Peter, tossed and assailed by continual storms, we refused to employ the vigorous and experienced rowers who volunteer their services in order to break the waves of a sea which threatens every moment ship-wreck and death."

The presumption is, that "these vigorous and experienced rowers who thus volunteer their services," have some moving principle, some hidden spring, which moves with that oneness and constancy under all discouragements. The watch does not show the spring that sets it in motion: who that looks at its face and observes the movement of the hands will doubt that it is there, and that they move in proportion to the strength or weakness of that spring?

The old Romans used to swear their soldiers: the Roman Church swears even her private members. Read the following from the creed: "I solemnly promise, vow, and *swear* true obedience to the Roman bishop," &c. "This true Catholic faith, out of which there is no salvation, &c.—I promise, vow, and *swear* most constantly to hold and profess the same, whole and entire, with God's assistance, to the end of my life, and procure, as far as lies in my power, that the same shall be held, taught, and preached by all who are under me," &c. "I also profess and undoubt-edly receive all other things delivered, defined, and declared by the sacred canons and general councils, and particularly by the holy Council of Trent; and, likewise, I also condemn, reject, and anathematize all things contrary thereto, and all heresies whatsoever, condemned, rejected, and anathematized by the Church."

CATHOLIC PERSECUTION.
HORRIBLE CRUELTIES BY CATHOLICS.

The Jesuits are more strict, subservient, devoted to the Vatican, than any other wing of the Catholic Church. In the second volume of the constitutions of the Jesuits, under the heading of *obedience to superiors*, is written:

"You shall always see Jesus Christ in the General."

"You shall obey him in every thing. Your obedience shall be boundless in the execution, in the will and understanding. You shall persuade yourselves that God speaks in his mouth: that when he orders, God himself orders. You shall execute his command immediately, with joy and with steadiness."

"You shall be in his hands a dead body, which he will govern, move, place, displace, according to his will."

Under these teachings, says ARNAULD, a student in a college of Jesuits stated, on hearing of the implicit obedience of another:

"I would have done still more. Were God to order me, through the voice of my superior, to put to death father, mother, children, brothers, and sisters, I would do it with an eye as tearless and a heart as calm as if I were seated at the banquet of the Paschal lamb."

Andrew B. Cross, of Baltimore, in a recent publication, says:

> "As early as 1624, the University of Paris charged them with being governed by 'secret laws.' In 1649, Palafox, Bishop of Angelopolis, in his letter to Innocent X., accuses them of having 'a secret constitution, hidden privileges, and concealed laws of their own.'"

What will our Democratic Protestant opposers of Know Nothing *secret lodges* say to this? What will our Democratic advocates of Popery say to the principles of such an organization, and to its "horrible oaths?" But hear the Roman Catholic King of Portugal, in his manifesto to his Bishops, in 1759, only ninety-seven years ago:

> "In order to form the union, the consistency, and the strength of the society, there should be a government not only monarchical, but so sovereign, so absolute, so despotic, that even the Provincials themselves should not have it in their power, by any act of theirs, to resist or retard the execution of the orders of the General. By this legislative, inviolable and despotic power; by the profound devotedness of the subjects of this company to mysterious laws with which they are not themselves acquainted; by the blind and passive obedience with which they are compelled to execute, without hesitation or reply, whatever their superiors command," &c.

But our Democratic anti-Know Nothings not only object to our having formerly kept our ritual concealed, but especially to our denial of the existence of our organization. Let them procure a copy of the secret instructions of the Jesuits, styled *"Secreta Monita,"* and in the preface they will find these *lovely* words:

> "The greatest care imaginable must be also taken that these instructions do not fall into the hands of strangers, &c.; if they should, *let it be positively denied that these are the principles of the society,"* &c.

But again:

> "Auquetil, in the fourth volume, page 333, of his History of France, gives an account of the celebrated case of the bankruptcy of the Rev. Father Jesuit La Valette, the Jesuit agent, for three million francs. Their ships had been taken by the English; the bankers in Marseilles, who had accepted bills of exchange to the amount of one and a half millions, required prompt payment. They wrote to De Sacy, the General Procurator of the Missions; he wrote to the General at Rome, but the General died at the same time; and before a new General could be elected, and an order sent to pay the money, the Fathers had become bankrupt, and suits were instituted. After delay and manœuvre on their part, the case came on unexpectedly in 1760. All the Jesuits were accused. They tried to lay the guilt upon La Valette, but the bankers charged that all the Jesuits were under the General, and La Valette was only agent. In this sad condition they proposed to prove, according

to their constitutions, that as a society their body possessed nothing, that all belonged to each college-house, convent, &c. The proposal of the Jesuits was accepted. On the 8th of May, 1761, after trial, the Parliament condemned the General and all the society to pay bills, costs, damages, &c., which they did without selling any of their property.

"It was in this evil hour to the Jesuits that their constitutions, which had been acted upon for two hundred years in secret, were brought to light. Rules and constitutions maybe in existence and acted upon, when it would be impossible to obtain a copy from any one who was sufficiently advanced in the order to be trusted with a copy."

It will astonish American Protestants to be told how numerous, influential, and strong the Catholics are in this land of liberty! They have 7 archbishops, 40 bishops, 1704 priests, 1824 churches, 21 colleges, 37 ecclesiastical institutions for the education of priests and Jesuits, 117 female academies, all of which are, in reality, *Convents*. Nuns, priests, and Jesuits are the professors, teachers, and matrons; and, strange to say, *Protestant* young ladies are their chief supporters!

The Romish Hierarchy is far more numerous in *Protestant* America, than in any Catholic country on earth. Their strength in America equals what it is in Ireland, Scotland, and England combined! How extensive is this religious organization in our land: how subtle! Its ramifications are all so many *arteries*, which receive their life's blood from the heart at Rome, and return it there by its regular palpitations! It is now concentrating its *arteries* at Washington City, and is promised "aid and comfort" from the great Democratic party—a party fast becoming the foe of true liberty, and of the evangelical Protestant faith.

THE CATHOLIC QUESTION—No. 6.

The Oath of a Bishop—Oath of a Priest—Oath of a Jesuit—Oath of a
San Fedisti—Oath of an Irish Ribbon-man—The Romish Curse!

In this chapter we will exhibit the *"horrible oaths"* of the various grades of Catholics, from a *Bishop* down to a *private member*—even to the "Irish Ribbon-men," thousands of whom swarm the United States. To these we will add the oath of the "Order of San Fedisti," an infamous secret society established in Italy, and introduced for the first time into this country by that prince of murderers, *Bedini*, the Pope's Nuncio; who was honored with a steamer at the expense of our government, Pierce at its head, to sail round our northern lakes, organizing these infamous societies. Last of all, we give the ROMISH CURSE, which is in full force and power in all Catholic countries, and is even pronounced publicly in our large cities, upon renegades from the Catholic faith.

These oaths will be found commencing on page 42 of "A Treatise of the Pope's Supremacy. By Rev. Isaac Barrow, D. D. Second American Edition, 1844." By this author, the Latin is given and then translated. The same, in part, will be found in the debate between Mr. Breckenridge, of the Presbyterian Church, and Archbishop Hughes, and by the latter publicly acknowledged to be genuine, before a Baltimore audience who heard the discussion!

But these particular forms of oaths in question, which reckless Catholics and unprincipled Democrats deny, were published in England by Archbishop Usher, whose correctness and reliability is equal to that of any man. These oaths will be found in a volume entitled "Foxes and Firebrands," from a collection of papers by Archbishop Usher, and it is there stated that "it remains on record at Paris, among the Society of Jesus," and was drawn up in that form to URBAN VIII., in 1642, when he revived the bull of Pious V., which had slumbered seventy-three years. These oaths, as published, contain nothing which is not taught by Popes and Councils, Priests and Jesuits. Examine these *oaths*, and this *curse*, and answer us the question, Can men taking them, and subscribing to their doctrines, make citizens of this Republic?

OATH OF THE BISHOPS.

"I, G. N., elect of the church of N., from henceforth will be *faithful* and obedient to St. Peter the Apostle, and to the holy Roman Church, and to our lord, the lord N. Pope N., and to his successors canonically coming in. I will neither advise, consent, nor do any thing that they may lose life or member, or that their persons may be seized or hands anywise laid upon them, or any injuries offered to them, under any pretence whatsoever. The counsel which they shall intrust me withal by themselves, their messengers, or letters, I will not knowingly reveal to any to their prejudice. I will help them to defend and keep the Roman Papacy and the royalties of St. Peter, saving my order against all men. The legate of the Apostolic see, going and coming, I will honorably treat, and help in his necessities. The rights, honors, privileges, and authority of the holy Roman Church, of our lord the Pope, and his aforesaid successors, I will endeavor to preserve, defend, increase, and advance. I will not be in any council, action, or treaty, in which shall be plotted against our said lord and the said Roman Church, any thing to the hurt or prejudice of their persons, right, honor, state, or power; and if I shall know any such thing to be treated or agitated by any whomsoever, I will hinder it all that I can; and as soon as I can, will signify it to our said lord, or to some other, by whom it may come to his knowledge. The rules of the Holy Fathers, the Apostolic decrees, ordinances, or disposals, reservations, provisions, and mandates, I will observe with all my might, and cause by others. Heretics, Schismatics, and Rebels to our said lord, or his aforesaid successors, I will to the utmost of my power persecute and oppose. I will come to a council when I am called, unless I am hindered by a canonical impediment. I will, by myself in person, visit the threshold of the Apostles every three years; and give an account to our lord, and his aforesaid successors, of all my pastoral office, and of all things anywise belonging to the state of my church, to the discipline of my clergy and people, and, lastly, to the salvation of souls committed to my trust; and will, in like manner, humbly receive and diligently execute the Apostolic commands. And if I be detained by a lawful impediment, I will perform all things aforesaid by a certain messenger hereto specially empowered, a member of my Chapter or some other in ecclesiastical dignity, or else having a parsonage; or in default of these, by a priest of the diocese; or in default of one of the clergy, (of the diocese,) by some other secular or regular priest of approved integrity and religion, fully instructed in all things above mentioned. And such impediment I will make out by lawful proofs, to be transmitted by the aforesaid messenger to the Cardinal proponent of the holy Roman Church, in the Congregation of the Sacred Council. The possessions belonging to my table, I will neither sell nor give away, mortgage nor grant anew in fee, nor anywise alienate, no, not even with consent of the Chapter of my Church, without consulting the Roman Pontiff. And if I shall make any alienation, I will thereby incur the penalties contained in a certain Constitution put forth about this matter.

"So help me God, and these holy Gospels of God."

OATH OF THE PRIESTS.

"I, A. B., do acknowledge the ecclesiastical power of his holiness; and the mother Church of Rome, as the chief head and matron above all pretended churches throughout the whole earth; and that my zeal shall be for St. Peter and his successors, as the founder of the true and ancient Catholic faith, against all heretical kings, princes, states, or powers repugnant to the same; and although I, A. B., may follow, in case of persecution or otherwise, to be heretically despised, yet in soul and conscience I shall hold, aid, and succor the mother Church of Rome, as the true, ancient, and apostolic Church. I, A. B., further do declare not to act or control any matter or thing prejudicial unto her, in her sacred orders, doctrines, tenets, or commands, without leave of its supreme power or its authority, under her appointed; and being so permitted, then to act and further her interests more than my own earthly good and earthly pleasure, as she and her Head, his Holiness, and his successors have, or ought to have, the supremacy over all kings, princes, estates, or powers whatsoever, either to deprive them of their crowns, sceptres, powers, privileges, realms, countries, or governments, or to set up others in lieu thereof; they dissenting from the mother Church and her commands."

OATH OF THE JESUITS

"I, A. B., now in the presence of Almighty God, the blessed Virgin Mary, the blessed Michael the Archangel, the blessed St. John the Baptist, the holy apostles St. Peter and St. Paul, and all the saints and hosts of heaven, and to you my ghostly father, do declare from my heart, without mental reservation, that his Holiness Pope — — is Christ's Vicar General, and is the true and only Head of the Catholic or universal Church throughout the earth; and by the virtue of the keys of binding and loosing, given to his Holiness by my Saviour Jesus Christ, he hath power to depose heretical kings, princes, states, commonwealths, and governments, all being illegal without his sacred confirmation, and that they may safely be destroyed: THEREFORE, to the utmost of my power, I shall and will defend this doctrine, and his Holiness' rights and customs, against all usurpers of the heretical (or Protestant) authority whatsoever; especially against the now pretended authority and Church of England, and all adherents, in regard that they and she be usurpal and heretical, opposing the sacred mother Church of Rome, I do renounce and disown any allegiance as due to Protestants, or obedience to any of their inferior magistrates or officers, I do further declare the doctrine of the Church of England, the Calvinists, Huguenots, and of others of the name Protestants, to be damnable, and that they themselves are damned, and to be damned, that will not forsake the same. I do further declare, that I will help, assist, and advise all or any of his Holiness' agents, in any place wherever I shall be, in England, Scotland, and Ireland, or in any other territory or kingdom I shall come to, and do my utmost to extirpate the heretical Protestant's doctrine, and to destroy all their pretended powers, regal or otherwise. I do further promise and declare, that notwithstanding I am dispensed with, to assume any religion heretical, for the propagating of the mother Church's interest, to keep secret and private all her agents' counsels, from time to time, as they intrust me, and not to divulge, directly or indirectly, by word, writing, or circumstance, whatever, but to execute all that shall be proposed, given in charge, or discovered unto me, by you my ghostly father, or any of this sacred convent. All which, I, A. B., do swear, by the blessed Sacrament I am now to receive, to perform, and on my part to keep inviolable; and do call all the heavenly and glorious host of heaven to witness these my real intentions to keep this, my oath. In testimony hereof, I take this most holy and blessed sacrament of the Eucharist, and witness the same further with my hand and seal, in the face of this holy convent this day — An. Dom., etc."

OATH OF THE SAN FEDISTI.

"I, Son of the Holy Faith, No. —, promise and swear to sustain the altar and the Papal throne, to exterminate heretics, liberals, and all enemies of the Church, without pity for the cries of children, or of men and women. So help me God."

OATH OF THE IRISH RIBBON-MEN.

"I, Patrick McKenna, swear by Saints Peter and Paul, and by the blessed Virgin Mary, to be always faithful to the Society (of Ribbon-men); to keep and conceal all the secrets, and its words of order; to be always ready to execute the commands of my superior officers, and, as far as it shall lie in my power, to extirpate all heretics, and ALL THE PROTESTANTS, and to walk in their blood to the knee! May the Virgin Mary and all saints help me! To-day, the 2d of July, 1852.

"PAT. McKENNA, *from Tydavenet.*"

The following are the curses pronounced by the Papal Church against all who leave it for any Evangelical Church:

THE ROMISH CURSE.

"By the authority of God Almighty, the Father, Son, and Holy Ghost, and the undefiled Virgin Mary, mother and patroness of our Saviour, and of all celestial virtues, Angels, Archangels, Thrones, Dominions, Powers, Cherubim, and Seraphim; and of all the Holy Patriarchs, Prophets, and of all the Apostles and Evangelists, of the Holy Innocents, who in the sight of the Holy Lamb are found worthy to sing the new song of the Holy Martyrs and Holy Confessors, and of all the Holy Virgins, and of all Saints together with the holy elect of God; may he, — —, be damned. We excommunicate and anathematize him from the threshold of the Holy Church of God Almighty. We sequester him, that lie may be tormented, disposed, and be delivered over with Dathan and Abiram, and with those who say unto the Lord: 'Depart from us, we desire none of thy ways:' as a fire is quenched with water, so let the light of him be put out for evermore, unless he shall repent him and make satisfaction. Amen!

"May the Father, who creates man, curse him! May the Son, who suffered for us, curse him! May the Holy Ghost, who is poured out in Baptism, curse him! May the Holy Cross, which Christ, for our salvation, triumphing over his enemies, ascended, curse him!

"May the Holy Mary, ever virgin and mother of God, curse him! May St. Michael, the advocate of the Holy Souls, curse him! May all the Angels, Principalities, and Powers, and all Heavenly Armies, curse him! May the glorious band of the Patriarchs and Prophets curse him!

"May St. John the Precursor, and St. John the Baptist, and St. Peter, and St. Paul, and St. Andrew, and all other of Christ's Apostles together, curse him! And may all the rest of the Disciples and Evangelists, who, by their preaching converted the universe, and the holy and wonderful company of Martyrs and Confessors, who by their works are found pleasing to God Almighty, curse him! May the holy choir of the Holy Virgins, who for the honor of Christ have despised the things of the world, damn him! May all the saints from the beginning of the world to everlasting ages, who are found to be beloved of God, damn him!

"May he be damned wherever he be, whether in the house, or in the alley, or in the water, or in the church! May he be cursed in living and dying!

"May he be cursed in eating and drinking, in being hungry, in being thirsty, in fasting, and sleeping, in slumbering, and in sitting, in living, in working, in resting, and * * * and in blood-letting.

"May he be cursed in all the faculties of his body!

"May he be cursed inwardly and outwardly! May he be cursed in his hair; cursed be he in his brains, and in his vertex, in his temples, in his eyebrows, in his cheeks, in his jaw-bones, in his nostrils, in his teeth and grinders, in his lips, in his shoulders, in his arms, in his fingers!

"May he be damned in his mouth, in his breast, in his heart, and purtenances, down to the very stomach!

"May he be cursed in his reins and his groins; in his thighs, in his genitals, and in his hips, and in his knees, his legs, and his feet, and toe-nails!

"May he be cursed in all his joints, and articulation of the members; from the crown of his head to the soles of his feet may there be no soundness!

"May the Son of the living God, with all the glory of His Majesty, curse him! And may heaven, with all the powers that move therein, rise up against him, and curse and damn him; unless he repent and make satisfaction! Amen! So be it. Be it so. Amen!"

Now, we ask all candid men whose eyes have not been blinded by the dust of Popery and Democracy, can a Bishop or Priest, a Jesuit or Catholic, with these oaths upon their souls, be true American citizens? Not without the guilt of perjury, as black as the altar of a Roman Confessional! And if guilty of such perjury, the penitentiary should be their canonical residence for life! Strange to say, however, the Chief Justice of the United States, Roger B. Taney, is a Roman Catholic! Gen. Pierce's Postmaster-General, James Campbell, is both a Roman Catholic, and a member of the Order of Jesuits, having taken this very oath! Roman Catholics are now on the Federal Bench in the United States: Roman Catholics fill the offices of Attorneys-general; Roman Catholics represent this Government abroad; and Roman Catholics fill post-offices, land-offices, and a variety of offices at home, out of which Protestants were driven by Pierce's Administration, to make room for them!

LETTER FROM THOMAS A. R. NELSON, ESQ.

This gentleman, an able lawyer of East Tennessee, a member of the Presbyterian Church, and a member of the American party, was nominated an Elector for the State of Tennessee at large, by the American State Convention at Nashville, in February last. Though an ardent American—a great friend of *Mr. Fillmore*—and a member of the late Philadelphia Convention, and aided in the nomination of *Maj. Donelson*, he has been reluctantly compelled to decline the position of Elector. Under date of May 30, 1856, he addressed a letter of nine columns, of great force and ability, to *Messrs. A. W. Johnson, Robert C. Foster, 3d., John H. Callender, William N. Bilbo, Sam'l. Pritchett, and E. D. Farnsworth, State Executive Committee of the American Party, Nashville, Tennessee*, declining the position. Although we regret his inability to serve, as do the whole party in this State, yet, if his letter could be placed in the hands of every voter in the State, we would be willing to risk the contest without further discussion. Such is our estimate of this document. For the benefit of "Old Line Whigs," and such Democrats as are disposed to excuse and apologise for Romanism, we give the four concluding columns of this letter. The five preceding columns are mainly occupied with an outline and defence of the action of the Philadelphia Nominating Convention, and a discussion of the slavery question—questions we had discussed in this work before this document came to hand. Mr. Nelson concludes thus:

> "The Foreigners and Catholics were directly appealed to in the Presidential elections of 1848 and 1852. Who does not remember that, immediately preceding the election in 1844, fraudulent naturalization papers were manufactured in New York? Who has forgotten the Plaquemines fraud in Louisiana? Who has not heard of the abuse of Mr. Frelinghuysen for no other cause than that he was the President of the American Bible Society?

> "But, without dwelling upon other illustrations, look to the Democratic platform of 1852, and read the 8th section of the third resolution, which is in the following words:

> "'That the liberal principles embodied by Jefferson in the Declaration of Independence and sanctioned in the Constitution, which makes ours the land of liberty and the asylum of the oppressed of every nation, have ever been cardinal principles in the Democratic faith, and every attempt to abridge the present privilege of becoming citizens and the owners of soil among us, ought to be resisted with the same spirit which swept the alien and sedition laws from our statute

books.'

"During the last election in Tennessee, it was often said by Democrats that they were just as much opposed to the immigration of foreign criminals and paupers as members of the American party, but would not attach themselves to the latter because of their objections to its organization. But the Democratic Platform of 1852 contains no exception against criminals and paupers. The naturalization laws have, in practice, been found inadequate to their exclusion, and the platform, in effect, avows unqualified adherence to them without *abridgement* or modification.

"These laws are, in substance, declared to have *'ever been cardinal principles* in the Democratic faith.' By its own avowal, the Democratic party is responsible for giving encouragement to the whole policy of foreign immigration. If that policy has flooded the country with criminals and paupers; if it has produced riots and bloodshed in our large cities; if it has endangered the religious as well as the civil liberty of Protestants; if it has swelled the ranks of Abolition and fanned the flame of Agitation—the Democratic party, by its own avowal, is amenable at the bar of public opinion for these astounding and deplorable results. Reckless of consequences, it has persevered in a system hazardous to the stability of our institutions, because that system has annually swelled the number of its adherents, and increased the chances of its perpetual ascendency.

"Without adverting to the census tables, or repeating those familiar facts connected with the statistics of immigration which have been so extensively published, it is sufficient to observe that, under this continued patronage of the Democratic party, the immigration of foreigners has increased from a few thousands, twenty years ago, to nearly half a million in 1854.

"But the Democratic party cannot justly claim the exclusive honor of projecting or carrying out the system. More than twenty years ago, the Duke of Richmond declared, in substance, that he had conversed with most of the sovereigns and princes of Europe; that they were jealous of the influence of our republican institutions upon their own Government; that they did not expect to conquer us as a nation, but designed the subversion of our Government by the introduction of the low and surplus population of Europe among us; that 'discord, dissension, anarchy, and civil war would ensue, and some popular individual would assume the government and restore order, and the sovereigns of Europe, the emigrants, and many of the natives, would sustain him.' He also said, in speaking of the United States, that 'the Church of Rome has a design upon that country, and it will, in time, be the established religion, and will aid in the destruction of that republic.'

"These statements of the Duke of Richmond are abundantly cor-
roborated by other declarations, as well as the most undeniable facts
which have occurred since their promulgation.

"I have in my possession, among various others, two small books
published by 'the American and Foreign Christian Union,' 156 Cham-
bers street, New York, the one entitled 'Foreign Conspiracy,' the other, 'Startling Facts,' both of which, as I infer from their contents, were
written in the year 1834, long before the American party had an existence. The work entitled 'Foreign Conspiracy' is composed of a series
of articles originally published, over the signature of Brutus, in the
New York Observer. They now appear with the name of the author,
SAMUEL F. B. MORSE. His object in writing the work was to arouse public attention to the efforts then being made in Europe to propagate the
Catholic religion in the United States, and to show its danger to our
republican institutions. He traces the origin of the Leopold Foundation in Austria, under the especial patronage of the Emperor at Vienna
on the 12th May, 1829, and shows that one of its leading objects was
'to promote the greater activity of Catholic missions in America.'

"The letter of Prince *Metternich* to Bishop Fenwich, of Cincinnati,
under date, Vienna, April 27, 1830, is set out at length; and, in that
letter, the Prince informs the Bishop, among other things, that the Emperor 'allows his people to contribute to the support of the Catholic
Church in America.' Numerous quotations are made from the letters
of Foreign Bishops in the United States to their patrons at home, and,
among the rest, on page 85, is the following statement, made by one of
them, in regard to the people of the United States: 'We entreat all European Christians to unite in prayer to God for the conversion of these
unhappy heathen and obstinate heretics.' But, forbearing to multiply
quotations from this little work, admirable in most of its positions,
my main object, in citing it, was to make the following extract, from
page 15 of the preface, taken by the author from the lectures of the
celebrated Frederick Schlegel, delivered at Vienna in 1828, where that
distinguished foreigner says, 'The true nursery of all these destructive
principles, the revolutionary school for France and the rest of Europe,
has been North America. Thence the evil has spread over many other
lands, either by national contagion or by arbitrary communication;'
and also the following quotation, from page 118 of Mr. Morse's book:
'Austria, one of the Holy Alliance of sovereigns, leagued against the
liberties of the world, has the superintendence *of the operations of Popery in this country.'*

"In the tract entitled 'Startling Facts for American Protestants,'
written in the year 1834, by REV. HERMAN NORTON, Corresponding
Secretary of the American Protestant Society, from pages 27 to 39, an
account is given of a London pamphlet entitled 'New Plan of Emigration,' the production of a Roman Catholic gentleman, a London Bank-

er; in which a project for occupying the North Western States with the Roman Catholic population of Europe, is unfolded, together with *a map of the country*, and, among other things, it is said, on page 29: 'The first settlements should be made in those fertile prairie districts situated on the southern sides of the Canadian lakes, *where slavery is unknown*. On page 28, the objects of this society, as set forth in this pamphlet, are stated to be,

"'1. To provide the means for colonizing the surplus Roman Catholic population of Europe in our Western States.

"'2. To do this in such a way as to create a large demand for articles of British manufacture.

"'3. *To make Romanism the predominant religion of this country.'*

"The census tables will show that, since these plans were set on foot, in England and in Europe, to break down our government, there has been an astonishing increase in the foreign immigration to this country. Great as it was prior to the Revolutions in Europe in 1848, it has been amazingly augmented since that time. Millions of foreign money have been collected in Europe and expended since the organization of the society for the propagation of the faith, at Lyons in France, about the year 1822, in the United States. While an Austrian Emperor has had the charge, in a good degree, of the propagation of the Catholic religion in the United States, the public authorities in various parts of Europe have defrayed the expenses of their criminals and paupers to this country, as was clearly shown by Congressional investigations.

"What do these facts prove? Why, that the declaration of the Duke of Richmond, that the crowned heads of Europe intended to subvert our government, was true. What more do they prove? Why, that the effort to establish the Catholic religion in this country has, for more than twenty years, been conducted with steady perseverance, until the Catholics, who, in 1850, were more numerous, as the census compendium shows, than any one denomination of Methodists, are now no doubt stronger than all the Methodists put together, and stronger than any other denomination of Protestants.

"While these publications have been before the American people for more than twenty years, Democratic leaders have received, with open arms, the swarms of foreigners who have settled upon our shores. What care *they* for the slavery question, when they have seen this foreign immigration, according to the plan concerted in England, settling in the non-slaveholding States, and every year increasing the Abolition power? What care they for the Protestant religion, if the Catholics can only give them the numerical strength at the ballot-box? What regard have *they* for the preservation of our liberties, when European despots are seeking to undermine them, if those despots only send such myrmidons as will shout hosannas to Democracy and drive from the polls peaceful American citizens who oppose them? Is the preservation of the Union a matter of any consequence to them? Do they not in vision behold its scattered fragments and contemplate new confederacies, with hosts of new offices and millions of spoil?

"Can any one doubt that the Democratic party is in league with all the dangerous elements that have disturbed and are continuing to disturb our once peaceful and happy country, and that they stickle at nothing when votes are at stake?

"Look to their conduct in running Mr. Polk as a tariff man in the North, and an anti-tariff man in the South! Look to the two lives of Cass. Look to their equivocal position as to slavery and the Union. Look to their appeals to foreigners and Catholics by name in the elections of 1844 and 1852, and probably in 1848. Look to their alliance with Free Germans and Fourierites, Free Soilers and Secessionists. And, above all, look to the miserable cant with which they raise the hue and cry of persecution in favor of the Catholics, and, indirectly, deny to Protestant ministers the right to make war upon a huge corporation, calling itself a church, dealing in human souls, reeking with the blood of martyrs, and begrimed with more than ten centuries of oppression.

"No wonder that they have vilified and denounced the American party with every term of opprobrium that our vocabulary can furnish. No wonder they talk of dark lanterns and secret oaths and midnight assemblies. No wonder that they strive to frighten their followers with the notion that the American party is a raw-head and bloody bones, which should be shunned and avoided. For, if honest men of that party will only take the trouble to shake off the control of their leaders: to think, examine, to read, reflect, and act for themselves, there are thousands of Democrats in the South who would scorn, like the American party, an alliance with Abolitionists, and there are tens of thousands of Protestant Union-loving Democrats everywhere, who have only confided in, to be deceived and betrayed by, their leaders, and, if they discover, as it is hoped they will, that they have brought them to the crumbling verge of an awful precipice, they have patriotism enough and Protestantism enough to break away from them rather than make the awful plunge.

"I regret that I am admonished by the length to which I have extended this communication, that I cannot now discuss the Catholic question, as I had hoped to do at the outset, and I shall present only a few disjointed remarks in connection with it.

"The American party does not seek to impose any religious test such as prevailed in the reign of Charles II., when two thousand Non-conformist ministers were driven from their pulpits, or such, as in the same reign, was imposed upon Roman Catholics and continued from 1673 to 1828. The American party does not propose that any religious test, of any kind, shall be imposed by law, upon any person whatever, but it does seek to organize a public sentiment on the Catholic question, just in the same mode that, in times past, parties have sought to organize public sentiment upon the tariff question—the bank question—the internal improvement question—the temperance question, and every other question which has been the subject of difference. If it is lawful to say, I will not vote for you because you are a Whig, it is equally lawful to say—I will not vote for you because you are a foreigner. If it is lawful to say, I will not vote for you because you are a Democrat, it is equally lawful to say, I will not vote for you because you are a Catholic.

"Neither does the American party propose, in the slightest degree, to interfere with any of the rights secured to Roman Catholics, in common with others, by the Constitution. If they choose to worship a great DOLL as the Virgin Mary—to burn tall wax-candles in daylight—to pray to God in an unknown tongue—to believe that a simple wafer is the actual body, and common wine the very blood of our Saviour—to enforce the celibacy of the clergy—to worship the host—to believe that old toe-nails and pieces of wood are precious relics—to prevent their people from reading the Bible—to refuse to send their children to Protestant schools—to retain the confessional and the nunnery—to pin their faith to unauthenticated traditions—to assert that theirs is the only true Church, and to perpetrate a thousand ridiculous mummeries—the members of the American party with one accord will say, molest them not, disturb them not, trouble them not; the religious privileges of this country are as free to them as they are to us, and we will not, by law or by violence, interrupt or interfere with them in the slightest degree. But knowing that the Catholic Church was for a thousand years allied to the State; that it claimed dominion, in temporal as well as spiritual affairs, over the kings of the earth; that it regards the Pope as the Vicegerent of the Almighty; that he wears the tiara as the symbol of his power in heaven, earth, and hell; that Romanists treat all other professions as heretics; that its Archbishops, Bishops and Priests are sworn to persecute all who differ with them; that the persecuting spirit of that Church has been displayed, for centuries, in the most odious acts of cruelty as well as the most despotic tyranny that ever cursed the earth; that fire and faggot, confiscation and torture have been its favorite weapons; that no age, or sex or condition has been exempt from its inhuman butcheries and demoniac lusts; that it exterminated the Albigenses and Waldenses; that it caused the gutters of Paris to run with human blood on St. Bartholomew's day; that it lighted the fires of Smithfield; that through the instrumentality of Tyrconnel and Catholic and Irish Rappadees, it perpetrated the inhuman atrocities of the Irish Massacres; that, it drove the Huguenots from France, and the

Puritans from England; that it has delighted in the chains and dungeons of the Inquisition, and shouted, with fiendish exultation, at the cries and groans of the victims in the *auto da fe*; that no republican government has ever flourished under its sway; that it regards ignorance as the mother of devotion, and denies the obligation of an oath; that it gave rise to the Order of Jesuits, the most detestable sect that the earth has ever seen; that, in the midst of the blaze of the nineteenth century, it has burned the Bible in America and imprisoned men and women in Europe for no other offence than that of reading it; that, abusing the freedom of the press and speech secured in the United States, it unblushingly avows that all Protestantism is heresy—that it is a crime—and punished in *Christian countries like Spain and Italy* as a crime; that it has banished the Bible from Protestant schools, when under its control; that it has intermeddled in political elections, and is struggling for political power; that it wears a mask and claims to be harmless in this country for present effect, although it has never renounced one of its dogmas in any authoritative mode; that it is typified, in the Bible, as the Man of Sin and the Great Whore of Babylon; that it comes to us as an angel of light, but is allied with the Prince of Darkness: knowing all these things, and believing that the Roman Catholic Church, now that it is covered with the broad wings of Modern Democracy, partakes of its meat and is pampered by its patronage, is, infinitely, the most dangerous political power with which the people of the United States have ever been compelled to grapple, the American party invites all who love national liberty more than Democracy; who prefer civil and religious freedom to the spoils of office; who revere the memory of Tyndale, Luther, and Calvin; of Cranmer, Latimer, and Ridley; of the seven Bishops; of Fox; of the Puritan fathers; of Wesley and Hall; of the Reformers and Protestants of every name, and, more than all, of our revolutionary ancestors, to burst the fetters of party and come to the rescue of their bleeding country, bleeding at every pore from wounds inflicted by Democratic hands, amidst the jeers of European despots, the shouts of foreigners in our midst, and the taunts and sneers of Catholics and Jesuits all around us!

"Let not Protestant ministers be intimidated by the impudent assaults of a venal press, or the fierce denunciations of infuriated politicians, from doing their whole duty in the pulpit and at the polls. No Presbyterian has ever denied to a Methodist the right to question his religious faith, and no Methodist will dispute the right of other denominations to impugn his creed. Methodists have assailed the Presbyterian doctrine of election. Presbyterians, in turn, have assailed their ideas of perfection and falling from grace. Both have controverted the Baptists' views of immersion, and all have denied the Episcopalians' doctrine of *apostolic succession*. These and many other points of difference have, from the foundation of our government, often been the subjects of earnest, protracted, and excited discussion; but when did any American Protestant ever deny to another American Protestant the constitutional right to differ with him in opinion, and to express that difference through the press, in the pulpit, or any other constitutional mode? Yet, it has been reserved for Democratic presses to attempt, for electioneering purposes, to curb the free spirit of Protestant ministers: to denounce them as "REVEREND HYPOCRITES;" and, when beholding at home and abroad, on the land and on the sea, among Christians and Pagans, in the halls of legislation, in churches and schools, in free speech, and in a free press, and in ten thousand other forms, the magnificent and glorious results of the Reformation, to ask, with impudent assurance, 'WHAT HAS PROTESTANTISM DONE FOR THE WORLD?' Not satisfied with the storm of execration which such an infamous interrogatory produced, the Nashville Union and American, the leading Democratic paper in Tennessee, in a very abusive article entitled '*What has it accomplished?*' under date of April 26, 1856, thus speaks, among other things, of what he styles 'the Know Nothing Organization:'

"'*It has done more than this: it has gone into the Church and* CONVERTED THE PULPIT INTO A POLITICAL ROSTRUM—*it has turned the attention of the ministry from* THE PEACEFUL PATHS OF CHRISTIANITY TO THE ARENA OF POLITICAL TURMOIL—*it has pulled down the banner of the Cross, and placed in its stead* THE RED FLAG OF INTOLERANCE AND PROSCRIPTION.'

"While Protestant ministers, in the enjoyment of the rights secured to them by the Constitution, have, as before stated, often engaged in controversies with each other as to their differences in matters of Church government and speculative faith, they have, with one accord, from the foundation of the government, preached and published their views against the Roman Catholic Church—which arrogates a superiority over them all, and stigmatizes them as sects—long before the American party ever had an existence. But because, in the course of events, it has become necessary for politicians to inquire what effect an acknowledgment of the temporal supremacy of the Pope may have upon our free institutions, the Democratic party—if it is to be judged of by its organ—would gag the Protestant clergy, deny to them a right which they have always exercised, and, if they dare to oppose the colossal strides of Rome, denounce them as having converted the pulpit into a *political rostrum,*' and as having raised '*the red flag of Intolerance and Proscription.*'

"It is not for me to prescribe, nor do I desire to dictate the duty of Protestant ministers; but if, in the combined efforts which the Catholics have been making under the patronage of European despots and noblemen, and the encouragement of Democratic demagogues in our own country, they see that this tremendous corporation has planted its footsteps in all our large cities—is possessing itself of the North-West and the Mississippi valley—and is encircling them, as it were, with a wall of fire: if they see that the newspapers and periodicals of that corporation have published doctrines in this free country which they would scarcely avow in the Roman Catholic countries of Europe: if, in one word, they believe that they are to be persecuted and exterminated by Catholics, or take care of themselves before it is too late—then Protestant ministers, agreeing as they do in all great doctrines, and differing only as to those which are not absolutely essential, will cease to disagree among themselves, at least until after they avert a common danger, and will rally as a band of brethren to resist, in such mode as they may deem proper, the encroachments and the insults of Rome, and all her satellites and allies.

"If I do not greatly err in the estimate which I place upon the Protestant clergymen of America, the Democratic party and the Catholics will discover, sooner or later, that the same spirit which caused the Protestant fathers to brave the perils of the BOOT and the STAKE: to stand, without flinching, before such miscreant judges as *Jeffreys* and *Scroggs*: to yield two thousand pulpits and look beggary and starvation in the face, rather than compromise with conscience; and, above all, to risk the untried dangers of the ocean and settle among savages—will nobly animate their descendants, and they will act in a manner worthy of themselves and of the great cause which is intrusted to their keeping.

"Never was a more unfounded charge made against any party than that of *proscription* against the American party. It is only the political feature—the allegiance to the Pope of Rome—which we have felt called upon especially to oppose: leaving it to Protestant ministers to expose, if they choose, the absurdity of Catholic theological tenets.

"It is a historical fact that the Romish clergy of France in 1682, under the lead of Louis XIV., made a declaration that 'Kings and sovereigns are not subject to any ecclesiastical power by the order of God in temporal things, and their subjects cannot be released from the obedience which they owe them, nor absolved from their oath of allegiance.' The doctrine of this declaration is called indifferently 'the Gallican, or the French, or the Cis-Alpine doctrine. That of the Court of Rome is called the Italian, or trans-Alpine doctrine."

"Under the solemn assurance of the Louisiana delegation that the native Catholics of Louisiana do not acknowledge the temporal supremacy of the Pope, they were admitted to representation in the American Council and Convention, and this fact abundantly proves that there is no desire to *persecute* Catholics for their religion, but only a determination to resist their political doctrine, which, although denied by Mr. Chandler in Congress, has been incontrovertibly established by the history of that Church for ages, the avowals of Mr. Brownson, the rebuke of Mr. Chandler by the Dublin Tablet, and other overwhelming proofs.

"In concluding this letter, it would, perhaps, be proper to dwell upon the claims of Messrs. Fillmore and Donelson to the support of the American people of all parties; but their characters are so well known, and I have already so extended my remarks, that I deem it unnecessary to observe any thing more than that Mr. Fillmore, by the faithful discharge of his duty, won the most cordial approbation of his political enemies as well as political friends, and had the confidence of the whole country when he retired from office, and has done nothing since to destroy it; while Maj. Donelson, as our Minister to Texas, to Prussia, and to Denmark, sustained the dignity of our country and ac-quitted himself with honor—denounced the unhallowed proceedings of the Southern Convention—struggled manfully, as the Democratic editor of the Washington Union, in behalf of the Compromise, and never withdrew from it until May, 1852, when, so far as I understand his course from his public acts, being unwilling to 'blow hot and cold' on the slavery question, and to aid the Democratic party in wearing a Northern and a Southern face, he indignantly retired from it, and subsequently attached himself to the American party in the hope that it could carry on his most cherished object—the preservation of the Union.

"The object of selecting an old-line Whig and an old-line Demo-crat, was to nail to the counter the charge that the American party is the Whig party in disguise, and to induce, if possible, conservative men of both the old parties to unite and rescue the country from Dem-ocratic misrule.

"Hundreds, thousands of Democrats in Tennessee, acting upon their own impulses and without concert with their leaders, attached themselves to the American party, but under the abuse of the leaders withdrew from it. Although, personally, I have no claims upon the Democracy, and have been always opposed to that party, yet I would respectfully observe that first impressions are often the best, and if such Democrats will take the trouble faithfully and honestly to exam-ine the questions of the day for themselves, uninfluenced by the dic-tation of party leaders on either side, they will, doubtless, find many and cogent reasons to return to their first love.

"But to such of the old-line Whigs as have not already gone over to the Democratic party, I do feel that I have the right through this or any other medium to address a few words. It is well known that I have been a Whig from my boyhood, and until I attached myself to the American party about twelve months ago; and that, in some form or other, I have labored in behalf of the Whig cause from my youth up—in good report and evil report, in prosperity and in adversity, and without fee or reward. And, with great deference to the opinions of others, I would inquire what has any old-line Whig to gain, either for his country or himself, by listening to the seductive flatteries of

Democracy, as he looks upon the dismembered fragments of the Whig party, or sits, like Marius, amid the ruins of Carthage? What party is it that has brought about the desolation you behold? To whose strategy was it owing that the once impregnable city was betrayed and surrounded, and its lofty battlements levelled with the dust? What foul coalition circumvented you, and whose pestilential breath is now whispering in your ear? Has that party against which you have fought for twenty years—which you have regarded as essentially corrupt and dangerous to the Union—all at once, and by some magical and unknown process, been cleansed of its impurities, and does it stand before you clothed in a white and spotless robe? What are some of the reasons why you opposed it?

"It denounced proscription for opinion's sake before it came into power, but kept the guillotine in continual motion afterwards. It rebuked any interference with the freedom of elections, and then denied its doctrine, and sought in countless ways to control them. It charged the administration of John Quincy Adams with reckless extravagance, and has expended as much, or nearly as much, of the public treasure in one year as he did in the course of his administration. It was favorable to *a* bank, a judicious tariff, and internal improvements by the general government, but has crushed beneath its iron heel the whole American system. It promised a gold and silver currency, and told the farmers that they and their wives should have 'long silken purses, through the interstices of which the yellow gold would shine and glitter,' but has given us instead more than thirteen hundred State bonds, with a capital of more than three hundred millions. It has united the purse and the sword by means of its odious Sub-Treasury. It trampled beneath its feet the broad seal of the State of New Jersey, and encouraged Dorr's rebellion.

"It annexed Texas and California, and has strengthened the Abolition power. It sustains the frequent use of the veto, and under the name of Democracy delights in the exercise of monarchical prerogative. It proclaimed in 1844 and 1845, that not a thimblefull of blood would be shed by any war growing out of the annexation of Texas, when that war sacrificed thousands of lives, and has cost us millions in money and land. It boasted, in regard to the Oregon question, that we must have '54° 40' or fight,' but swallowed its own words, and in later times has attempted to retrieve its courage by the sublime and magnificent bombardment of Greytown! It ordered General Taylor into the heart of the Mexican country with a feeble force, and when his victories had won the grateful plaudits of his countrymen, it had the unparalleled meanness, while he was still fighting our battles, to censure the capitulation of Monterey. It had the baseness to call General Scott from the head of a victorious army, and to attempt to disgrace him in the eyes of his own country and the world. It denounced

Judge White as a renegade, General Harrison as a coward, Mr. Clay as a blackguard, and General Scott as a fool. And, without repeating what has been already urged in regard to its attitude upon the slavery question and the other topics that have been discussed, I submit to the old-line Whigs that there is no principle which the Democratic party sincerely holds in common with them, and that they should unite with us in the effort to man the ship of State with officers and men devoted to the Constitution and true to the Union, in the hope that it may be rescued from the whirlpools and breakers among which it has been so recklessly conducted.

"Having expressed myself with the independence which should characterize a freeman, I cannot expect that a party which has dealt in the most unmitigated denunciation of wiser and better men than myself, will permit my observations to pass with impunity, but I shall be amply compensated for their abuse if abler tongues and pens will improve upon these hurried remarks, and teach our Democratic traducers that they cannot continue, without just retaliation, their unjustifiable assaults upon the American party.

"Yours respectfully,
"THOS. A. R. NELSON."

PROSCRIBING FOREIGNERS—FOREIGN IMMIGRATION—FOREIGN PAUPERS AND CRIMINALS—FOREIGNERS ELECTED GEN. PIERCE—OPINIONS OF GREAT MEN.

The issue which most disturbs the Sag-Nicht Foreign Catholic Locofoco Dry-rot *patriots*, of the present day, in connection with the principles of the American party, is their *proscription* of foreign-born citizens. If the reader will turn back to the Philadelphia Platform, and consult the 3d, 4th, 5th, and 9th sections of that instrument, it will be seen that the American party really proscribe only those who are proscribed by the *Constitution of the United States*, and the laws defining the rights of foreign-born citizens. The American party demand the enactment of laws upon this subject more *definite*, and in accordance with the provisions of the Constitution.

The only *positive* work which the Constitution does, in regard to foreigners, is to *proscribe*. It contains but five clauses touching the subject: four of these are PROHIBITORY, and the other is simply *permissive*. There is no guaranteeing clause whatever. We must be pardoned for recalling the very language of the Constitution—for in this *progressive* age, our "Young American" generation is fast losing sight of the plainest features of that document: which, with Fillibustering, Fire-eating agitators, is *Old Fogyism*! Let the Constitution speak for itself:

Section 5, Article II. of the Constitution says: "No person, except a natural-born citizen, or a citizen of the United States at the time of the adoption of this Constitution, shall be eligible to the office of President." That is proscription.

Section 3, Article XII., says: "No person constitutionally ineligible to the office of President shall be eligible to the office of Vice-President of the United States." That is proscription.

Section 8, Article I., says: "No person shall be a Senator who shall not have attained the age of thirty years, and been nine years a citizen of these United States." That is proscription.

Section 2, Article I., says: "No person shall be a Representative who shall not have attained the age of twenty-five years, and been seven years a citizen." This is proscription.

These are the disabilities imposed upon Foreigners after they have been made citizens. But, more than this, the Constitution leaves it discretionary whether to make them citizens at all. It simply confers the power—*simply permits*. Here is the remaining clause, to which we have alluded:

Section 8, Article I., says: "Congress shall have power to establish a uniform rule of naturalization, and uniform laws on the subject of bankruptcies throughout the United States."

But let us notice the matter of foreign emigration to this country. In that fragment of a nation, composed of three and a quarter millions, which accomplished the American Revolution, there were in the United Colonies, in the year 1775, just 20,000 more foreigners than now come into this country in six months!

The progress of emigration into this country, as shown from the State Department at Washington, is after this fashion:

In the year 1852,	375,000
In the year 1853,	368,000
In the year 1854, the returns of the first six months warrant the estimate for the entire year of	500,000
The aggregate, for the first four and a half years of this decennial term, is	1,801,000

There is no reason for believing that the vast immigration of this year will diminish. In fact, there is no limit to its rate of progress but the means of conveyance. Now, then, we have upon this basis an aggregate for the six years and a half intervening between this period and 1860, of   3,250,000

Making for the current ten years, the astounding aggregate of   5,051,000

Let Americans charge continually that the righteous ground upon which it plants itself is, THAT AMERICANS SHALL RULE AMERICA. Let them point the voters of the country to solid facts, from which there is no escape. Tell them that the emigration to this country, according to the Census records at Washington, was:

From	1790 to 1810	120,000
From	1810 to 1820	114,000
From	1820 to 1830	203,979
From	1830 to 1840	778,500
From	1840 to 1850	1,542,850

—and that statistics show that during the present decade, from 1850 to 1860, in regularly increasing ratio, nearly four millions of aliens will probably be poured in upon us.

Point to the fact, that from this immigration spring nearly four-fifths of the beggary, two-thirds of the pauperism, and more than three-fifths of the crime of our country; that more than half the public charities, more than half the prisons and alms-houses, more than half the police and the cost of administering criminal justice, are for foreigners,—and let the demand be made, that national and State legislation shall interfere, to direct, ameliorate, and control these elements, so far as it may be done within the limits of the Constitution.

Let Americans everywhere, and at all times, charge home and force upon the attention of the people the alarming fact that if immigration continues at the above rates, in thirty years from this time the population of this country will exceed that of France, England, Spain, Portugal, Sweden, and Switzerland, all combined; that in fifteen years the foreign will outnumber the native population; that in 1854 the number of foreign immigrants was 500,000, of which 307,639 arrived at the port of New York; that the white population of North Carolina is only a little over 500,000—so that enough come to settle a State as populous as North Carolina in a year. Set forth the statistical facts, as shown by the last Census, that the immigration of 1854 was more than equal to the white population of either one of eighteen States of this Union; and in proof, point them to the following startling facts:

A. Table comparing the white population of the States therein enumerated, with the foreign immigration of 1854, and showing the excess of foreign immigrants for this year above the respective population of the several States.

States.	White population.	Excess of immigrants.
Arkansas	162,189	337,811
Alabama	426,514	73,486
California	91,635	418,365
South Carolina	274,563	226,437
Connecticut	363,099	136,901
Delaware	71,169	328,831
Florida	47,203	452,717
Iowa	191,881	308,119
Louisiana	225,491	374,509
Maryland	417,943	82,057
Michigan	395,071	104,929
Mississippi	295,718	204,282
New Hampshire	317,456	182,514
New Jersey	465,509	34,491
Rhode Island	143,875	356,125
Texas	154,034	345,946
Vermont	213,402	186,598
Wisconsin	304,756	195,244

Analyze this table, and show from it that the foreign immigration of 1854 was sufficient to have settled three States equal to Arkansas, three equal to Iowa, three equal to Texas, two to Louisiana, four to Rhode Island, five to California, seven to Delaware, or ten to Florida; so that under the principle of the Kansas and Nebraska act, while immigrants continue pouring in upon us at the present rate, we may have within one year ten new States applying for admission into the Union, entitled to their twenty Senators in the United States Senate; and yet this would be but the Senatorial representation of 500,000 foreigners.

Let the light of truth be heard upon the great question of immigration, and let the people see that if the ratio of immigration continues as it has been since 1850, during the ten years from 1850 to 1860 there will have come four millions of foreigners into this country—enough to settle eighty States equal to Florida, thirty-two equal to Rhode Island, sixteen equal to Louisiana, or eight equal to Maryland, North Carolina, South Carolina, Georgia, Michigan, Mississippi, Vermont, Alabama, New Hampshire, or New Jersey. So the Senatorial representation of foreigners may reach one hundred and sixty members in the United States Senate, and cannot be less than twenty in a body composed of but sixty-two members representing thirty-one States.

UNITED STATES COAST SURVEY—FOREIGNISM AND NATIVEISM.

The reader will find below a list of the names of the employees in the Coast Survey, classified according to birth, and their respective salaries:

Natives.	Salary.	Foreigners.	Salary.
E. Nutty	$1,200	J. E. Hilgard	$2,200
J. T. Hoover	600	S. E. Werner	1,419
J. H. Toomer	519	C. A. Schott	1,500
J. E. Blackenship	500	J. Main	1,100
R. Freeman	350	G. Rumpf	1,000
H. Mitchell	1,000	J. Weisner	900
H. Heaton	700	L. F. Pourtales	1,500
R. S. Avery	660	S. Hein	2,500
J. Kincheloe	339	J. Welch	1,565
G. C. Blanchard	339	A. Brschke	1,408
R. E. Evans	339	— — Balback	639
R. L. Hawkins	1,200	— — Lendenkehl	782
W. McPherson	700	W. P. Schultz	704
W. M. C. Fairfax	1,800	G. McCoy	2,000
M. J. McClery	1,600	A. Rolle	1,700
— — Poterfield	1,000	G. B. Metzenroth	1,095
L. Williams	860	J. C. Koudnip	939
John Key	782	J. Rutherdall	526

— — Martin	751	J. Barrett	375
B. Hooe	419	J. Vierbunchen	1,095
F. Fairfax	500	P. Vierbunchen	281
H. McCormick	156	T. Hunt	704
E. Wharton	1,100	J. Missenson	626
J. Knight	1,700	R. Schelpass	469
F. Dankworth	1,700	C. Ramkin	313
J. V. N. Throop	1,252	F. White	960
R. Knight	939	D. Flyn	600
C. A. Knight	626	T. Kinney	525
G. Mathiot	1,800	C. Kraft	420
S. Harris	519	B. Neff	526
S. D. O'Brien	1,059	A. Maedell	1,095
A. Geatman	704		$31,867
H. Tine	626		
C. B. Snow	1,000		
J. Smith	593		
G. Hitz	313		
J. Cronion	519		
A. W. Russell	1,300		
— — Tansill	660		
V. E. King	720		
F. Holden	500		
J. Mitchell	331		
W. Bright	216		
	$24,429		

The whole number of natives, 43; number of foreigners, 31. Amount paid natives, $24,429; amount paid foreigners, $31,867. The average salary of the natives is $568 12 per year; of the foreigners, $1,029 98 per year—nearly double that of the natives. Is not this *favoritism* to the foreigner, and *discrimination* against the native? The disbursing officer, S. Hein, receives $2,500.

The result of the last Presidential election was controlled by *foreign votes*, beyond all question. Look at the figures—see how they foot up—and see that the country is controlled by foreigners:

States.	Foreign population.	Foreign vote.	Pierce's majority.	Electoral vote for Pierce.
New York,	655,224	93,317	27,201	35
Pennsylvania,	303,105	43,300	19,446	27
Maryland,	51,011	7,287	4,945	8
Louisiana,	67,308	9,615	1,392	6
Missouri,	76,570	10,938	7,698	9
Illinois,	111,860	15,980	15,653	11
Ohio,	218,099	31,157	16,694	23
Wisconsin,	110,471	15,781	11,418	5
Iowa,	20,968	2,995	1,180	4
Rhode Island,	23,832	3,404	1,109	4
Connecticut,	38,374	5,482	2,870	6
Delaware,	5,243	749	25	3
New Jersey,	59,804	8,543	5,749	7
California,	21,628	10,000	5,694	4
	——	——	——	——
	258,548	120,094		152

RECAPITULATION.

Pierce's vote,	1,602,663
Scott's vote,	1,385,990
	216,673
Foreign vote,	367,320
Pierce's majority,	216,673
	150,647

The foreign vote exceeded Pierce's majority over Scott, 150,647 votes.

It is thus demonstrated that in each of these fourteen States the foreign vote was larger than the majority given for General Pierce; and it is also demonstrated that the aggregate foreign vote of these fourteen States is more than twice the whole number of General Pierce's majorities in said States. If even one-half of the foreign vote had been given to General Scott, he would have been elected instead of General Pierce!

The following New York City statistics set forth the amount of *crime* committed in that city for six months ending in June, 1855:

"It appears that the number of arrests made during that time were 25,110. Of these, no less than 9,755 were for intoxication and disorderly conduct combined; and 7,025 for crimes that had their origin in the dram-shops, to wit:

"Assault and battery, disorderly conduct, vagrancy, &c. The greatest number of arrests were in June, showing that during the hot weather, as is generally the case, more liquor was drank. The birth-place of the criminals, for two months, was as follows:

United States,	1,750
Ireland,	5,117
Germany,	1,010
All other places,	4,847

"It needs no argument to prove if there had been no intoxicating liquor sold in that city, a large portion of the crimes and the misery resulting therefrom would have been prevented."

MORE INSTRUCTIVE STATISTICS.—The Jersey City Sentinel of the 22d ult. publishes statistics of crime and pauperism in Jersey City and Hudson County, as follows:

"Number of inhabitants in Jersey City, 21,000, viz.: natives, 13,000; Irish, 5,000; other foreigners, 4,000. Number of persons who have been confined in the city prison, 4,100, viz.: natives, 75; Irish, 3,550; other foreigners, 475. Number of persons confined in the county jail at present, 68, viz.: natives, 2; Irish, 58: other foreigners, 8. Of 188 persons who have been inmates of the Almshouse, none have been natives, and no foreigners except Irish. Of 723 who received aid from the Poor-master, 2 were natives, and 721 were Irish."

We will now submit, as authorities, some names which ought to have weight with the American people, and which demonstrate, beyond all contradiction, that we have had "Know Nothings" in our country in former days, if they were not called by that name! Here are the words and sentiments of these "dark-lantern patriots:"

"Against the insidious wiles of foreign influence, (I conjure you to believe me, fellow-citizens,) the jealousy of a free people ought to be constantly awake. It is one of the most baneful foes of a Republican government." —WASHINGTON.

"I hope we may find some hope in future of shielding ourselves from foreign influence, in whatever form it may be attempted. I wish there were an ocean of fire between this and the old world." —JEFFERSON.

"Foreign influence is a Grecian horse to the republic: we cannot be too careful to exclude its entrance." —MADISON.

"There is an imperative necessity for reforming the Naturalization Laws of the United States." —DANIEL WEBSTER.

"It is high time we should become a little more Americanized, and instead of feeding the paupers and laborers of England, feed our own; or else, in a short time, by our present policy, we shall become paupers ourselves." — ANDREW JACKSON.

"I agree with the father of his country, that we should guard with a jealousy becoming a free people, our institutions, against the insidious wiles of foreign influence." — HENRY CLAY.

"Our naturalization laws are unquestionably defective, or our alms-houses would not now be filled with paupers. Of the 134,000 paupers in the United States, 68,000 are foreigners, and 66,000 natives. The annals of crime have swelled as the jails of Europe have poured their contents into the country, and the felon convict, reeking from a murder in Europe, or who has had the fortune to escape punishment for any other crime abroad, easily gains naturalization here, by spending a part of five years within the limits of the United States. Our country has become a Botany Bay, into which Europe annually discharges her criminals of every description." — JOHN M. CLAYTON, United States Senator.

Forty years ago, this subject came up in the Congress of the United States, and that far-seeing statesman and patriot, JOHN RANDOLPH, of Virginia, made a speech, from which we take the following extract:

"How long the country would endure this foreign yoke in its most odious and disgusting form he could not tell, but this he would say, that if we were to be dictated to and ruled by foreigners, he would much rather be ruled by a British Parliament than by British subjects here. Should he be told that those men fought in the war of the Revolution, he would answer, that those who did so were not included by him in the class he adverted to. That was a civil war, and they and we were at its commencement alike British subjects. Native Britons, therefore, then taking arms on our side, gave them the same rights as those who were born in this country, and his motion could be easily modified so as to provide for any that might be of this description, but no such modification, he was sure, would be found necessary, for this plain reason, to wit:

"Where were the soldiers of the Revolution who were not natives? They were either already retired or else retiring to that great reckoning where discounts were not allowed. If the honorable gentleman (opposing the proposition) would point his finger to any such kind of person now living, he would agree to his being made an exception to the amendment. It was time that the American people should have a character of their own, and where would they find it? In New England and in Virginia only, because they were a homogeneous race—a peculiar people. They never yet appointed foreigners to sit in that house (of Congress) for them, or to fill their high offices. In both States this was their policy: it was not found in, nor was it owing to their paper constitutions, but what was better, it was interwoven in the frame of their thoughts and sentiments, in their steady habits, in their principles from the cradle—a much more solid security than could be found in any abracadabra which constitution-mongers could scrawl upon paper.

"It might be indiscreet in him to say it, for, to say the truth, he had as little of that rascally virtue, prudence, he apprehended, as any man, and could as little conceal what he felt as affect what he did not feel. He knew it was not the way for him to conciliate the manufacturing body, yet he would say that he wished with all his heart that his bootmaker, his hatter, and other manufacturers, would rather stay in Great Britain, under their own laws, than come here to make laws for us, and leave us to import our covering. We must have our clothing home-made, (said he,) but I would much rather have my workmen home-made, and import my clothing. Was it best to have our own unpolluted republic peopled with its own pure *native* republicans, or erect another Sheffield, another Manchester, and another Birmingham, upon the banks of the Schuylkill, the Delaware, and the Brandywine, or have a host of Luddites amongst us—wretches from whom every vestige of the human creation seemed to be effaced? Would they wish to have their elections on that floor decided by a rabble? What was the ruin of old Rome? Why, their opening their gates and letting in the rabble of the whole world to be their legislators!"

"If (said he) you wish to preserve among your fellow-citizens that exalted sense of freedom which gave birth to the Revolution—if you wish to keep alive among them the spirit of '76, you must endeavor to stop this flood of immigration! You must teach the people of Europe that if they do come here, all they must hope to receive is protection—but that they must have no share in the government. From such men a temporary party may receive precarious aid, but the country cannot be safe nor the people happy where they are introduced into government, or meddle with public concerns in any great degree."

"This (said Mr. Randolph) is a favorable time to make a stand against this evil (immigration,) and if not *this* session, he hoped that in the *next* there would be a revisal of the naturalization laws."

A few short epistles from the pen of Gen. WASHINGTON, and we will close this chapter. These we take from the "Papers of Washington by Sparks." George Washington, justly styled the "father of his country," was a great and good man—a primitive Know Nothing—a praying Protestant—and withal, the man who was "first in war, first in peace, and first in the hearts of his countrymen." Here are the honest sentiments of this man:

TO RICHARD HENRY LEE.

"MORRISTOWN, May 17, 1777.

"DEAR SIR:—I take the liberty to ask you what Congress expects I am to do with the many foreigners they have at different times promoted to the rank of field-officers, and, by the last resolve, two to that of colonels.... These men have no attachment nor ties to the country, further than interest binds them. Our officers think it exceedingly hard, after they have toiled in this service and have sustained many losses, to have strangers put over them, whose merit, perhaps, is not equal to their own, but whose effrontery will take no denial.... It is by the zeal and activity of our own people that the cause must be supported, and not by a few hungry adventurers....

"I am, &c.,
"G. WASHINGTON."

[Vol. IV., p. 423.]

TO THE SAME.

"MIDDLEBROOK, June 1, 1777.

"You will, before this can reach you, have seen Monsieur Ducoudray. What his real expectations are, I do not know; but I fear, if his appointment is equal to what I have been told is his expectation, it will be attended with unhappy consequences. *To say nothing of the policy of intrusting a department, on the execution of which the salvation of the army depends, to a foreigner who has no other tie to bind him to the interests of this country than honor*, I would beg leave to observe that by putting Mr. D. at the head of the artillery, you will lose a very valuable officer in General Knox, who is a man of great military reading, sound judgment, and clear conceptions, who will resign if any one is put over him.... I am, &c.,

"G. WASHINGTON."

[Vol. IV., p. 446.]

TO GOUVERNEUR MORRIS, ESQ.

"WHITE PLAINS, July 24, 1778.

"DEAR SIR:—The design of this is to touch cursorily upon a subject of very great importance to the well-being of these States: much more so than will appear at first view. I mean *the appointment of so many foreigners to offices of high rank and trust in our service.*

"The lavish manner in which rank has hitherto been bestowed on these gentlemen, will certainly be productive of one or the other of these two evils—*either to make us despicable in the eyes of Europe, or become a means of pouring them in upon us like a torrent, and adding to our present burden.*

"But it is neither the expense nor trouble of them that I dread: there is an evil more extensive in its nature and fatal in its consequences to be apprehended, and that is the driving of all our own officers out of the service, and throwing not only our army but our military councils entirely into the hands of foreigners.

"The officers, my dear sir, on whom you must depend for the defence of this cause, distinguished by length of service, their connections, property, and military merit, will not submit much, if any longer, to the unnatural promotion of men over them who have nothing more than a little plausibility, unbounded pride and ambition, and a perseverance in application not to be resisted but by uncommon firmness, to support their pretensions: men who, in the first instance, tell you they wish for nothing more than the honor of serving in so glorious a cause as volunteers, the next day solicit rank without pay, the day following want money advanced to them, and in the course of a week want further promotion, and are not satisfied with any thing you can do for them. The expediency and the policy of the measure remain to be considered, and whether it is consistent with justice or prudence to promote these military fortune-hunters at the hazard of your army.

"Baron Steuben, I now find, is also wanting to quit his inspectorship for a command in the line. This will be productive of much discontent to the brigadiers. In a word, although I think the Baron an excellent officer, *I do most devoutly wish that we had not a single foreigner among us, except the Marquis de Lafayette*, who acts upon very different principles from those which govern the rest. Adieu.

"I am most sincerely yours,
"G. WASHINGTON."

[Vol. VI., p. 13.]

TO JOHN ADAMS, VICE-PRESIDENT OF THE UNITED STATES.

"PHILADELPHIA, Nov. 27, 1794.

"DEAR SIR:—... My opinion with respect to immigration is, that except of useful mechanics and some particular description of men or professions, there is no need of encouragement.

I am, &c.,
"G. WASHINGTON."

[Vol. XI., p. 1.]

TO J. Q. ADAMS, AMERICAN MINISTER AT BERLIN.

"MOUNT VERNON, Jan. 20, 1799.

"SIR:—... You know, my good sir, that it is not the policy of this country to employ aliens where it can well be avoided, either in the civil or military walks of life.... There is a species of self-importance in all foreign officers that cannot be gratified without doing injustice to meritorious characters among our own countrymen, who conceive, and justly, where there is no great preponderancy of experience or merit, that they are entitled to the occupancy of all offices in the gift of their government.

"I am, &c.,
"G. WASHINGTON."

[Vol. XI., p. 392.]

SAME DATE, TO A FOREIGNER APPLYING FOR OFFICE.

"DEAR SIR:—... It does not accord with the policy of this government to bestow offices, civil or military, upon foreigners, to the exclusion of our own citizens. Yours, &c.,

"G. WASHINGTON."

[Vol. XI., p. 392.]

INSTRUCTIONS OF THE SECRETARY OF WAR
TO THE INSPECTOR-GENERAL.

"WAR DEPARTMENT, Feb. 4, 1799.

"... For the cavalry, for the regulations restrict the recruiting officers to engage none *except natives* for this corps, and those only as from their known character and fidelity may be trusted."

Cass and other distinguished Democrats said his career had been one of genuine patriotism, honor, and usefulness; and Gov. Wise, upon the stump in Virginia, characterized it as "Washington-like;" while the Democratic papers and orators, from Maine to California, declared that he ought to have been nominated in lieu of Gen. Scott, because he was one of the best men in America.

He is now in Europe, familiarizing himself with the workings of the despotic governments of that country. Before leaving, almost one year ago, he told his friends, in answer to questions relating to the presidency, not to start any newspapers for his benefit—not to publish any documents—not to make any speeches, or even electioneer—and added, that if the American people nominated him, of their own free will and accord, he would accept their nomination, and if elected, he would serve them to the best of his abilities. His nomination, therefore, under the circumstances, is a great honor, and shows the implicit confidence the real people have in the integrity, patriotism, and qualifications of the man. That he will go into the presidential chair almost by acclamation, we have not the shadow of doubt.

As to Mr. Fillmore's chances, we consider them excellent, and growing brighter every day. The indications are now very clear that he will obtain a *plurality*, if not a *majority* vote, in most of the Northern States; and under the most unfavorable circumstances, he will be sure to divide the electoral vote of the South, so as to carry more States than Mr. BUCHANAN. Virginia, South Carolina, Mississippi, and Alabama, are the only four States we concede to the Cincinnati nominee and *one* of these, we confidently expect to carry. Georgia and Arkansas we set down as doubtful, and we contend that Buchanan can't get either of them without a severe struggle.

We then make this estimate, and claim as certain for FILLMORE and DONELSON the following States, viz.:

Massachusetts	13
Rhode Island	4
New York	35
New Jersey	7
Pennsylvania	27
Maryland	8
Kentucky	12
Tennessee	12
North Carolina	10
Louisiana	6
Missouri	9
California	4
Delaware	3
Florida	3

This makes a total of 157—*eleven,* more than is necessary to an election. This is not an extravagant, but a very fair estimate. The friends of the American ticket have a right to feel encouraged. With proper exertions our ticket will carry. Let every American consider himself a sentinel upon the watch-tower—let every friend of the party do his duty, and the result will not be doubtful. And let all who believe that "Americans ought to rule America," take courage—"the skies are bright and brightening."

As it regards Mr. Fillmore's Americanism, *that* is settled—he has been a Protestant American *fifteen years in advance* of the party, as it now exists. The Hon. J. T. Headley, Secretary of State of New York, delivered a speech at the Capital of his State, March 7th, 1856, in which he spoke of Mr. Fillmore in the following language:

> "Now, in the first place, he was an American years before those who denounce him ever thought of Americanism. The Police constable of Newburg elected last year on the American ticket, told me, that years ago, when that well-known conflict occurred between the citizens of Buffalo and the foreign population, that a combination was formed called the *"American League."* The members of this League entered into *a solemn compact to stand together and fight together for the rights of Americans.* This constable was at the time an humble mechanic in Buffalo, and he said that *he constantly met Mr. Fillmore (who was a member of that League with him) at the Council Room.* Thus you see that those who would arrogate to themselves the title of Americans, and yet carp at Mr. Fillmore as wanting in American sentiment, are really recent volunteers compared with him. Mr. Fillmore carried his American principles still farther and became (so an officer in the same order informs me) *a member of the United Americans.* He has always been a true American, *he is now, and ever will be,* and is worthy to move at the head of the glorious column over which floats the flag bearing the inscription, 'Americans shall rule America.'"

After the defeat of Mr. Clay, in 1844, Mr. Fillmore addressed him this noble *American* letter:

> "Buffalo, Nov. 14, 1844.

> "My Dear Sir:—I have thought for three or four days that I would write to you, but really I am unmanned. I have no courage or resolution. All is gone. The last hope, which hung first upon the city of New York, and then upon Virginia, is finally dissipated, and I see nothing but despair depicted upon every countenance.

> "For myself, I have no regrets. I was nominated for Governor much against my will, and though not insensible to the pride of success, yet I feel a kind of relief at being defeated. But not so for you or the nation. Every consideration of justice, every feeling of gratitude conspired in the minds of honest men to insure your election, and though always doubtful of my own success, I could never doubt

yours, till the painful conviction was forced upon me.

"The Abolitionists and *Foreign Catholics have defeated us in this State.* I will not trust myself to speak of the vile hypocrisy of the leading Abolitionists now. Doubtless many acted honestly and ignorantly in what they did. But it is clear that Birney and his associates sold themselves to Locofocoism, and they will doubtless receive their reward.

"*Our opponents, by pointing to the Native Americans and to Mr. Frelinghuysen, drove the Foreign Catholics from us and defeated us in this State.*

"But it is vain to look at the causes by which this infamous result has been produced. It is enough to say that all is gone. I must confess that nothing has happened to shake my confidence in our ability to sustain a free government so much as this.

"MILLARD FILLMORE."

But here is one other letter, written to ISAAC NEWTON, just before MR. FILLMORE left the United States for Europe. A more patriotic letter, breathing more of the genuine American spirit, we have never met with:

"BUFFALO, N. Y., Jan. 3, 1855.

"RESPECTED FRIEND ISAAC NEWTON:—It would give me great pleasure to accept your kind invitation to visit Philadelphia, if it were possible to make my visit private, and limit it to a few personal friends whom I should be most happy to see; but I know that this would be out of my power, and I am therefore reluctantly compelled to decline your invitation, as I have done others to New York and Boston, for the same reason.

"I return you many thanks for your information on the subject of politics. I am always happy to hear what is going forward, but, independent of the fact that I feel myself withdrawn from the political arena, I have been too much depressed in spirit to take an active part in the late elections. I contented myself with giving a silent vote for Mr. Ullman, for Governor.

"While, however, I am an inactive observer of public events, I am by no means an indifferent one, and I may say to you in the frankness of private friendship, that I have for a long time looked with dread and apprehension at the corrupting influence which the contest for the foreign vote is exerting upon our elections. This seems to result from its being banded together, and subject to the control of a few interested and selfish leaders. Hence it has been a subject of bargain and sale, and each of the great political parties of the country have been bidding to obtain it, and, as usual in all such contests, the party which is most corrupt is most successful. The consequence is, that it is fast demoralizing the whole country; corrupting the very fountains of political power; and converting the ballot-box—that great palladium of our liberty—into an unmeaning mockery, where the rights of native-born citizens are voted away by those who blindly follow their mercenary and selfish leaders. The evidence of this is found not merely in the shameless chaffering for the foreign vote at every election, but in the large disproportion of offices which are now held by foreigners at home and abroad, as compared with our native citizens. Where is the true-hearted American whose cheek does not tingle with shame and mortification to see our highest and most coveted foreign missions filled by men of foreign birth to the exclusion of native-born? Such appointments are a humiliating confession to the crowned heads of Europe that a Republican soil does not produce sufficient talent to represent a Republican nation at a monarchical court. I confess that it seems to me—with all due respect to others—that, as a general rule, our country should be governed by American-born citizens. Let us give to the oppressed of every country an asylum and a home in our happy land, give to all the benefits of equal laws, and equal protection; but let us at the same time cherish, as the apple of our eye, the great principles of constitutional liberty, which few who have not had the good fortune to be reared in a free country know how to appreciate and still less how to preserve.

"Washington, in that inestimable legacy which he left to his country—his farewell address—has wisely warned us to beware of foreign influence as the most baneful foe of a republican government. He saw it to be sure in a different light from that in which it now presents itself; but he knew it would approach us in all forms, and hence he cautioned us against the *insidious wiles of its influence*. Therefore, as well for our own sakes, to whom this invaluable inheritance of self-government has been left by our forefathers, as for the sake of unborn millions who are to inherit this land—foreign and native—let us take warning of the Father of his Country, and do what we can justly to preserve our institutions from corruption and our country from dishonor, but let this be done by the people themselves in their sovereign capacity by making a proper discrimination in the selection of officers, and not by depriving any individual—native or foreign-born—of any constitutional or legal right to which he is entitled.

"These are my sentiments in brief; and although I have sometimes almost despaired of my country when I have witnessed the rapid strides of corruption, yet I think I perceive a gleam of hope in the future, and I now feel confident, that when the great mass of intelligence in this enlightened country is once fully aroused, and the danger manifested, it will fearlessly apply the remedy, and bring back the government to the pure days of Washington's administration. Finally, let us adopt the old Roman motto, '*Never despair of the Republic.*' Let us do our duty, and trust in that Providence which has so signally watched over and preserved us for the result. But I have said more than I intended, and much more than I should have said to any one but a trusted friend, as I have no desire to mingle in political strife.

"Remember me kindly to your family, and believe me truly your friend,

"MILLARD FILLMORE."

In March, 1851, LEWIS CASS, than whom there is not a more devoted partisan in the Democratic ranks, delivered a speech on the floor of the United States Senate, in the course of which he paid the following just compliment to Mr. Fillmore's integrity, and to his efficiency in *"pacifying the country,"* while he was President. We quote from the Congressional Globe, and hold it up as a withering rebuke to those "lesser lights" of Democracy, who are now defaming this pure and patriotic statesman:

> "The Administration has placed itself high in the great work of *pacifying the country*, and they received the meed of approbation from political friends and political foes. *I partake of the same sentiment.* I do them justice. But I am a Democrat, and, God willing, I mean to die one. This is a Whig administration, but there is no reason I should not do them justice; and I do it with pleasure, in this great matter of *the salvation of this country*—if I may say so. I have done so; shall continue to do so, whatever sneers their papers may contain; for I do it not for their sake, but *for the sake of their country.*"

The *Democratic Review*—the highest Democratic authority in the United States—for December, 1855, commenting upon the Compromise Measures of 1850, thus spoke of Mr. Fillmore, in a moment of candor, long before Mr. Fillmore was nominated by the American party for the Presidency:

> "Momentous events were transpiring. The agitation of the question of slavery was paramount in the public mind. In this crisis, it was well that so reliable a man as Mr. Fillmore was found in the Presidential chair. The safety and perpetuity of the Union were threatened. Already had fanaticism raised its hydra-head. Schemes and 'isms' leaped from a thousand ambuscades. The enemies of the Union started forth on every side—Abolitionism here; secessionism there; acquisition and filibusterism elsewhere. These were the formidable elements of misrule with which the Executive had to cope. How well he met, and how entirely he for the time overcame these enemies of the peace of the republic, we leave the historian to relate; but our retrospect would be incomplete and disingenuous, did we not accord the meed of praise justly due to high moral excellence and intellectual and administrative honesty and talent, as developed in the administration of Mr. Fillmore."

Since the foregoing was prepared for the press, Mr. Fillmore's letter of acceptance has come to hand, greatly to the annoyance of the Democratic and anti-American fuglemen and politicians. We congratulate the country upon the patriotic, national, and *truly American* spirit which pervades this chaste and well-written document. It is just what we expected from *one of the very first men in the Nation.*

His reference to his past course as a guaranty for the future is well-timed. *Sectional* legislation he is opposed to; and sectional agitation he will use his influence to suppress. We ask every man into whose hands this work shall fall, to read this admirable letter for himself: it is worthy of the man and the times; nay, it is the letter of a patriot and a statesman—

> "Who for his country feels alone,
> And loves her weal, beyond his own."

[COPY.]

Philadelphia, Feb. 26th, 1856.

To the Hon. Millard Fillmore:

Sir:—The National Convention of the American party, which has just closed its session in this city, has unanimously chosen you as the candidate for the Presidency of the United States in the election to be held in November next. It has associated with you Andrew Jackson Donelson, Esq., of Tennessee, as the candidate for the Vice-Presidency.

The Convention has charged the undersigned with the agreeable duty of communicating these proceedings to you, and of asking your acceptance of a nomination which will receive not only the cordial support of the great national party in whose name it is made, but the approbation also of large numbers of other enlightened friends of the Constitution and the Union, who will rejoice in the opportunity to testify their grateful appreciation of your faithful service in the past, and their confidence in your experience and integrity for the guidance of the future.

The undersigned take advantage of this occasion to tender to you the expression of their own gratification in the proceedings of the Convention, and to assure you of the high consideration with which they are yours, &c.

Alexander H. H. Stuart,
Andrew Stewart,
Erastus Brooks,
E. B. Bartlett,
Wm. J. Eames,
Ephraim Marsh.
Committee, &c.

Paris, May 21st, 1856.

Gentlemen:—I have the honor to acknowledge the receipt of your letter informing me that the National Convention of the American party, which had just closed its session at Philadelphia, had unanimously presented my name for the Presidency of the United States, and associated with it that of Andrew Jackson Donelson for the Vice-Presidency. This unexpected communication met me at Venice on my return from Italy, and the duplicate, mailed thirteen days later, was received on my arrival in this city last evening. This must account for my apparent neglect in giving a more prompt reply.

You will pardon me for saying that when my administration closed in 1853, I considered my political life as a public man at an end, and thenceforth I was only anxious to discharge my duty as a private citizen. Hence I have taken no active part in politics. But I have by no means been an indifferent spectator of passing events; nor have I hesitated to express my opinion on all political subjects when asked; nor to give my vote and private influence for those men and measures I thought best calculated to promote the prosperity and glory of our common country. Beyond this I deemed it improper for me to interfere. But this unsolicited and unexpected nomination has imposed upon me a new duty, from which I cannot shrink; and therefore, approving, as I do, of the general objects of the party which has honored me with its confidence, I cheerfully accept its nomination, without waiting to inquire of its prospects of success or defeat. It is sufficient for me to know that by so doing I yield to the wishes of a large portion of my fellow-citizens in every part of the Union, who, like myself, are sincerely anxious to see the administration of our government restored to that original simplicity and purity which marked the first years of its existence; and, if possible, to quiet that alarming sectional agitation, which, while it delights the Monarchists of Europe, causes every true friend of our own country to mourn.

Having the experience of past service in the administration of the Government, I may be permitted to refer to that as the exponent of the future, and to say, should the choice of the Convention be sanctioned by the people, I shall, with the same scrupulous regard for the rights of every section of the Union which then influenced my conduct, endeavor to perform every duty confided by the Constitution and laws to the Executive.

As the proceedings of this Convention have marked a new era in the history of the country, by bringing a new political organization into the approaching Presidential canvass, I take the occasion to reaffirm my full confidence in the patriotic purposes of that organization, which I regard as springing out of a public necessity, forced upon the country, to a large extent, by unfortunate sectional divisions, and the dangerous tendency of those divisions towards disunion. It alone, in my opinion, of all the political agencies now existing, is possessed of the power to silence this violent and disastrous agitation, and to restore harmony by its own example of moderation and forbearance. It has a claim, therefore, in my judgment, upon every earnest friend of the integrity of the Union.

So estimating this party, both in its present position and future destiny, I freely adopt its great leading principles as announced in the recent declaration of the National Council at Philadelphia, a copy of which you were so kind as to enclose me, holding them to be just and liberal to every true interest of the country, and wisely adapted to the establishment and support of an enlightened, safe, and effective American policy, in full accord with the ideas and the hopes of the fathers of our Republic.

I expect shortly to sail for America; and, with the blessings of Divine Providence, hope soon to tread my native soil. My opportunity of comparing my own country and the condition of its people with those of Europe, has only served to increase my admiration and love for our own blessed land of liberty, and I shall return to it without even a desire ever to cross the Atlantic again.

I beg of you, gentlemen, to accept my thanks for the very flattering manner in which you have been pleased to communicate the results of the action of that enlightened and patriotic body of men who composed the late Convention, and to be assured that

I am, with profound respect and esteem,
Your friend and fellow-citizen,
MILLARD FILLMORE.

Messrs. Alex. H. H. Stuart, Andrew Stewart, Erastus Brooks, E. B. Bartlett, Wm. J. Eames, Ephraim Marsh, *Committee*.

WHO IS ANDREW J. DONELSON?

This gentleman being now the nominee of the American party for the office of Vice-President, naturally attracts much of public attention; and as a matter to be looked for, and not at all to be regretted, draws down upon him great abuse and slander from the hireling editors of the corrupt party opposing him. We will let a neighbor of Major Donelson, who has had access to his papers, and who has prepared and published in the *Nashville Banner* a sketch of his life, answer the question propounded at the head of this chapter:

"MR. DONELSON is the second son of Samuel Donelson, deceased, who was the brother of the late Mrs. Jackson. His eldest brother died in 1817, soon after the Creek War, in which he participated as a soldier under General Jackson. His death was announced to Mr. Donelson by General Jackson in the following terms: 'Whilst we regret his loss, he has left us the endearing recollection that there was not a stain upon his character. He has performed his duty here below, and has taken his flight to realms above, as unspotted as an angel. What a lesson he has given us! How delightful to dwell upon the idea that he has walked in the paths of virtue during his whole life, without a blemish on his character, and that all his friends may recount his acts with pride and pleasure!' The younger brother is still living in the paternal mansion, and was a member of the last Legislature of Tennessee. The mother of these children afterwards married Mr. James Sanders, of Sumner county, Tennessee, and is still enjoying good health. She is the only daughter of Gen. Daniel Smith, who was one of the surveyors of the line between Virginia and North Carolina, and succeeded Gen. Jackson in the Senate of the United States.

"General Smith had an important agency in shaping the early history of Tennessee—having represented a portion of the people in the North Carolina Legislature, and in the Convention which ratified the Constitution of the United States. He was also Secretary of the Territory, and a member of the Convention of 1796. He was a native of Virginia, and emigrated to Tennessee soon after he had surveyed the line between that State and North Carolina, having, while in the execution of that service, seen the fine lands in Middle Tennessee. He settled the lands upon which his grandson, Henry Smith, now resides; and built the mansion, which is still there, at a period when the men engaged in quarrying the rock had to be guarded from the attacks of the Indians.

"The father of Samuel Donelson, Col. John Donelson, was also a native of Virginia, and at onetime a Representative of one of her oldest counties, Pittsylvania, in the House of Burgesses. He possessed in an eminent degree the respect of the Provincial Governor of that Commonwealth, from whom he received the appointment of Indian Commissioner about the year 1770; and it is to his bold and enterprising spirit that we are in a great measure indebted for the Indian Treaties which extended the settlements of Virginia through Kentucky to the Ohio river. He left Port Patrick Henry in 1779, descending the Tennessee river with all his family, in boats built on the Holston, and came up the Cumberland in those boats as high as the Clover Bottom, encountering incredible toils and dangers. Three years afterwards, in 1793, in conjunction with Col. Martin, he concluded an Indian Treaty, by which the settlements on the Cumberland river were greatly benefited; but he had, previously to his departure from Virginia, under a contract with Georgia, explored the country, and run the line between that State and North Carolina, as far west as the Mississippi river. After settling his family near the present site of the Hermitage, he was killed by the Indians, on a journey to Kentucky, near the Big Barren River, at the advanced age of 75.

"Samuel Donelson was a lawyer by profession, and the intimate friend and associate of Gen. Jackson, after whom he named his son Andrew, who was born on the 25th of August, 1800. On the second marriage of his mother, this son was taken into the family of the General, who became his guardian and patron; and he remained the most of his time with him until he was prepared to enter the Cumberland College. After finishing his studies at this school, Gen. Jackson obtained for him a Cadet's warrant, which enabled him to enter the Military Academy at West Point, in 1816. He was one of the first class which was graduated under the superintendence of Col. Thayer—finishing the course of studies in three, instead of four years; as is customary. Throughout his service at West Point, he was distinguished for his proficiency in mathematics, and for the facility with which he mastered all the studies which appertain to military science. No higher proof need be adduced of this fact, than the position assigned to him by the Board of Examiners and Visitors, when he graduated. He was placed No. 2, in a class of great merit, notwithstanding he had the studies of two years to pass through in one year, and was recommended to the Department of War for a commission in the Engineer Corps—a compliment accorded only to the most distinguished of the class.

"After obtaining his commission, Mr. Donelson was ordered to the Western frontier to build a fort; but before he reached this destination, the War Department, on the application of Gen. Jackson, allowed him to accept the appointment of Aide-de-camp in the staff of the General.

In this capacity he attended the General when he took possession of the Floridas, and remained with him until the latter resigned his commission in the army.

"At this period, Mr. Donelson seeing no prospect for rapid promotion in the corps of Engineers, and sharing the conviction then so prevalent in the army, that the conclusion of the war with England had shut the door for a long time to come against those military enterprises which are so tempting to the officer and soldier, and feeling also that he could be more useful in the pursuits of civil life, turned his attention to the study of law. He accordingly resigned his commission; and after attending the course of law lectures in the Transylvania University, then under the presidency of Dr. Holly, he received his license, and appeared at the Nashville bar in 1823, having formed a partnership with Mr. Duncan. Circumstances, however, soon occurred, which withdrew him in a great degree from the practice. General Jackson was again in the field as a candidate for the Presidency, and needed the services of a confidential friend to aid him in repelling the bitter assaults which were made upon his character and services. Animated by a deep sense of gratitude, no duty could be more pleasing to Mr. Donelson than that of contributing his labor to advance the great popular movement which aimed, by the elevation of his benefactor and friend, to promote the highest interests of the country. He therefore cheerfully entered again into the General's family, and travelled with him to Washington City after the elections in 1824. Those elections devolved the choice of President upon the House of Representatives. Mr. Adams was the successful candidate, although Gen. Jackson had a much larger popular vote, and was evidently the favorite of the people.

"As is well known to the country, the result of that election gave increased force to the sentiment which had placed Gen. Jackson in nomination. The efforts of his friends throughout the Union became more active, and were never abated until the decision of the House of Representatives in 1824 was reversed, and Gen. Jackson placed in the Presidential chair. During these four years, Mr. Donelson, who had married in 1824, settled upon his plantation adjoining the Hermitage, and continued there to promote the cause he had espoused so warmly in the beginning.

"When the elections of 1828 were over, Gen. Jackson insisted upon the acceptance by Mr. Donelson of the post of private Secretary. Mr. D. accordingly set out with him in the winter of 1828 for the city of Washington, taking with him his wife, whom he had married in 1824. This lady was the youngest daughter of Capt. John Donelson, and was invited by Gen. Jackson to do the honors of the White House—a position which she held throughout the greater portion of his Presidency.

"It was in this capacity that Mr. Donelson endeared himself still more than ever to the Hero of the Hermitage. He spent the prime of his life, from 1828 to 1836, in his service, and he felt himself amply rewarded by the knowledge he thus acquired of public men and measures.

"At the close of Gen. Jackson's Presidency, Mr. Donelson declined to take office under Mr. Van Buren, being anxious for a respite from public affairs, and to enjoy the pleasures of his farm; upon which he remained until he was called unexpectedly to take a part in the negotiation which brought Texas into our Union. It was upon this theatre that he displayed the judgment and tact which brought him prominently before the country as a man that understood the public interests, and knew how to take care of them.

"The commission appointing Mr. Donelson Minister to Texas is dated the 16th of September, 1844. Mr. Calhoun, then Secretary of State, in the letter enclosing the commission, says:

"'The state of things in Texas is such as to require that the place (Charge d'Affaires) should be filled without delay, and to select him who, under all circumstances, may be thought best calculated to bring to a successful decision the great question of annexation pending before the two countries. After full deliberation, you have been selected as that individual; and I do trust, my dear sir, that you will not decline the appointment, however great may be the personal sacrifice of accepting. That great question must be decided in the next three or four months; and whether it shall be favorable or not, will depend on him who shall fill the mission now tendered you. I need not tell you how much depends on its decision for weal or woe to our country, and perhaps the whole continent. It is sufficient to say that, viewed in all its consequences, it is one of the first magnitude; and that it gives an importance to the mission at this time, that raises it to the level with the highest in the gift of the Government.

"Assuming, therefore, that you will not decline the appointment, unless some insuperable difficulty should interpose, and in order to avoid delay, a commission is herewith transmitted, without the formality of waiting your acceptance, with all the necessary papers.'"

President Polk, after this, confided an important and most critical foreign negotiation to Major Donelson; and his estimate of the prudence, discretion, and ability with which Major Donelson discharged his trust, appears from a letter to Major D. from the Hon. John Y. Mason, President Polk's Secretary of War, dated August 7th, 1845. From that letter, complimentary from beginning to end, we copy only this portion:

"The services which you have rendered your country in the delicate negotiations intrusted to you, are justly appreciated. *Your prudence, discretion, and ability have inspired the President with a confidence which would make him feel much more at ease if that delicate task could be in your hands.*

"It gives me great pleasure to assure you that *the publication of your official correspondence will give you a most enviable reputation for the highest qualities of a statesman and diplomatist.*

"The President unites in the kindest regards, with your friend,

"J. Y. MASON."

PRESIDENT PIERCE's opinion of Major Donelson may be learned from the following letter, written by him to the Major when the latter was the editor of the *Washington Union*, the National Organ of the Democratic party:

"CONCORD, May 30, 1851.

"MY DEAR SIR: I rejoice that the leading organ of our party is now under your control, and regard the change as most auspicious at this juncture. There is a great battle before us—a battle for the Union—a battle for the ascendency of the principles, the maintenance of which so nobly signalized the administration of General Jackson. THE TONE, VIGOR, AND STATESMANLIKE GRASP *which you have brought to the columns of the Union are not merely important, they are* ABSOLUTELY INDISPENSABLE *in this crisis.*

"With great respect, your friend and servant,
"FRANK. PIERCE."

The following article is from the *Nashville Union*, of October 15, 1844, the Tennessee Organ of Democracy, published within a few miles of where Major Donelson lives, and has passed most of his life. This article shows what opinion was entertained of him before he became a *Know-Nothing*:

"The diplomatic agency of this government in Texas is, at this moment, the most important mission abroad; although it ranks with those of the second class, its high and important duties require the talents of one every way qualified for the first foreign mission on the globe.

"*We congratulate the administration on having been able to secure the services of one so eminently qualified in all respects for the station, whose thorough knowledge of the relations subsisting between the two countries, and whose intimate acquaintance with the prominent statesmen of this and that government, will place him in the enjoyment of advantages which cannot fail to secure to us the most desirable results.*

"Major Donelson leaves his plantation near the Hermitage today—proceeding overland to the Mississippi river on his way to the Texan Capital—and we cannot but participate in the painful emotions with which the word 'farewell' will be exchanged between himself and his venerable patron, friend, and relative, 'The Sage of the Hermitage.'

"In view of the advanced age of General Jackson, it is more than probable that they may never meet again. A relationship next to that of father and son, if, indeed, it be not equally near and dear, will be severed perhaps for ever. And we feel assured that nothing short of a sense of DUTY TO HIS COUNTRY could have induced an acceptance of the mission. Nor, for this patriotic reason, would the aged veteran advise him to decline it.

"Major D. leaves a host of good and true friends, who will continue to have an abiding solicitude for his health and happiness, and for his early and complete success in 'extending the area of freedom.'"

Mr. Clayton, Secretary of State under Gen. Taylor, wrote to Major Donelson, announcing the expiration of the diplomatic relations between the United States and Germany, (where the Major was stationed,) and closed with the following complimentary expressions:

"I am directed by the President to express to you his entire approbation of your conduct, and I cannot take leave of you in your public character without adding my testimony to that of the President to the ability and faithfulness with which you have discharged the arduous and delicate duties which your mission imposed upon you.

"JOHN M. CLAYTON."

The Democratic party having always boasted that Gen. Jackson was unsurpassed in his keen and unerring insight into the characters of men, we must be permitted to call their attention to a clause in the *Last Will and Testament* of Gen. Jackson, as recorded in the county of Davidson. This clause sets forth the estimate placed upon Mr. Donelson by the old General, after this fashion:

"HERMITAGE, June 7, 1843.

... "I bequeath to my well-beloved nephew, Andrew J. Donelson, son of Samuel Donelson, deceased, the elegant sword presented to me by the State of Tennessee, with this injunction, that he fail not to use it when necessary in support and protection of our glorious Union, and for the protection of the constitutional rights of our beloved country, should they be assailed by foreign enemies or *domestic traitors*. This, from the great change in my worldly affairs of late, is, with my blessing, all that I can bequeath him, doing justice to those creditors to whom I am responsible. This bequest is made as a memento of the high regard, affection, and esteem I bear for him as a *high-minded, honest, and honorable man*."

And now, to show that Gen. Jackson had not changed his opinion of the Major, we give about the last epistle he ever wrote to him, as it bears date but a few days previous to his death:

"HERMITAGE, May 24, 1845.

"MY DEAR ANDREW: I received last night your affectionate letter of the 15th inst., with the enclosed for your dear Elizabeth, which I sent forthwith, and your kind letter of the 13th this morning. Your family were here yesterday. All well, but looking out for you hourly. I assured Elizabeth that you could not leave your mission before the Texan Congress acted upon the subject with which you were charged. I shall admonish her to be patient and await your return, which will be the moment your honor and duty will permit.

"My dear Andrew:—What may be my fate God only knows. I am greatly afflicted—suffer much, and it will be almost a miracle if I shall survive my present attack. I am swollen from the toes to the crown of the head, and in bandages to my hips.

"How far my God may think proper to bear me up under my weight of afflictions, he only knows. But, my dear Major, live or die, you have my blessing and prayers for your welfare and happiness in this world, and that we may meet in a blissful immortality.

"Your affectionate uncle,
"ANDREW JACKSON."

While editor of the *Washington Union*, Major Donelson frankly admitted, in his account of the election in Tennessee, between Gov. Campbell and Gen. Trousdale, that the latter owed his defeat to his opposition to the Compromise measures, and his sympathies with the Disunionists. In the *Hartford* Convention held in Nashville, the Major appeared in person, and denounced the whole concern as a blow at the Union, and its prime movers and advocates as *traitors to their country and to the Constitution*. These *Secession* Democrats, headed by A. V. Brown, Eastman & Co., are uncompromising in their hatred of the Major, and they never will forgive him, while he remains true to the Union of these States, and the Constitution as it is, which will be to the latest hour of his earthly existence! Had he never opposed the *treasonable* designs of the Nashville Convention—and had he not advocated the doctrines of the American party, these same men would now be loud in his praise, as the relative, the political student, and the *successor* of the Sage of the Hermitage!

BUCHANAN NOMINATED AT CINCINNATI.—DISPERSION OF FALSTAFF'S ARMY!

From the Knoxville Whig of June 14, 1856.

The Cincinnati Anti-American, Anti-Protestant, Foreign Catholic, Locofoco Pow Wow, has met—transacted its appropriate business—nominated old Federal James Buchanan, of Pennsylvania, for the Presidency, and Robert C. Breckenridge, of Kentucky, for the Vice Presidency—and dispersed: dealing largely in the old game of *brag*, as to the *nationality, soundness,* and *ability* of their ticket; when it is notorious, that they have at the head of their ticket one of the most vulnerable men in the nation; an old political hack, who has been "every thing by turns and nothing long;" advocating and opposing all the leading measures which have agitated the country for the last forty years, as we shall show in the sequel!

They had an awful time at Cincinnati! They organized by calling to the chair, temporarily, the notorious *Sam'l. Medary,* the Abolition editor of the Ohio Statesman. Either the anti-slavery forces were in the majority, or the "odds and ends" of all parties represented in the Convention desired to conciliate the Abolition and Black Republican wings of their *Foreign Corporation*!

The Missouri Delegation were refused their seats, and they openly rebelled, forcing their way into the Convention with *clubs,* knocking down and cruelly mangling the head and shoulders of the poor doorkeeper! From this, it would seem that they were doing business with *closed doors*! Wonder if they had a *password*! Had they "signs and grips," other than those by which they made themselves known to the *doorkeeper*?

Did they carry with them "dark-lanterns?" Not they—they are opposed to all *secrecy*—they are opposed to all disorderly conduct—they are the "harmonious Democracy," and labor alone for the good of the country, and of posterity! What a farce their Cincinnati Convention was! And what hypocrites they are!

But two full sets of Delegates appeared from New York, and claimed their seats; these were *Hards* and *Softs*—Pierce and *anti*-Pierce—Nebraska and *anti*-Nebraska—pro-Slavery and *anti*-Slavery, *Filibustering Foreign Catholic Democrats*! Being unable to agree among themselves, and the Convention not wishing to *offend* either of these wings of the "great Harmonious Democratic Party," they rejected both delegations! This was having a bad effect, as a portion of each delegation was out of doors cursing the majority, and making threats as to what they would do. So the Convention reconsidered their cases, and ADMITTED BOTH DELEGATIONS TO SEATS. They then progressed "harmoniously," much after the style of a rickety old cart on a hill-side, drawn by a balky horse, whose driver curses him when at fault, and curses him when faultless.

Frequently the scenes of confusion and excitement were alike disgusting and alarming. The friends of Douglass, Pierce, and Buchanan, were alike bitter, and each disposed to ruin the party if they should fail to get their man nominated. The anti-slavery portion of the Convention were much incensed against the South for the *"lam-basting"* given to *Senator Sumner* by *Representative Brooks*, for words spoken in debate. One of Buchanan's men boasted that the assault of Brooks on Sumner had gained *twenty* votes for "Old Buck!" And others of the Buchanan wing, out of doors, were stating that they had reliable evidence that "Old Buck" did not approve the assault, while Pierce and Douglass did! We have no doubt that this sort of influence, added to Buchanan's *known hostility to slavery*, secured for him the nomination. And, as if desirous to atone for the sin against the South of nominating an old *Anti-Slavery Federalist*, they came into a Southern State, Kentucky, and selected a young and inexperienced politician, Mr. Robert C. Breckenridge, for the Vice Presidency. As Breckenridge is brave, and has challenged his man for a *duel*, they can now turn about and appeal to the Church-going folks to sustain their ticket *for what* they implored them to repudiate the Whig ticket in 1844! Besides, Breckenridge *approves* the basting of Sumner by Brooks, and this will *offset* Buchanan's opposition to that *Southern Democratic measure!* Breckenridge has another virtue, which aided in securing his nomination. Though the nephew of those *able Know-Nothing Presbyterian Preachers* of that State, he has the independence to come out in opposition to them, and the insulting claims set up by *Protestants generally*, and to advocate and defend the Roman Catholics.

The "rich and racy" scenes that came off in the Convention, we will leave our several friends from Nashville, who were there as reporters in the Convention for the American papers, to set forth. With more truth than poetry, the "unterrified Democracy" convened at Cincinnati can say, "Our army swore terribly in Flanders!" And how could it have been otherwise? The Convention was large—composed of several hundred delegates, drawn together from all sections of the country, East, West, North, and South—"held together by the cohesive power of public plunder"—and representing every variety and shade of opinion known and held under the much abused but comprehensive name of Democracy! Nor was the moral and personal character of the Convention less mixed and many-colored than was its politics.

In looking over the proceedings of this coalition and combination of Bogus Democrats, Foreign Pauper Advocates, and anti-Protestant lovers of Religious Liberty, we have looked in vain for the names of distinguished Tennesseeans, who ought to have been second best, to say the least of it, in the ballots for a nomination! It was that Aaron V. Brown, "the son of a now sainted father," was put in nomination for the office of Vice President, by a Mr. Brown, supposed to be his nephew; but making no run at all, he was taken off the track instantly—rubbed down and salted away!

But Andrew Johnson, who was to have been nominated for the first office within the gift of the American people and no mistake, (!) was not even named, and some say he was not even thought of for the position. We had supposed that there existed among the leaders of the self-styled Democracy, a determination to doom to utter extinction the light that has guided the children of Political Reform in Tennessee, and throughout the known world, and now we know it! The opposers of intellectual emancipation, of "Jacob's Ladder Democracy," so superior to Christianity, have triumphed at Cincinnati, and trampled under foot, with impunity, the soul-stirring doctrine of "converging lines." The next steps with these "enemies of righteousness" will be the rack, the gibbet, and a second edition of the infernal inquisition! Will the friends of the "White Basis" Governor of Tennessee tamely surrender their dearest rights to these Cincinnati *crusaders*, without a single struggle? Will they allow the saddle of Federal domination to be quietly thrown on their backs? Ye Greene county delegates forbid it!

But Johnson is doomed to an inglorious retirement from public life. He can console himself with the reflection, that rank only degrades—wealth only impoverishes—ornaments but disfigure him! The man who discovered that the Bogus Democracy of the nineteenth century leads fallen sinful man to the throne of God, needs no office to elevate him. These Johnson Democrats enjoy the pure religion of Democracy—a religion which enters the closet—pours forth its supplications in private, feeds the poor, clothes the naked—inflames not the prejudices of Protestant sects—is modest and unassuming in its demeanor—is charitable and kind to the persecuted and pious Catholics—bears with the infirmities of Foreign Paupers—is not ambitious and designing, seeking to accomplish vast schemes by doubtful means!

While Old Federal Buck was nominated on the seventeenth ballot, after much excitement, wrangling and abuse, young Breckenridge, whose only merit is his having challenged the Hon. Francis B. Cutting, of New York, to fight a duel, two years ago, was nominated on the second ballot. The ballot for a candidate for the Vice Presidency resulted as follows:

John C. Breckenridge, of Kentucky,	55
John A. Quitman, of Mississippi,	59
Linn Boyd, of Kentucky,	33
Benjamin Fitzpatrick, of Alabama,	11
Aaron V. Brown, of Tennessee,	29
Herschel V. Johnson, of Georgia,	31
Thomas J. Rusk, of Texas,	2
Wm. H. Polk, of Tennessee,	5
J. C. Dobbin, of North Carolina,	13

A second ballot was entered into, when Hon. John C. Breckenridge, of Kentucky, was unanimously chosen.

Tennessee, in voting for a Presidential candidate, voted SIX times for Pierce, and EIGHT times for Douglass, and never came over to old Federal Buck until they could do nothing for Pierce or Douglass. Buck seems to have been a fill for

Tennessee! But now, the Tennessee Democracy say:

> "With hounds and horn,
> At rosy morn,
> We *Bucks* a hunting go!"

Well, we Americans will get after Old Buck's venison too, and between this and November next, many will be the steak we shall eat out of his old Federal carcass. It is venison worthy of the chase, for

> — —"Finer or fatter
> Ne'er roamed in the forest,
> Or smoked in a platter."

So—

> "Hi, ho, Chevy,
> Hark away, hark away, tantivy,
> Here rests the burthen of my song,
> This *time* a stag must die."

But Democracy have commenced their old game of brag, by puffing their ticket as a national and conservative ticket, the very thing they denied. Now let us look into the soundness and nationality of the HEAD of the ticket. We have before us a copy of a work published in 1839, by Robert Mayo, M. D., entitled, "Political Sketches of Eight Years in Washington, in four parts." This work has gone through various editions, having been published by Fielding Lucas, Jr., of Baltimore; Garret Anderson, of Washington; J. R. Smith, of Richmond; Carey, Hart & Co., of Philadelphia, and by others in New York and Boston. On page 38 of this work, which Mr. Buchanan has never contradicted, he is reported to have denounced the visions, patronage, and corruptions of the Democratic Administrations, while he, Buchanan, was a member of the Old Federal Party.

On page 6 of this work, in the preface, the author says, in speaking of Buchanan before he turned Democrat:

> "The declarations of some of these new disciples of Democracy in past times are striking enough. MR. BUCHANAN of PENNSYL-VANIA, while he acted in his true character, DECLARED THAT IF HE HAD A DROP OF DEMOCRATIC BLOOD IN HIS VEINS, HE WOULD LET IT OUT! He put his royal declaration on paper, and it has risen up against him."

A recent brief memoir of Mr. Buchanan, put forth in Pennsylvania, states that he was elected to the Legislature in 1815, where he distinguished himself by those exhibitions of intellect which gave promise of future eminence. The Lancaster *Register*, published in the immediate vicinity of Mr. Buchanan's residence, asks *by whom* was he elected? and thus supplies the record for 1815:

ASSEMBLY.

For   JAMES BUCHANAN,   Federal   3051

For   Molton O. Rogers,   Democrat   2502

The memoir sets forth that Mr. Buchanan was elected to Congress in 1820, and that he retained his position in that body for ten years, voluntarily retiring.

The Lancaster *Register* inquires if he were elected as a *Democrat*, and answers the inquiry by the following historical facts:

CONGRESS.

1820—	James Buchanan, Federal	4642
1820—	Jacob Hibsman, Democrat	3666
1822—	James Buchanan, Federal	2153
1822—	Jacob Hibsman, Democrat	1940
1824—	James Buchanan, Federal	3560
1824—	Samuel Houston, Democrat	3046
1826—	James Buchanan, Federal	2760
1826—	Dr. John McCamant, Democrat	2307
1828—	James Buchanan, Jackson	5203
1828—	William Hiester, Adams	3904

The Lancaster *Register* then pursues its criticism as follows:

"On the 4th of July, 1815, Mr. Buchanan, when he was a candidate for Assembly on the *Federal ticket*, delivered 'an oration' in Lancaster, in which he showed his *love* of Federalism and *hatred* of Democracy, by attacking the Administration of James Madison. He said:

"'Time will not allow me to enumerate all the other evils and wicked projects of the Democratic administration.'

"And again, in the same oration, he said:

"'What must be our opinion of an opposition whose passions were so dark and malignant as to be gratified in endeavoring to blast the character and imbitter the old age of Washington? After thus persecuting the saviour of his country, *how can the Democratic party dare to call themselves his disciples?*'"

And who does not recollect, in Tennessee, with what force and effect JAMES C. JONES used to point out JAMES BUCHANAN as one of the *rank old Federalists* who had come over to the Democratic ranks, and was battling with *Col. Polk*, side by side, while he was consuming half his time in abuse of the Federal party? When the Democratic candidate for Congress in this District, JULIUS W. BLACKWELL, charged *Federalism* upon the Whig party, who does not recollect with what effect and spirit JOHN H. CROZIER ran over the list of ODIOUS OLD FEDERALISTS, then fighting under the Democratic flag, among them naming out JAMES BUCHANAN? And will not the files of the KNOXVILLE POST, edited by Capt. JAMES WILLIAMS, show how he held up JAMES BUCHANAN and others as an *old Federalist of the first water*?

On the subject of *Slavery* the memoir is not definite, and the Lancaster Register comes to its aid by publishing the following proceedings of a public meeting held in that city on the 23d of November, 1819:

"WHEREAS, the people of this State, pursuing the maxims and animated by the beneficence of the great founder of Pennsylvania, first gave effect to the gradual abolition of slavery by a national act, which has not only rescued the unhappy and helpless African within their territory from the demoralizing influence of slavery, but ameliorating his state and condition throughout Europe and America; and whereas, it would illy comport with those humane and Christian efforts to be silent spectators when this great cause of humanity is about to be agitated in Congress, by fixing the destiny of the new domains of the United States: therefore,

"*Resolved*, That the representatives in Congress from this district be and they are hereby most earnestly requested to use their utmost endeavors, as members of the National Legislature, to prevent the existence of slavery in any of the Territories or new States which may be created by Congress.

"*Resolved*, As the opinion of this meeting, that as the Legislature of this State will shortly be in session, it will be highly deserving of their wisdom and patriotism to take into their early and most serious consideration the propriety of instructing our representatives in the National Legislature to use the most zealous and strenuous exertions to inhibit the existence of slavery in any of the Territories or States which may hereafter be created by Congress; and that the members of Assembly from this county be requested to embrace the earliest opportunity of bringing this subject before both Houses of the Legislature.

"*Resolved*, That, in the opinion of this meeting, the members of Congress who at the last session sustained the cause of justice, humanity, and patriotism, in opposing the introduction of slavery into the State then endeavored to be formed out of the Missouri Territory, are entitled to the warmest thanks of every friend of humanity.

"*Resolved*, That the proceedings of this meeting be published in the newspapers in this city.

"JAMES HOPKINS,
WM. JENKINS,
JAMES BUCHANAN."

"The foregoing resolutions being read were unanimously adopted, after which the meeting adjourned. (Signed)

WALTER FRANKLIN, Ch'n.

"Attest—WM. JENKINS, Sec'y."

The "Perry County Democratic Press," for April 9th, 1856, an able paper published at Bloomfield in Pennsylvania, shows up the *Federal anti-slavery, anti-Democratic, turn-coat character* of Mr. Buchanan, after this fashion:

JAMES BUCHANAN'S SOMERSETS.

"No man in the United States has turned his political coat as often as James Buchanan. He has espoused the principles of every party that has had an existence since the memorable Hartford Convention, and has been on all sides of political questions.

"A brief reference to his history will establish conclusively our assertions."

HIS FEDERALISM.

"He entered political life in 1814 as a rank Federalist, and by the Federal party he was elected to the Legislature of the State. He was re-elected in 1815, defeating Molton C. Rogers, the Democratic candidate, and afterwards one of the Supreme Judges of the State.

"In 1820, he was the Federal candidate for Congress, and was elected over Jacob Hibsman, the Democratic candidate, by 976 majority. In 1822, he was reëlected over the same man by 813 majority. In 1824, he was the Federal candidate for Congress, and elected over Samuel Houston, the Democratic candidate, by 519 votes. In 1826, he was re-elected over Dr. John McCamant, the Democratic candidate, by 453 votes. His majorities were becoming less each time, and in order to satisfy his Federal friends of his fidelity to the party, he had to declare that 'if he had a drop of Democratic blood in his veins, he would open them and let it out.'"

HE BECOMES A DEMOCRAT.

"Two years after this, he changed his coat and became a full-blooded Democrat, and ran for Congress as the Democratic candidate, and was elected by virtue of General Jackson's popularity. He was afraid to run a second term, and he declined."

HIS TEN CENT SPEECH.

"In 1843, in the United States Senate, he made a speech advocating the principle that ten cents is a sufficient compensation for a day's labor. Hence he is called 'Ten Cent Jimmy.'

"In 1845, he became Secretary of State under Polk's administration, and consented to give away about half of the Territory of Oregon to the British government, after he had proven that they had not a spark of title to it.

"He extolled the Federal administration of John Adams, and endorsed the abominable Alien and Sedition laws of the Federal reign of terror. He bitterly denounced the administration of that pure Democrat, James Madison, and ridiculed what he termed the follies of Thomas Jefferson."

HIS SLAVERY SOMERSETS.

"In 1819, at a meeting in Lancaster, he reported resolutions favoring resistance to the extension of slavery and the admission of the State of Missouri as a slave State.

"In 1847, he wrote to the Democracy of Berks county, saying that the Missouri Compromise had given peace to the country, and that instead of repealing it he was in favor of its extension and maintenance.

"In 1850, in a letter to Col. Forney, he rejoiced over the settlement of the slavery agitation by the passage of the compromise measures during Fillmore's administration, and hoped that before a dissolution of the Union he might be gathered to his fathers, and never be permitted to witness the sad catastrophe.

"In 1852, he wrote to Mr. Leake, of Virginia, concerning Fillmore's compromise measures of 1850, which had been passed by Congress, and said, 'that the volcano has been extinguished, and the man who would apply the firebrand to the combustible materials still remaining, will produce an eruption that will overwhelm the Constitution and the Union."

BUCHANAN'S LAST SOMERSET.

"On the 28th of December, 1855, about three months ago, Mr. Buchanan, in a letter to John Slidell, of Louisiana, says: 'The Missouri Compromise is gone, and gone for ever. It has departed. The time for it has passed away, and the best, nay, the only mode now left of *putting down* the fanatical and reckless spirit of the North is to adhere to the existing settlement without the slightest thought or appearance of wavering, and without regarding any storm which may be raised against it."

Here, then, is an authentic record—if the reader please, a GILT-FRAME PENNSYLVANIA LOOKING-GLASS, in which the Democracy of the South who admire the nominee of the late Cincinnati Convention can *see him as he is!* Heretofore, to use the language of Holy Writ, they have seen him "through a glass darkly, but now face to face." Here they see him standing erect upon the floor of the United States Senate, in all the pride of that *aristocracy* which has characterized his course in life, and giving vent to the old and bitter feelings of the *royalists* in Pennsylvania, by advocating the *oppressive British doctrine*, that TEN CENTS PER DAY *is enough for a poor white man as a day-laborer*! And here, too, our hard-fisted working-men, North and South, can see what sort of a man the Democracy are asking them to vote for for the Presidency!

In his Fourth of July oration in 1815, delivered in the hearing of an immense crowd, and afterwards published in all the leading papers of Pennsylvania, Mr. Buchanan came out as a *Know-Nothing*, which he has now to repudiate in stepping upon the *Anti-American Catholic Platform* prepared for him at Cincinnati! Here is what he said in that celebrated oration:

"The greater part of those foreigners who would not be thus affected by it, have long been the warmest friends of the party. They had been *one of the great means of elevating the present ruling* (Democratic) party, and it would have been ungrateful for that party to have abandoned them. To secure this foreign feeling has been the labor of their leaders for more than twenty years, and well have they been paid for their trouble, for it has been one of the principal causes of introducing and continuing them in power. Immediately before the war this foreign influence had completely embodied itself with the majority, particularly in the West, and its voice was heard so loud at the seat of government, that President Madison was obliged either to yield to its dictates or retire from office. The choice was easily made by a man who preferred his private interests to the public good, and therefore hurried us into a war for which we were utterly unprepared."

And then again:

"We ought to use every honest exertion to turn out of power those weak and wicked men whose wild and visionary theories have been tested and found wanting. Above all, we ought to drive from our shores foreign influence, and cherish American feeling. Foreign influence has been in every age the curse of republics—its jaundiced eye sees every thing in false colors—the thick atmosphere of prejudice by which it is ever surrounded, excluding from its sight the light of reason. Let us then learn wisdom from experience, and for ever banish this fiend from our country."

And here is what JACKSON thought of BUCHANAN. The Democratic Washington correspondent of the New York Evening Post, who was favorable to the nomination of Pierce, makes this statement—a statement we have often heard before, and never heard contradicted:

"On the night before leaving Nashville to occupy the White House, Mr. Polk, in company with Gen. Robert Armstrong, called at the Hermitage to procure some advice from the old hero as to the selection of his cabinet. Jackson strongly urged the President-elect to give no place in it to Buchanan, as he could not be relied upon. It so happened that Polk had already determined to make that very appointment, having probably offered the situation to the statesman of Pennsylvania. This fact induced Gen. Armstrong subsequently to tell Jackson that he had given Polk a rather hard rub, as Buchanan had already been selected for Secretary of State. 'I can't help it,' said the old man: 'I felt it my duty to warn him against Mr. Buchanan, whether it was agreeable or not. Mr. Polk will find Buchanan an unreliable man. I know him well, and Mr. Polk will yet admit the correctness of my prediction.'

"It was the last visit ever made by Mr. Polk to the old hero when this unavailing remonstrance was delivered, but the new President, long before the end of his administration, had reason to acknowledge its propriety and justice, and in the diary kept by him during that period may still be read a most emphatic declaration of his distrust of Mr. Buchanan. Every one is aware of two marked instances in which, as Secretary of State, the latter failed to support the policy of the administration, viz., on the question of the tariff of 1846, and the requisition of the ten regiments voted by Congress for the Mexican war. On both of these measures he was known to be opposed to the wishes of Mr. Polk."

Mr. Charles Irving, the Democratic editor of the Lynchburg Republican, and a delegate at Richmond in the State Convention, thus disposes of Mr. Buchanan in a long and able letter, dated May 7th, 1856:

"If silence during the battle constitutes a claim for office, how can the South expect Northern statesmen to uphold her banner, when abolitionists are seeking to tear it to tatters? If an ability to get free-soil votes makes a candidate available, and that species of availability is recognized as a merit at the South, Northern statesmen should court free-soilers, and not struggle with them, if they wish to be Presidents. Such availability may be very desirable to those who wish success alone, but those who look to the interests of the country may well be excused if they prefer a different standard. I certainly *prefer* that the South shall PREFER the selection, not only of a sound man, but that she shall vote for the nomination of no man upon any such ground of availability. The coming election must settle the slavery agitation. I do not wish a single free-soiler to vote the Democratic ticket, nor will I willingly afford them the slightest excuse for so doing. A prominent North-West Democrat told me to-day, that the nomination of Mr. Buchanan would enable Trumbull, Wentworth, and other free-soilers to come back into the party. I am not anxious to get back such characters. These are some reasons for not preferring Mr. Buchanan.

"But there is still another reason. That reason is in his record. To carry the entire South, we must have not only a sound man, but one who is above impeachment—whose record is as stainless as the principles he advocates. Is such the case with Mr. Buchanan? Let the record answer.

"On the 27th of December, 1837, Mr. Calhoun submitted to the Senate that celebrated series of resolutions, the great objects of which were to set forth with precision and force the constitutional rights of the slaveholding States, and to attract to their support an enlightened public opinion against the attacks of Northern fanaticism. The second resolution was in these words: (Calhoun's Works, volume 3, page 140.)

"'*Resolved*, That in delegating a portion of their powers to be exercised by the Federal Government, the States retained severally the exclusive and sole right over their own domestic institutions and police, and are alone responsible for them, and that any intermeddling of any one or more States, or a combination of their citizens, with the domestic institutions and police of the others, on any ground or under any pretext whatever, political, moral, or religious, with a view to their alteration or subversion, is an assumption of superiority not warranted by the Constitution, insulting to the States interfered with, tending to endanger their domestic peace and tranquillity, subversive of the objects for which the Constitution was formed, and, by necessary consequence, tending to weaken and destroy the Union itself.'

"Mr. Morris of Ohio, who was then the only avowed Abolitionist in the Senate, moved to strike out the words 'moral and religious.' Had the motion prevailed, the effect would have been to encourage agitation in the form in which it would be most likely to be fatal to the South. It would have been a direct encouragement to the Abolitionized clergy of the North to take the very course which was taken by the 'three thousand and fifty divines' who, in 1854, sacrilegiously assumed, 'in the name of Almighty God, and in his presence,' to denounce the repeal of the Missouri Compromise as 'a violation of plighted faith and a breach of a national compact.' Subsequent events have abundantly attested the truth of what Mr. Calhoun said, when arguing against the motion, 'that the whole spirit of the resolution hinged upon that word *religious*.'

"The vote taken on Mr. Morris's amendment stood as follows: (Congressional Globe, volume 6, page 74.)

"Yeas—Messrs. Bayard, BUCHANAN, Clayton, Davis, McKeon, Morris, Prentiss, Robbins, Ruggles, Smyth of Indiana, Southward, Swift, Tipton, and Webster—14.

"Nays—Messrs. Allen, Black, Brown, Calhoun, Clay of Alabama, Clay of Kentucky, Cuthbert, Fulton, Hubbard, King, Knight, Linn, Lumpkin, Lyon, Nicholas, Niles, Norvell, Pierce, Preston, Rives, Roane, Robinson, Sevier, Smyth of Connecticut, Strange, Walker, Wall, White, Williams, Wright, and Young—31.

"The fifth resolution to which Mr. Calhoun here referred, and which he justly regarded as the most important of all, and struggled most perseveringly to have passed without amendment, was strictly as follows:

"'*Resolved*, That the intermeddling of any State or States, or their citizens, to abolish slavery in this District, or in any of the Territories, on the ground, or under the pretext, that it is immoral or sinful, or the passage of any act or measure of Congress, with that view, would be a direct and dangerous attack on the institutions of all the slaveholding States.'

"This resolution covered the whole premises. It met the issue boldly and fully. No Southern Democrat can hesitate to say that it embodied a great truth, to which events have borne emphatic testimony. Mr. Clay, of Kentucky, moved to strike it out, and insert the following as a substitute:

"'Resolved, That when the District of Columbia was ceded by the States of Virginia and Maryland to the United States, domestic slavery existed in both of those States, including the ceded territory; and that, as it still continues in both of them, it could not be abolished within the District without a violation of that good faith which was implied in the cession, and in the acceptance of the territory, nor unless compensation were made for the slaves, without a manifest infringement of an amendment of the Constitution of the United States, nor without exciting a degree of just alarm and apprehension in the States recognizing slavery, far transcending, in mischievous tendency, any possible benefit which would be accomplished by the abolition.' (Congressional Globe, vol. 6, page 58.)

"The utter insufficiency of this temporizing amendment scarcely need be pointed out. Objectionable as it was in conceding to Congress the constitutional power to abolish slavery in the District of Columbia, and declaring against the exercise of that power only on the ground of inexpediency, it was still more so in this, that it made no reference whatever to the territories of the United States. The passage of Mr. Calhoun's resolution would have committed the Senate, not only against the abolition of slavery in the District of Columbia, but against the application of the Wilmot Proviso and kindred measures to the Territories. Mr. Clay's amendment was entirely silent on the subject. It is true, that in another resolution which he proposed to have adopted as an additional amendment, it was declared that the abolition of slavery in the Territory of Florida would be highly inexpedient, for the principal reason 'that it would be in violation of a solemn compromise made at a memorable and critical period in the history of this country, by which, while slavery was prohibited north, it was admitted south of the line of thirty-six degrees thirty minutes north latitude.' The defect in the first amendment can hardly be considered by Southern men as remedied by another which recognized the binding force of the Missouri Compromise.

"On the question to strike out Mr. Calhoun's resolution, and insert Mr. Clay's as an amendment, after it had been modified by striking out the part relating to compensation for slaves, the vote stood—yeas 19, nays 18. (Congressional Globe, vol. 6, page 62.) *Mr. Buchanan's name stands recorded in the affirmative.*

"On a subsequent occasion, Mr. Calhoun, with a view to infuse vitality into Mr. Clay's amendment, moved to insert that any attempt of Congress to abolish slavery in the Territories, 'would be a dangerous attack upon the States in which slavery exists.' Mr. Buchanan opposed the amendment, and it was in reply to his speech that Mr. Calhoun made the remarks which may be found in the third volume of his works, pages 194 to 196, and which he commenced by saying that 'the remarks of the Senator from Pennsylvania were of such a character that he could not permit them to pass in silence.'

"From these votes, and this language of Mr. Buchanan, it is clear:

"1st. That he was not opposed to the *religious* agitation of the slavery question—a species of agitation which Mr. Calhoun justly regarded as more fatal than any other.

"2d. That he recognized the constitutional power of Congress to abolish slavery in the District of Columbia, opposing its existence only on the ground of its inexpediency—a proposition which the position of Mr. Van Buren shows affords no reliable protection to Southern institutions.

"3d. That he refused to commit himself fully on the great question as to the power of Congress over the Territories of the United States, and as far as he did go, evidently left it to be understood that the abolition of slavery by Congress in those Territories would be no attack on the States in which it exists.'

"If his opinions, in these respects, have undergone any material change, the country has not yet been authoritatively apprised of the fact. The reflections cast by him on the institution of slavery, in one of his speeches in England, and the studied design he has manifested to keep aloof from the excitement growing out of the repeal of the Missouri Compromise, are not well calculated to inspire confidence, that if his views have undergone any change, it has been a change for the better."

After thus disposing of the *slavery issue*, Mr. *Irving* thus turns to the *Tariff Question*:

"So much for the slavery issue. How does Mr. Buchanan stand upon the tariff? Will the Sentinel say that he is sound, or justify his 'low wages' speech? How does he stand upon the French Spoliation bill, which President Polk and President Pierce vetoed? Everybody knows that he was in favor of it. How does he stand upon the Pacific Railroad? He declared himself in favor of an appropriation of public money to build it, as is notorious. In fact, is there a single Federal measure except that of the United States Bank, upon which he is not recorded against Democratic principles? How can we hope to carry the united South with such a record? Will Southern Democrats overlook this record? Will Northern Nebraska men overlook this ignoring of Pierce and Douglass? Is there no danger that in admitting the abolitionist Trumbull, we may not dishearten the gallant Douglass? Is there no fear that in reinstating the free-soil Hickman, who is in favor of Reeder, we may not palsy the arm of Richardson? In fine, is there no fear that in hoping for free-soil aid, we may not lose the few real friends the South has in the North? It is evident to the commonest understanding, that the first step of Northern Black Republicanism is to kill off all those influential men at the North, like Pierce or Douglass, who have actively participated in the fight for our rights. Is not the South aiding them in this first step, when it not only ignores its own sons, but also ignores, upon the ground of availability, those Northern men identified with the late Kansas-Nebraska bill? This is a question the South would do well to ponder. If Mr. Buchanan is to be nominated, and Pierce and Douglass in the North ignored, let the responsibility rest elsewhere than upon the State of Virginia. He may be, and probably is sound, but these are times when more than ordinary caution is necessary. It may become the duty of the South to support him. When that time arrives I can discharge the duty; but I do think that the reasons above stated exempt me from any blame for not advocating him until that responsibility devolves upon me. Very respectfully, CHAS. IRVING.

The Southern Dough-faces of the Foreign Catholic party pretend to hold Mr. Fillmore responsible for a letter he wrote more than twenty years ago, in which he answers certain interrogatories in reference to slavery, *affirmatively*, and in opposition to the extension of slavery! The *latest* record of Buchanan is in 1844, and proves him to be an ABOLITIONIST OF THE BLACKEST DYE. About the last speech he ever made in Congress, was IN OPPOSITION TO SLAVERY, in secret session of the Senate, just before Mr. Polk, in opposition to the wishes of Gen. Jackson, gave him a seat in his cabinet. This speech will be found in the Congressional Globe for 1844, an extract from which is in these *explicit* and *memorable* words:

"In arriving at the conclusion to support this treaty, I had to encounter *but one serious obstacle*, AND THAT WAS THE QUESTION OF SLAVERY. Whilst I have ever maintained, and ever shall maintain, in their full force and vigor, the constitutional rights of the Southern States over their slave property, I yet feel a strong repugnance by any act of mine to extend the limits of the Union over a new slaveholding territory. After mature reflection, however, I overcame these scruples, and now believe that the acquisition of Texas will be the means of limiting, not enlarging, the dominion of slavery.

"In the government of the world, Providence generally produces great changes by gradual means. There is nothing rash in the counsels of the Almighty. May not, then, the acquisition of Texas be the means of gradually drawing the slaves far to the South to a climate more congenial to their nature; and may they not finally pass off into Mexico, and THERE MINGLE WITH A RACE WHERE NO PREJUDICE EXISTS AGAINST THEIR COLOR? The Mexican nation is composed of Spaniards, Indians, and Negroes, blended together in every variety, who would receive our slaves on terms of perfect social equality. To this condition they never can be admitted in the United States.

"That the acquisition of Texas would ere long convert Maryland, Virginia, Kentucky, Missouri, and probably others of the more Northern Slave States, into free States, I entertain not a doubt....

"But should Texas be annexed to the Union, causes will be brought into operation which must inevitably remove slavery from what may be called the farming States. From the best information, it is no longer profitable to raise wheat, rye, and corn, by slave labor. Where these articles are the only staples of agriculture, in the pointed and expressive language of Randolph, if the slave does not run away from his master, the master must run away from the slave. The slave will naturally be removed from such a country, where his labor is scarcely adequate to his own support, to a region where he can not only maintain himself, but yield large profits to his master. Texas will open an outlet; and slavery itself may thus finally pass the Del Norte, and be lost in Mexico. One thing is certain, the present number of slaves cannot be increased by the annexation of Texas.

"I have never apprehended the preponderance of the slave States in the councils of the nation. Such a fear has always appeared to me visionary. But those who entertain such apprehensions need not be alarmed by the acquisition of Texas. More than one-half of its territory is wholly unfit for the slave labor; and, therefore, in the nature of things must be free. Mr. Clay, in his letter of the 17th of April last, on the subject of annexation, states that, according to his information—

"'The Territory of Texas is susceptible of a division into five States of convenient size and form. Of these, two only would be adapted to those peculiar institutions (slavery) to which I have referred; and the other three, lying west and north of San Antonio, being only adapted to farming and grazing purposes, from the nature of their soil, climate, and productions, would not admit of these institutions. In the end, therefore, there would be two slave and three free States probably added to the Union.'

"And here permit me to observe, that there is one defect in the treaty which ought to be amended if we all did not know that it is destined to be rejected. The treaty itself ought to determine how many free and how many slave States should be made out of this territory."

On the 11th of April, 1826, James Buchanan, who is now being supported by *Southern slaveholders*, made a speech in Congress, *eleven years after* his Fourth of July oration, from which the following is taken:

"Permit me here, Mr. Chairman, for a moment, to speak upon a subject to which I have never before adverted upon this floor, and to which, I trust, I may never again have occasion to advert. I mean the subject of slavery. I BELIEVE IT TO BE A GREAT POLITICAL AND A GREAT MORAL EVIL. I THANK GOD, MY LOT HAS BEEN CAST IN A STATE WHERE IT DOES NOT EXIST.... IT HAS BEEN A CURSE ENTAILED UPON US BY THAT NATION WHICH MAKES IT A SUBJECT OF REPROACH TO OUR INSTITUTIONS." (See Gales and Seaton's Register of Debates, page 2180, vol. ii., part 2.)

MORE BUCHANAN ANTECEDENTS.

When a *"Uniform Bankrupt Law"* was enacted by Congress, after the election of General Harrison, there were on the files of the Judiciary Committee of the Senate *fifty-one petitions*, praying for the passage of such a law. Twenty-nine of these were from New York, five from New Jersey, three from Ohio, two from Indiana, two from Massachusetts, and *one* from each of the States of Tennessee and Mississippi. There were *twenty-five* other petitions praying for *"A General Bankrupt Law;"* *fifteen* of which were from New York, and eight from Pennsylvania; and how will the Democracy like to see it hereafter proven that BUCHANAN presented these petitions, and voted for the law? If it shall turn out that "Old Buck" did really go for the "odious Bankrupt Law," let his friends defend him on the ground that his *State* desired it, and had always favored the measure!

In the House of Representatives, in Congress, January 3, 1815, *Mr. Ingersoll*, a notorious Democrat from Pennsylvania, and a *Boy Tory* of the war of the Revolution, from the Committee on the Judiciary, reported a bill to establish *a uniform law of Bankruptcy throughout the United States!* If these facts should not turn out to be a sufficient justification of *Mr. Buchanan's course*, provided he went for this Bankrupt Law, let his friends present these facts, and show that he was in good old Federal Democratic *company*:

NUMBER 1. On the 5th of September, 1837, Mr. Van Buren's *Democratic* Secretary of the Treasury made a report to Congress, praying the passage of a *uniform Bankrupt Law*, which was referred to the Committee on the Judiciary.

NUMBER 2. On the 13th day of January, 1840, *Mr. Norvell*, a Democratic Senator from Michigan, moved that the Judiciary be instructed to inquire into the expediency of reporting a bill for the establishment of a *General Bankrupt Law*.

NUMBER 3. On the 22d of April, 1840, *Garret D. Wall*, a flaming Democratic Senator in Congress, reported certain amendments to a Bankrupt Law, from a minority of the Committee; which were referred to the Senate's select Committee, and reported by Mr. Wall, and passed—21 to 19—and sent to the House.

NUMBER 4. In the Senate, July 23, 1841, *Mr. Nicholson*, a Democratic Senator from Tennessee, delivered an able speech in favor of a uniform system of Bankruptcy, and moved to amend the bill then pending, by inserting "BANKS AND OTHER CORPORATIONS;" which motion was lost by a vote of 34 to 16.

NUMBER 5. That great light of Democracy, *Col. Richard M. Johnson*, late Vice-President of the United States, wrote and spoke in favor of a General Bankrupt Law. In a letter of his, now before us, dated Washington, January 18, 1841, he says, speaking of such a law: "*My opinion is that it will redound to the honor of our country.*"

But we will do Mr. Buchanan justice, by stating that he said he would vote *against* the Bankrupt Law of 1840, because he did not like its features. When Mr. Webster spoke in favor of the law, and of the character of the *petitioners*, many of whom presented their petitions through Mr. Buchanan, the latter spoke on the 24th of February, 1840; and, to satisfy Mr. Webster and others that he was not opposed to the *principle* in former days, stated, "*He came to the other House of Congress, many years since*, A FRIEND OF A BANKRUPT LAW. The subject was before the House when he entered the body twenty years ago." He added, "He was *open to conviction*, and might change his purpose!"

Thus, it will be seen that Mr. Buchanan, in this, as in every thing else, *was on both sides*! And how does it look in a Presidential candidate, to have supported a *General Bankrupt Law* for the relief of *rich, extravagant, and aristocratic* gentlemen, and then to turn round and advocate "ten cents per day" for poor folks and laboring men? It will look rather bad; but, then, Sag Nicht Democracy can go any thing! This old "ten cents per day" champion of Democracy advocated, in so many words, the reduction of all paper money prices to the real Cuba standard of solid money! We take extracts from his speech, which will be found in the Appendix to the Congressional Globe, page 135:

> "In Germany, where the currency is purely metallic, and the cost of every thing is REDUCED to a hard money standard, a piece of broadcloth can be manufactured for fifty dollars; the manufacture of which in our country, from the expansion of paper currency, would cost one hundred dollars. What is the consequence? The foreign French and German manufacturer imports this cloth into our country, and sells it for a hundred. Does not every person perceive that the redundancy of our currency is equal to a premium of one hundred per cent. in favor of the manufacturer?"

> "No tariff of protection, unless it amounted to prohibition, could counteract this advantage in favor of foreign manufactures. I would to heaven that I could arouse the attention of every manufacturer of the nation to this important subject."

> "What is the reason that, with all these advantages, and with the protective duties which our laws afford to the domestic manufacturer of cotton, we cannot obtain exclusive possession of the home market, and successfully contend for the markets of the world? It is simply because we manufacture at the nominal prices of our inflated currency, and are compelled to sell at the real prices of other nations. REDUCE OUR NOMINAL STANDARD OF PRICES THROUGHOUT THE WORLD, and you cover our country with blessings and benefits."

"The comparative LOW PRICES of France and Germany have afforded such a stimulus to their manufactures, that they are now rapidly extending themselves, and would obtain possession, in no small degree, even of the English home market, IF IT WERE NOT FOR THEIR PROTECTING DUTIES. While British manufactures are now languishing, those of the continent are springing into a healthy and vigorous existence."

How will the *Free Trade Democracy* of the South relish these "protecting duties" of an old Federal politician? They are about as consistent in their support of the Cincinnati nominee as "Clay Whigs" are, when they know that Buchanan was the only man living who had it in his power to do Clay justice, in reference to the "bargain and intrigue" calumny, and obstinately refused!

CLAY AND BUCHANAN.

In 1825, Mr. Buchanan, then a member of the House, entered the room of Mr. Clay, who was at the time in company with his only messmate, Hon. R. P. Letcher, also a member of the House, and since Governor of Kentucky. Buchanan introduced the subject of the approaching Presidential election, Letcher witnessing what was said; and after that, when Mr. Clay was hotly assailed with the charge of "bargain, intrigue, and corruption," notified Mr. Buchanan of his intention to publish the conversation, but was induced, by the *earnest entreaties of Buchanan*, to forbear. And Mr. Clay died with a letter in his possession, from Buchanan, which, if published, as it should be, would place Buchanan without the pale of Democracy, and disgrace him in the eyes of all honorable men. *That* letter, too, would explain why Gen. Jackson had no confidence in him, and was opposed to his taking a seat in Polk's cabinet. Let it come!

Keep it before the People, That it was the vote of James Buchanan which, in the Senate, in 1832, secured the passage of the "Black Tariff," so offensive to the "Free Trade" Democracy of Tennessee, South Carolina, and other Southern States, and which Gov. JONES threw up to Col. Polk with so much effect in their race of 1843!

Keep it before the People, That the Cincinnati Platform unblushingly affirms that "the Constitution does not confer upon the Federal government authority to assume the debts of the several States, contracted for local internal improvements, or for other State purposes;" while the Democratic members of Congress annually violate this principle by voting away hundreds of acres of public lands to the States, for purposes of railroads and other improvements.

Keep it before the People, That the same Platform hypocritically asserts, that "it is the duty of every branch of our Government to enforce and practice the most rigid economy in conducting our public affairs;" when the expenditures of Pierce's administration are TWENTY MILLIONS PER ANNUM over that of MILLARD FILLMORE!

Keep it before the People, That the 8th of the series in this Platform declares, that "the attempt to abridge the privilege of becoming citizens and owners of soil amongst us ought to be resisted with the same spirit which swept the alien and sedition laws from our statute book:" and then the hypocritical builders of the platform turned about and nominated James Buchanan, who commenced public life as the advocate of the "alien and sedition laws," and sustained, in and out of Congress, the Federal party, who passed these laws.

Keep it before the People, That the Cincinnati Platform, which prates so loudly about the privilege of becoming "owners of the soil," and which rebukes all efforts to amend our naturalization laws as oppressive to foreigners, nominated a man for the Presidency who spoke publicly in this language: "Above all, we ought to drive from our shores foreign influence, which has been in every age the curse of republics!"

Keep it before the People, That this Cincinnati Platform pledges itself to the "Acts known as the Compromise Measures," and then resolves "to resist all attempts at renewing, in Congress or out of it, the agitation of slavery;" while the second best nags before the Convention were Douglass and Pierce, who brought forward the bill repealing the Missouri Compromise line, and opening up anew the slavery agitation, while Pierce signed the bill and adopted it as an Administration measure!

Keep it before the People, That this same Platform asserts, as an indispensable article of the Democratic faith, that "the proceeds of the public lands ought to be sacredly applied to the national objects specified in the Constitution;" and yet a majority of the Democracy, in one branch of Congress, unhesitatingly voted for a bill introduced by Robert M. T. Hunter, a leader of "the most straitest sect" of Democratic Pharisees, which proposed to give away the whole body of the public lands to squatters, at the nominal price of ninepence an acre, and at five years' credit!

Keep it before the People, That this same platform deprecates a policy which legislates for the few at the expense of the many; yet its builders nominated a man for the Presidency who has avowed himself on the floor of the Senate in favor of reducing the wages of poor white men to the Cuban standard of TEN CENTS per day!

Keep it before the People, That this Cincinnati Platform utterly fails to come up to that high Southern standard, which the country looked for from a party so lavish of promises, and that it has deliberately and completely shirked the slavery issue, the only apology for which is found in their having nominated an old anti-slavery Federalist.

Keep it before the People, That JAMES BUCHANAN was opposed to the war of 1812, but is in favor of the next war—while a Federalist he was conservative in his views, but is now square upon a Filibustering Platform—his nomination, an overture to the Sumner Wing of Democracy, is the very nomination for the Nullifiers, Fire-eaters, and Disunionists of the South—that while we cry North, shout South, every faction is united.

THE CINCINNATI
VICE PRESIDENTIAL CANDIDATE.

John C. Breckenridge, of Kentucky, is now the Democratic candidate for the Vice Presidency; and in our devotion to the *head* of the ticket, we do not wish to neglect the *tail*. Mr. Breckenridge is a good speaker, and is about as good a selection as his party could make. He has not been long enough in public life to attain any experience as a statesman, nor has he been guilty of any great indiscretion in his short Congressional career. He will be unable to carry Kentucky for his party, though he has some elements of strength. Standing out in violent opposition to his relatives upon the *Know Nothing* issues, he will be acceptable to all Foreigners, and the Catholics in particular! Being on the very best of terms with *Cassius M. Clay*, and voting with the Emancipationists of Kentucky, he will be rather acceptable to the Anti-Slavery men than otherwise! He was a zealous supporter of the bill in Congress appropriating a million or two dollars to works of Internal Improvement, which was *vetoed* by Pierce. That bill provided $50,000 for the improvement of the Kentucky River, to which he urged an amendment insisting on $150,000. This will give him strength with the Democracy of the North and North-West, who advocated the doctrine of Internal Improvements by the General Government!

On May 20th, 1856, the *Charleston Mercury* came out advising the South as to the selection of candidates, which advice, if adhered to, would prove ruinous alike to Buchanan and Breckenridge. A brief extract from that article is in these words:

> "A man unsound on Slavery, Free Trade, and Internal Improvements, or whose opinions are shrouded in treacherous ambiguity — such a man, be he Black Republican or Democrat, is unworthy of her support. To vote for either, is to give away her influence, to be used against her. It is to stultify principle, and be the instrument of her own undoing."

This doctrine would get very much in the way of such men as *Toombs and Stephens*, of Georgia, and other Anti-Internal Improvement Democrats, but they can excuse Breckenridge on the ground that he acquiesced in the veto of Pierce, and was possibly only trying to make a little capital at home, which is common with Democracy. Besides, Mr. Breckenridge being raised a *Clay Whig*, and representing the Ashland District as a Democrat, should be allowed to pass over the *Jordan* of Democracy by degrees!

His name can be used advantageously in this contest in another respect. While Mr. Buchanan was Mr. Clay's most vindictive enemy, traducer, and calumniator, Mr. Breckenridge can be held up to the Clay Whigs, as having announced to the House of Representatives the death of Mr. Clay, in language and sentiments branding Buchanan as a malignant slanderer, without mentioning his name, by the character he gave to Clay! Closing his eulogy upon Mr. Clay in these words, Mr. Breckenridge evidently looked with the eye of prophecy at the slanders of Buchanan, the recollection of which would "cluster" around his grave:—

"Every memorial of such a man will possess a meaning and value to his countrymen. His tomb will be a hallowed spot. Great memories will cluster there, and his countrymen as they visit it may well exclaim:

"Such graves as his are pilgrim shrines—
Shrines to no creed or code confined;
The Delphian vales, the Palestines,
The Meccas of the mind."

If we mistake not, this young Breckenridge is the nephew of the Rev. John Breckenridge, formerly of Baltimore, and pastor of the Presbyterian Church. If so, he is the nephew of the Rev. Robert Breckenridge, the talented and staunch advocate of the American party. The venerable uncle of this young man, whilst pastor of the Church in Baltimore, was a most formidable opponent of the Roman Catholic religion, and is the man who conducted the debate with Archbishop Hughes, in 1836, which we now have before us, in a large volume of 550 pages. Of course *Bishop Hughes* will require the young man to repudiate his uncle's views and charges in opposition to the Papal religion; and this, we should think, he will do for the sake of the Catholic vote in America!

PROGRESSIVE DEMOCRACY—ITS LEGITI-MATE FRUITS.

From the Knoxville Whig of June 14, 1856.

The following important document we take from the National Intelligencer, of January 22, 1851. It was signed and published by gentlemen irrespective of parties—FORTY-FOUR Senators and Representatives in Congress. It will be a *curiosity* to those of our readers who may have forgotten its well-timed and patriotic pledges. How unfortunate it has been for the country, and especially the public tranquillity, that the determination and counsels of these men were, in an evil hour, departed from, and flagrantly violated by the demagogues of the self-styled Democratic party! To the violation of this solemn pledge by the repeal of the Missouri Compromise line, and the reöpening of the Slavery agitation by the introduction of the Kansas-Nebraska bill, intended to elevate that miserable little demagogue, *Stephen A. Douglass*, to the Presidency, we are indebted for all the scenes of bloodshed in Kansas, to the angry slavery discussions in Congress, and the disgraceful scenes of riot being almost daily enacted there!

Several copies of the following Declaration were circulated in Congress, and obtained a number of signatures in both halls; but no other list was ever published, that we know of, besides this, which, it will be seen, was headed by the illustrious HENRY CLAY:

"The undersigned, members of the thirty-first Congress of the United States, believing that a renewal of sectional controversy upon the subject of slavery would be both dangerous to the Union and destructive of its objects; and seeing no mode by which such controversy can be avoided, except by a strict adherence to the settlement thereof effected by the Compromise Acts passed at the last session of Congress, do hereby declare their intention to maintain the said settlement inviolate, and to resist all attempts to repeal or alter the acts aforesaid, unless by the general consent of the friends of the measure, and to remedy such evils, if any, as time and experience may develop. And, for the purpose of making this resolution effective, they further declare that they will not support for the office of President, Vice-President, Senator, or Representative in Congress, or as a member of a State Legislature, any man, of whatever party, who is not known to be opposed to the disturbance of the settlement aforesaid, and to the renewal, in any form, of agitation upon the subject of slavery.

"Henry Clay,	C. S. Morehead,	Robt. L. Rose,
W. C. Dawson,	Thos. J. Rusk,	Jere. Clemens,
James Cooper,	Thos. C. Pratt,	Wm. M. Gwin,
Samuel A. Elliot,	David Outlaw,	O. H. Williams,
J. Philips Phœnix,	A. M. Schemerhorn,	Jno. R. Thurman,
D. A. Bokee,	Geo. R. Andrews,	W. P. Mangum,
Jeremiah Morton,	R. I. Bowie,	E. C. Cabell,
Alex. Evans,	Howell Cobb,	H. S. Foote,
Wm. Duer,	Jas. Brooks,	A. H. Stephens,
R. Toombs,	M. P. Gentry,	H. W. Hilliard,
F. E. McLean,	A. G. Watkins,	H. A. Bullard,
T. S. Haywood,	A. H. Shephard,	Daniel Breck,
Jas. L. Johnson,	J. B. Thompson,	J. M. Anderson,
John B. Kerr,	J. P. Caldwell,	Ed. Deberry,
H. Marshall,	Allen F. Owen."	

The *rowdyism* and *treachery* of Democracy never intended to abide by this pledge—and hence their "disturbance of the settlement aforesaid," by opening up anew this villainous "agitation upon the subject of slavery." This violation of a solemn pledge has introduced into Kansas civil war, caused bloodshed, the shooting down of men in cold blood, and overrun that country with contending parties, called *"Friends of Freedom"* and *"Border Ruffians,"* armed with Sharpe's rifles, Colt's revolvers, bowie-knives, and clubs, mixed with Bibles!

All this really affords an illustration of the domineering insolence of Democratic Abolitionism—an element in our Federal Government which will stop at no extremity of violence, in order to subdue the people of the Slave States, and force them into a miserable subservience to its fanatical dominion. And it is worthy of note, that the shooting of Sheriff Jones and others in Kansas, occurred immediately after the arrival of the *New Haven Emigrant Rifle Company*! This, too, calls to mind forcibly the very delectable *conversational speechifying* that took place at the New Haven Rifle Meeting, among the pious villains who figured most conspicuously. As it is short, we give it entire:

Rev. Mr. Dutton (pastor of the church.)—One of the deacons of this church, Mr. Harvey Hall, is going out with the company to Kansas, and I, as his pastor, desire to present him a Bible and a Sharpe's rifle. (Great applause.)

E. P. Pie.—I will give one.

Stephen D. Purdee.—I will give one for myself, and also another one for my wife.

Mr. Beecher.—I like to see that—it is a bold stroke both right and left. (Great laughter.)

Charles Ives.—Put me down for three.

Thomas R. Trowbridge.—Put me down for four. (Continued laughter.) Dr. J. I. Howe.—I will subscribe for one.

A gentleman said that Miss Mary Dutton would give one.

Dr. Stephen G. Hubbard.—One.

Mr. Beecher here stated that if twenty-five could be raised on the spot, he would pledge twenty-five more from the church at Plymouth—fifty being a sufficient number for the whole supply. (Clapping of hands all over the house.)

Prof. Silliman now left Mr. Beecher to speak for the bid, and sat down to enjoy the occasion.

Mr. Killem.—I give one.

Mr. Beecher.—*Killem*—that's a significant name in connection with a good Sharpe's rifle. (Laughter.)

After this, this clerical vagabond, Beecher, blessed the weapons, and encouraged the party to go forth and "do or die" in the sublime "cause of nigger freedom!" In all human probability, sweet Mary Dutton's rifle may have sped the ball that pierced the side of Sheriff Jones, the officer of the law, while in the honest discharge of a sworn duty! Subsequent murders, where pro-slavery men were shot down with these rifles, we attribute to the *omen* that Beecher found in his name "*Killem*"—it is a significant name in connection with Sharpe's rifle. The real assassins shoot down their men, and with their *rifles* and *Bibles* flee; but *she* who unfrocked herself by furnishing a rifle, and *he* who gave and blessed the weapon of death, are here to accept the thanks of their admirers and partisans. Let sweet Mary and her *beloved* pastor be crowned with wreaths of deadly night-shade, and consigned to one cell in Sing Sing prison!

But the success of Ruffianism in Kansas, in the hands of those vile Abolition Democrats, has emboldened members of the same party to introduce it in the Federal Capital. But the other day, MR. SUMNER, of Massachusetts, made, in his place in the U. S. Senate, one of the most incendiary and inflammatory speeches ever uttered on the floor of either House of Congress! The vocabulary of Billingsgate was exhausted in denouncing all who dared to justify the institution of slavery—using, over and over again, such terms as "hireling, picked from the drunken spew of an uneasy civilization in the form of men," &c. The language made use of was disgraceful to the vile Abolitionist himself, and to the Senate, of which he never ought to have been a member. There was no limit to the personal abuse in which the villainous Senator indulged, no restraint to the vile epithets coined in his insane head; and the very natural consequence was, a personal chastisement of Mr. Sumner, in the Senate chamber, by Mr. Brooks, a Representative from South Carolina, and a relative of Judge Butler, the gentleman abused in his absence, which, for its severity, never was equalled in Washington. Mr. Sumner was the aggressor, because he poured out the vials of his wrath upon not only Judge Butler, a distinguished Senator, but upon the whole State of South Carolina.

We do not justify the selection of a *time* and *place* by *Mr. Brooks*, for punishing this Massachusetts Abolitionist; but we should despise the son of South Carolina who could hear his native State arraigned in such temper and language, without feeling intensely, and *manifesting* that feeling at a proper time and place. Indeed, it would be strange if a South Carolinian did not resent the arrogant, insulting, and contemptuous tone which Mr. Sumner saw fit to indulge in towards South Carolina in general, and her Senator in particular! We know Judge Butler—we have seen him on the Bench, in the discharge of the duties of a Circuit-Judge—we have seen and heard him in the Senate Chamber, where he has served for years, with credit to himself and honor to his State. He is an accomplished man, and a most amiable and honorable gentleman. His character is unblemished; he stands deservedly high; he is a gentleman of urbane and courteous demeanor, and is beloved, esteemed, and respected, by all *gentlemen* who know him or associate with him. Besides, he is an old man, gray-haired, and palsied; and, whether present or absent, deserved to be treated as a gentleman.

Northern men may not expect to vilify the South in this way, without having to atone for it. Men who profess to belong to the peace party, ought not to employ language that will provoke a fight, and then shield themselves behind their non-resistant defences. They voluntarily put themselves upon the platform of *resistance*—they pass insults, and they must submit to the consequences. We have just finished the perusal of a case in Æsop's Fables, exactly in point. It is the case of a *trumpeter* taken prisoner in battle. He claimed exemption from the common fate of prisoners of war, in ancient times, on the ground that he carried no weapons, and was, in fact, a non-combatant, belonging to the peace party! "Non-combatant, the Devil!" exclaimed the opposing party, pointing to his trumpet, as preparations were being made to put him to death, "Why, Sir, you hold in your hands the very instrument which incites our foes to tenfold furies against us!"

But this fight between the parties has to come, and it should begin at Washington, and if not in the halls of Congress, at least in the *streets* of the Federal city. Let the battle be fought there, and not in *Kansas*, and let it fall upon the villainous agitators of the Slavery question, and the *Democratic* disturbers of the Compromises of the Constitution. Let it come *now*, that it may be fought out and settled, and not left to *posterity*, to curse and crush the rising generation!

Mr. Brooks is a Democrat, and an anti-Know Nothing. Mr. Sumner is a Democrat—was elected by the votes of the Democrats, over that noble and dignified Whig, Mr. Winthrop, and his election was hailed throughout the Union as a Democratic triumph!

Massachusetts, irrespective of parties, seems to have taken great offence at this occurrence, and to have held indignation meetings, and was to have had *Legislative* action upon the subject. We tell Massachusetts that she is alone to blame, for sending such a man to the United States Senate. There was a great debate in the Senate twenty-five years ago, in which Daniel Webster and Gov. Hayne met each other and grappled like giants, as they were. The State of South Carolina, in that day, though represented by an able, patriotic, and great man, came off *second best*. The Senator from Massachusetts, of that day, was an able statesman, a Constitutional lawyer of unsurpassed abilities, and, withal, a cautious gentleman, and rose above the low blackguardism of a Sumner and a Wilson. When *taunted* by the Senator from South Carolina with *Federalism*, and opposition to some of the features of the War of 1812, the great Webster presented Massachusetts before the Senate and the Union, in such a manner that men of all sections bowed down and worshipped her. Standing erect with the flash of his eagle eye, he exclaimed, "There is Boston, and Concord, and Lexington, and Bunker Hill"—let them testify to the loyalty of Massachusetts to this glorious Union! Not only did Mr. Webster come out of that controversy with South Carolina with the admiration of every man in the country, but with the respect and admiration of Calhoun, Hayne, McDuffie, and all the high-toned statesmen of the South. And why? Because he was not a Sumner, a Wilson, or an *Abolition Blackguard*. Times have changed—a different man takes the place of a Webster, with only the memory of an insulting speech and a broken head! Let Massachusetts send men to the United States Senate who can and will demean themselves like gentlemen, and gentlemen from the South will appreciate them, while they differ honestly with them on great questions.

What wonderful *progress* Democracy is making in the country! *First*, Democracy quarrelled and jowered over the election of a Speaker two months, and finally, by the introduction of the *Plurality Rule*, caused Banks, a Black Republican, to be elected. And as if determined to atone for this wear of time and money, they have brought about a series of fights, which, before they are disposed of, will cost the government half a million of dollars!

First then, William Smith, an ex-Governor of the State of Virginia, and member of the House of Representatives, assailed and beat the editor of the *Evening Star*, in December last, in the street.

Second, Albert Rusk, a member of the House of Representatives from Arkansas, assailed and beat the editor of the New York *Tribune* in the grounds of the capitol, immediately after leaving the House of Representatives.

Third, Philip T. Herbert, of Alabama, a member of Congress from California, shot down and killed an Irish Catholic waiter at Willard's, and is now under bonds to appear before the Court and await his trial for such crime as they may adjudge him to have committed.

Fourth, Preston S. Brooks, a member of the House of Representatives from South Carolina, assails and beats unmercifully a Senator from Massachusetts, when occupying his seat in the Senate of the United States.

Fifth, Mr. Bright knocked down the doorkeeper, for an inconsiderable offence. Here, then, we have five breaches of the peace in five months, by Democrats upon Democrats, although the "Boston Pilot," a Catholic organ, falsely charges that some of the parties making these assaults are "Know Nothings." We congratulate the Democratic party upon the progress of its leading members! They are sinking by swift descent into barbarism, and bringing the country to ruin. And in keeping with all this, they have tried to nominate for the Vice-Presidency a man who openly proposed in Congress the repeal of our neutrality laws, so as to bring a general fight!

It will not do to say that *Sumner* is not of the Democratic party, because he is a regular-built Free-Soiler and Black Republican: the Washington *Union* settled this point in 1852, when it uttered these memorable words:

> "The Free-soil Democratic leaders of the North are a regular portion of the Democratic party, and General Pierce, if elected, will make no distinction between them and the rest of the Democracy in the distribution of official patronage, and in the selection of agents for administering the government."

The rules of the Senate forbid personalities in debate, and it was the sworn duty of its Locofoco President, Mr. Bright, to have called Mr. Sumner to order for his abuse of Judge Butler. But as far back as thirty years ago, under the auspices of JOHN C. CALHOUN as presiding officer, a decision was made to the effect that the presiding officer of the Senate was neither bound nor had he the power to call Senators to order! That power, according to his decision, belonged wholly to the Senate itself— —thus delivering over the minority of that body to "the tender mercies" of the majority! The object of Mr. CALHOUN at the time was to play into the hands of a combination which had been formed to break down the Administration of John Quincy Adams, and to cripple Henry Clay. The instrument used was the sarcastic, irritating, and personal rhetoric of John Randolph, then a member of the Senate. To this end, Randolph was suffered to deliver in the Senate a long succession of tirades, disgraceful to the Senate, abusive of New England and of Henry Clay. Here is a specimen of Randolph's abuse, which led to a duel between him and Mr. Clay:

> "This man, (mankind, I crave pardon,) this worm, (little animals, forgive the insult,) was raised to a higher life than he was born to, for he was raised to the society of blackguards. Some fortune—kind to him, cruel to us—has tossed him to the Secretaryship of State. Contempt has the property of descending, but stops far short of him. She would die before she would reach him: he dwells below her fall. I would hate him, if I did not despise him. It is not WHAT he is, but WHERE he is, that puts my thoughts into action. The alphabet which writes the name of Thersites, blackguard, squalidity, refuses her letters for him. That mind which thinks on what it cannot express, can scarcely think on him. An hyperbole for MEANNESS would be an ellipsis for CLAY."

This was pleasing to Mr. Calhoun and the dominant party in the Senate, and his decision which tolerated it never was questioned by any authoritative precedent, until MILLARD FILLMORE was elected Vice-President. With characteristic independence, he determined that a precedent so unreasonable and absurd should not be binding on him as the presiding officer of the Senate. He therefore, on assuming the duties of his office, delivered an address to the Senate, in which he informed that body that he considered it his sworn duty to preserve decorum, and would *reverse* the rule which had so long prevailed, that Senators were not to be called to order for words spoken in debate! The Senate ordered this address to be entered at large on their journals, as an evidence of their endorsement of its doctrines; and there it is now, recorded evidence of the patriotism, high sense of decorum, and senatorial dignity of that great and good man, MILLARD FILLMORE.

STRENGTH OF PARTIES IN TENNESSEE.

OFFICIAL VOTES OF THE STATE.

The following tables exhibit the official vote of Tennessee for President in 1852, for Governor in 1853, and for Governor in 1855, as compared at the capital of the State, and will be valuable as a table for reference. In the last contest, when the *Know Nothing issues* were fully made, causing all the *latent blackguardism in the Democratic ranks to be fully developed*, it will be seen that *Andrew Johnson* received 67,499 votes, and *Meredith P. Gentry* 65,342, leaving Johnson a majority of 2,157, a falling off of 104 votes from his majority over *Maj. Henry* two years before that. It will also be perceived that the vote of the State at this last election is an increase of 8,260 over the vote two years previous. Of this increase, *Col. Gentry* gets 4,182, his vote exceeding *Maj. Henry's* by that much, while Johnson's increase upon his own vote two years previous was 4,078.

It is a moderate calculation to say that Johnson received at least two thousand *foreign and illegal votes*; while we are within bounds when we say that at least 5,000 old-line Whigs refused to vote for *Col. Gentry*—demonstrating beyond all doubt that a majority of the legal voters of the State were opposed to Johnson and his party.

In the contest now being waged, *Fillmore and Donelson* will carry the State by a majority ranging from *three* to *five* thousand votes, despite the low Billingsgate slang and vile blackguardism that may be heaped upon them and their supporters. And as this calculation is made in *June*, five months in advance of the election, we must ask those into whose hands this work shall fall without the limits of Tennessee, to bear it in mind, and when they get the returns in November, to give us credit for our sagacity or our want of sagacity!

The contest will be fierce and bitter, exceeding any former political battle witnessed in the State. If the orators and editors of the self-styled Democratic party have not greatly reformed in the space of one year, but little argument will be adduced, but little gentlemanly courtesy manifested; and instead of facts, figures and arguments, bitter invective, low blackguardism, and Billingsgate abuse of secret organizations, dark lanterns, and Protestant clergymen, will be the order of the day. In this *congenial* work, all the conglomeration of ignorant men, foreign paupers, and fag-ends and factions, styling themselves *Democrats*, will engage!

But to the official vote of the State:

POPULAR VOTE OF TENNESSEE—OFFICIAL.

EAST TENNESSEE.

Counties.	1852.		1853.		1855.	
	Scott.	Pierce.	Henry.	Johnson.	Gentry.	Johnson.
Anderson	602	267	648	379	772	333
Bledsoe	464	209	469	303	404	361
Blount	827	566	1146	734	1069	789
Bradley	547	778	562	1085	644	1021
Campbell	313	251	356	445	507	383
Carter	585	139	721	294	768	238
Claiborne	503	519	620	707	756	744
Cooke	743	196	867	383	929	422
Grainger	852	477	998	767	1327	621
Greene	780	1301	902	1915	989	1985
Hawkins	778	831	805	1180	887	1158
Hamilton	774	648	786	972	966	1044
Hancock	241	336	221	532	264	589
Jefferson	1168	307	1396	639	1697	444
Johnson	365	93	392	184	400	215
Knox	1863	565	2279	770	2560	695
McMinn	796	866	799	965	909	953
Meigs	141	442	118	561	97	588
Marion	453	292	476	357	554	468
Monroe	805	847	739	900	851	1005
Morgan	240	222	229	260	219	358
Polk	272	470	249	527	385	676
Rhea	300	307	270	358	298	415
Roane	820	678	912	755	1002	769
Sevier	621	80	824	133	964	120
Scott	199	127	186	182	121	259
Sullivan	260	1114	361	1407	601	1403
Washington	565	853	967	1069	847	1338
	— — —	— — —	— — —	— — —		
			19,298	18,763	21,787	19,394

MIDDLE TENNESSEE.

Counties.	Scott.	Pierce.	Henry.	Johnson.	Gentry.	Johnson.

Bedford	1390	1356	1359	1257	1630	1293
Cannon	453	727	445	803	458	859
Coffee	205	722	274	824	294	880
Davidson	2617	2058	2597	1963	3132	1783
De Kalb	559	588	632	610	560	738
Dickson	323	607	357	743	388	745
Fentress	153	411	166	504	129	616
Franklin	330	1133	356	1224	394	1302
Giles	1303	1447	1301	1468	1312	1439
Grundy	44	327	58	374	22	425
Hardin	643	808	671	827	745	775
Hickman	241	839	263	812	223	1053
Humphreys	263	471	341	501	354	543
Jackson	1170	803	1154	995	1122	1131
Lawrence	547	583	523	731	524	845
Lewis	43	186	66	182	34	243
Lincoln	606	2297	617	2322	402	2521
Maury	1324	1799	1238	1731	1444	1793
Montgomery	1260	993	1309	1004	1502	881
Marshall	666	1340	671	1282	678	1310
Macon	617	374	553	341	540	424
Overton	345	1039	431	1282	290	1528
Robertson	1013	769	1183	763	1256	804
Rutherford	1495	1313	1407	1243	1435	1288
Smith	1742	520	1735	546	1572	644
Stewart	533	725	479	718	563	785
Sumner	825	1563	806	1425	780	1740
Van Buren	107	165	110	205	90	228
Warren	344	922	402	1093	393	1153
Wayne	666	380	709	430	687	535
White	949	518	974	634	978	694
Williamson	1583	763	1502	710	1621	688
Wilson	2248	923	2241	995	2290	937
			— — —	— — —	— — —	— — —
			26,930	30,550	27,842	32,623

WEST TENNESSEE.

Counties.	Scott.	Pierce.	Henry.	Johnson.	Gentry.	Johnson.
Benton	340	485	393	465	475	453
Carroll	1498	649	1469	663	1567	694
Decatur	400	315	408	285	353	429
Dyer	508	411	476	373	442	483
Fayette	1006	1034	1011	1006	1151	940
Gibson	1570	901	1514	1024	1618	1213
Hardeman	717	1024	651	1025	619	1123
Henderson	1193	511	1301	593	1230	734
Henry	899	1516	891	1496	871	1738
Haywood	790	732	726	785	803	762
Lauderdale	330	277	319	252	354	297
McNairy	921	872	1016	984	915	1059
Madison	1426	819	1261	795	1448	788
Obion	431	644	547	792	407	865
Perry	325	314	387	329	320	450
Shelby	1824	1628	1545	1435	1831	1477
Tipton	357	565	284	527	424	566
Weakley	783	1149	733	1279	885	1411
	———	———	———	———	———	———
	58,802	57,123	14,932	14,108	15,713	15,482
	57,123					
	———					
Scott's majority,	1,679					
East Tennessee,			19,298	18,763	21,787	19,394
Middle Tennessee,			26,930	30,550	27,842	32,623
			———	———	———	———
			61,160	63,421	65,342	67,499
				61,160		65,342
				———		———
Johnson's majority				2,261		2,157

FILLMORE AND DONELSON ELECTORAL TICKET.

As a matter of reference, and that none may mistake the American Ticket on the day of the election, we give it as agreed upon and matured by our party:

FOR THE STATE.

HON. NEILL S. BROWN, of Davidson.

HORACE MAYNARD, of Knox.

FOR THE DISTRICTS.

1st   District—   N. G. TAYLOR, of Carter.

2d   District—   MOSES WHITE, of Knox.

3d   District—   REESE B. BRABSON, of Hamilton.

4th   District—   W. P. HICKERSON, of Coffee.

5th   District—   ROBERT HATTON, of Wilson.

6th   District—   W. H. WISENER, of Bedford.

7th   District—   C. C. CROWE, of Giles.

8th   District—   J. M. QUARLES, of Montgomery.

9th   District—   ISAAC R. HAWKINS, of Carroll.

10th   District—   JOSEPH R. MOSBY, of Fayette.

This is an able ticket, and greatly superior to the opposing ticket, as our readers will bear us witness when they hear the parties in debate. Most of these gentlemen have consented to serve on the ticket at great personal sacrifices; and like their chief, Mr. FILLMORE, they have undertaken to serve their party and country "without waiting to inquire of its prospects of success or defeat." And all the reward they seek is to be able to conduct the struggle to a victorious consummation in Tennessee, and this we feel confident they will do. The battle in Tennessee will be hotly contested, but it is by no means doubtful. Tennessee for the last twenty years, and in five preceding presidential contests, has refused to range herself under the black banner of Locofocoism; and now that that banner is doubly infamous by being raised and cheered by Catholics, foreigners, and paupers of every clime, it is fair to presume she will spurn the flag!

THE BLACK REPUBLICAN NOMINEES.

The Black Republican Party, in their recent Convention at Philadelphia, have nominated JOHN CHARLES FREMONT, of California, for the Presidency, and Ex-Senator WILLIAM L. DAYTON, of New Jersey, for the Vice Presidency!

This man Fremont is no statesman—has no experience in political life—has not the first qualification for this eminent and responsible station—and his nomination has not been made upon any plausible pretext whatever. He is an Engineer by profession—once penetrated with his companions to the Pacific coast, across the Rocky Mountains—is the son-in-law of *Tom Benton*—is a Free Trade Locofoco, and an avowed Free Soiler.

The following letter addressed by Fremont to the great Tabernacle Abolition meeting in New York, last spring, is full and explicit, and defines his position on the slavery question:

"NEW YORK, April 29, 1856.

"GENTLEMEN: I have to thank you for the honor of an invitation to a meeting this evening at the Broadway Tabernacle, and regret that other engagements have interfered to prevent my being present.

"I heartily concur in all movements which have for their object 'to repair the mischiefs arising from the violation of good faith in the repeal of the Missouri Compromise.' I am opposed to slavery in the abstract and upon principle, sustained and made habitual by long-settled convictions.

"While I feel inflexible in the belief that it ought not to be interfered with where it exists under the shield of State sovereignty, I am as inflexibly opposed to its extension on this continent beyond its present limits.

"With the assurance of regard for yourselves,

"I am very respectfully yours,
"J. C. FREMONT."

"Messrs. J. D. Morgan and others."

In addition to this, Fremont is the representative of *aggression*: he is a *Filibuster*, and the exponent of a civilization above all constitutions, and all laws. The fact that Seward, Chase, Giddings, and such men—able anti-slavery men, and experienced politicians, were passed over, is proof that they were not governed by *principle*, but seek to shift the issue, and to make it personal and sectional. Take into the account, moreover, the fact that Dayton, a man of moderate talents, is a sort of *Protective Tariff Locofoco*, the advocate of Foreign Pauper labor, and the largest liberty for *Catholics*, and it gives to the ticket a considerable degree of interest.

The leading men in the Convention were reckless and unprincipled demagogues, of the Locofoco school of politics, including the British Free Trade policy, Filibusterism, etc., whose only aim is place and plunder. Their Free-soil principles, outside of their radical purposes, are scarcely skin deep!

By many well-informed men, no doubts are entertained now, that the nomination of Fremont and Dayton has been the result of an intrigue between Seward and Archbishop Hughes; and from a resolution of their platform, as reported by the Committee on Resolutions, we attach credit to this inference. It will bring the Buchanan party at the North to terms, as they are likely to be the only sufferers from this ticket. It will be managed in future alone with an eye to the *aid* of Buchanan!

We take the following notice of Fremont from the Charleston (S. C.) Standard, and consider it every way reliable:

"Mr. Fremont will be destined to play a distinguished part in the drama, and his history and character therefore will, doubtless, become subjects of considerable importance. He is generally regarded as a native of Charleston, but of this we have occasion to doubt. Many gentlemen here, who knew him in early life, concur in saying that he was born in Savannah. Up to within a short time prior to his birth, his mother was a resident of Norfolk, in Virginia, and it is generally asserted that his parents resided in Savannah before they became settled in Charleston; however this may have been, it is at least conceded that he first came into notice in this city. His prospects here were not particularly promising, but he attracted the attention of some philanthropic gentlemen, who provided the means for his entrance and instruction in the Charleston College. His progress there was not remarkable, and when his class graduated he was not considered entitled to a diploma. He was afterwards recommended as a proper person to take charge of the night-school of the Apprentices' Library Association; but, though his attainments were sufficient, and his address particularly acceptable to the Directors of that Institution, he was not as attentive as he might have been, and the school fell through. He afterwards procured, through Mr. Poinsett, a situation as instructor of junior officers on board a vessel of war bound to the Pacific, and in this condition is said to have acquitted himself well. He afterwards acquired some knowledge of civil engineering, and filling unimportant positions in connection with one and another public work, was at length brought to notice and distinction by his connection with Mr. Nicholet in his Survey of the Mississippi Valley, and from that marched steadily on to the Rocky Mountains, and a renown that has placed his name before the country.

"From the records of his early life, it would seem that he had talent, and was quite addicted to naval reading, but was wayward, and if not indolent, was inefficient in the tasks undertaken at the instance of other people, and up to the time of his entrance upon his duties as instructor in the naval school, had hardly made up his mind whether he would be a man of character or a blackguard. He was fond of dress, however, and the records of the court still show that he wore a suit of clothes which he was afterwards compelled to declare on oath his inability to pay for, in order to avoid inconvenient restrictions upon his personal liberty; but chance gave a proper direction to his abilities; he had the latent energy of character to act up to his opportunities, and he has really presented a career which any one might regard with satisfaction. It is certainly to be regretted that he should lend himself to the uses of a party so reckless and subversive, not only of the Union but of the rights of that section to which, if capable of sentiments of patriotism, he might be supposed to feel attachment; but the prospect of the Presidency would be a sore trial to the probity of most men, and we find nothing in the antecedents of Mr. Fremont to cause a feeling of disappointment that he should yield to the allurements of power.

"He is commended for his attentions to his mother, and they were certainly exemplary. She was poor, and after he determined to behave himself and work like a man, he made her as entirely comfortable as there was the reason to believe his circumstances permitted."

Postscript. — Mr. Fremont turns out to be a Roman Catholic, and to have been raised one, and this explains the readiness of Bishop Hughes to abandon Buchanan, and go over to Fremont. It also explains why it is that so many *German Catholic papers* are coming out for Fremont, in the large cities, and in the North-Western States.

In 1850, Fremont held a seat in the United States Senate, for the space of about three months, and during that time sought to introduce a Catholic Priest to open their services with prayers, and was successful to some extent. He also attended service at the Catholic Church. The *Washington Star*, of the 19th June, 1856, gives the following exposition of facts, in reference to Fremont and his religion:

"A sort of a Catholic. — We take it for granted that among the informal pledges extracted by delegations in George Law's Convention, from Col. Fremont, there was not one against the Catholic Church; insomuch as, up to the recent birth of his aspirations for the Presidency, he always passed in Washington for a good enough outside Roman Catholic; that being the Church in which he was reared. He was married in this city, it will be remembered, by Father Van Horseigh, a clergyman of his Church — not of that of his wife's family."

The Republicans sought to incorporate into their platform a plank in opposition to the *Religious Proscription* of the American party, so as to suit the taste of Romanists generally; but Thaddeus Stevens, who knows Pennsylvania as well as any man living, implored them not to do so, and stated that such a course, with

Fremont as their nominee, would lose them Pennsylvania by 50,000 votes!

It turns out, however, that Fremont, as the anti-American, anti-Protestant candidate, with Mr. Dayton on the ticket, equally anti-American, and devoted to Romanism, will sweep the Catholic vote in the United States. Catholics may favor Buchanan in such Southern States as do not run a Fremont ticket, but in all the Northern and North-Western States, the Fremont ticket will ruin the Buchanan ticket.

This question, taken in connection with the Slavery issue, and the Filibustering issue, narrows the contest down to one between Fillmore and Fremont. Buchanan is defeated, and the Southern fire-eaters see and feel it! The *Atlanta* (Ga.) *Intelligencer* comes out and states, that if Buchanan can't be elected, it prefers Fremont to Fillmore! And the South Carolina and Mississippi Disunionists openly avow, that they wish this to be the last contest of the kind. They are for Buchanan or Fremont, over Fillmore, because they believe the election of either will have the glorious effect to bring about a dissolution of the Union! In the same breath they admit that Fillmore will labor to perpetuate the Union, and that his election will have the effect to prolong its existence a few brief years!

Southern men, and Northern men, Union men, and national, conservative men, of all parties, can now see *where* we are driving to, and *who* they should support for the Presidency. Let them guard against these demons of Popery—these incarnate fiends of the Free Soil faith—these fanatics of a sectional cast—these slimy vultures of Secession—these bogus Democrats—and these infinitely infernal traitors to the Constitution and the Union!

> "Col. Fremont was educated in and graduated from St. Mary's College, in Baltimore, a Roman Catholic Institution. He was brought up in the Catholic Faith, and is a Catholic. He married a daughter of Col. Benton. Miss Benton was a Presbyterian. They were married by a clergyman of that denomination; but a Catholic priest made a fuss about it as being null, void, and heretical, and the ceremony was re-performed by him!" —*Auburn American.*

The *American* might have added, that Fremont is the son of a *Catholic Frenchman*, the son of a *Catholic mother*, and was reared under Catholic influence. Nay, Fremont educates his children at the Roman Catholic Institution at Georgetown, in the District of Columbia! The placing of such a candidate before the public, seems especially designed to defy public sentiment, and mock the Protestant American feeling of the country! We had expected the Catholics, with Bishop Hughes at their head, in a few years more, to come out openly, and run a Catholic for the Presidency, but we had not supposed them bold enough to attempt it in 1856. To show beyond all doubt that the nomination of Fremont was the result of a coalition between Seward and Hughes, more in reference to the *Catholic question* than the *Slavery issue*, we present the record of Fremont in the United States Senate—his *ultra-Pro-Slavery course*—his voting against justice to the Colonization Society, and *seven hundred and fifty* captured slaves—his opposition to the abolition of Slavery in the District of Columbia!

HE IS EXTREME SOUTHERN AND PRO-SLAVERY.

John C. Fremont held a seat in the United States Senate, in 1850, for the space of a few months. During that time he made no speeches; indeed, he has scarcely ever been known to utter any sentiments, or sanction any opinions. Yet his votes, as a member of the Senate, did make for him a record; and it is this record that will stare him in the face as long as he lives—a record in direct conflict with his present professions and position before the country:

LOOK AT IT!—JOHN C. FREMONT'S STATESMANSHIP.

[From the Congressional Globe—Vol. 21, part 2d, p. 1803, etc.]

"IN SENATE OF UNITED STATES, Sept. 11, 1850.

"Mr. Underwood, of Kentucky, called up the bill for the relief of the American Colonization Society. The slaves that were recaptured on the barque Pons were turned over to the Colonization Society, by the authority of the United States, sent to Liberia, and there kept at the expense of the society for one or two years. Most of them were children of twelve, fifteen, and sixteen years of age. The society thinks that the expense of feeding, clothing, and educating these people, which was thus devolved on them by the action of the Government, ought to be repaid them. It was certainly an expense incurred by the society, through the action of the Government in throwing these young negroes upon them for maintenance, instead of taking them, as the Government was bound to do by law, and providing for them. That is the nature of the claim. They simply ask that so much shall be paid them as the society, from its own experience, pays in reference to its own emigrants. The claim was reported upon favorably two years ago. A similar report has again been made; and as the necessities of the society require that they should have the money, I hope, said Mr. U., the Senate will consent to take up the bill. The Senate agreed to take up the bill, and proceeded to consider it as in Committee of the Whole.

"Mr. Turney asked for the reading of the report of the Committee.

"The Secretary read the report accordingly. It sets forth that a liberal construction of the act of Congress of March 3d, 1819, would require that the Government should provide for the support of these recaptured Africans, for a reasonable time after they had been landed in Liberia, and that it is beneath the dignity of the Government to devolve this duty upon the society. The petition of the executive committee of the society which the Committee incorporated in their report, states that on the 16th of December, 1845, the United States Ship Yorktown, Commodore Bell, landed at Monrovia, in Liberia, from the slaver Pons, seven hundred and fifty recaptured Africans, in a naked, starving, and dying condition, all of them excepting twenty-one being under the age of twenty-one. The United States made no provision for their support after they were landed....

"The services of providing for the destitute negroes were not required to be performed by the society under their constitution, but the alternative was to leave these recaptured Africans to starve and die, and the society therefore cheerfully took charge of them, relying upon the Government of the United States to refund the cost to them."

The question was discussed at length as to whether the United States would pay these just and legal demands; and on the vote being taken for the engrossment of the bill to a third reading, Mr. Fremont's name is found recorded in the negative—as follows:

"YEAS—Messrs. Badger, Baldwin, Bell, Chase, Clayton, Davis of Mass., DAYTON, Dodge of Wis., Dodge of Iowa, Douglass, Ewing, Felch, Greene, Hale, Hamlin, Jones, Mangum, Pearce, Pratt, Seward, Shields, Smith, Spruance, Sturgeon, Underwood, Wales, Walker, Whitcomb, and Winthrop—29.

"NAYS—Messrs. Atchison, Barnwell, Benton, Butler, Dawson, Dickinson, Downs, FREMONT, Hunter, King, Mason, Rusk, Sebastian, Soule, Turner, and Yulee—16."

LOOK AGAIN!—On the 18th day of September, 1850, the bill to prevent persons from enticing away slaves from the District of Columbia was under consideration, and John P. Hale "moved that it be committed to the Committee on the District of Columbia, with instructions *to so amend it as to* ABOLISH SLAVERY IN THE DISTRICT OF COLUMBIA." On the vote being taken, FREMONT'S name was recorded in the NEGATIVE. (See Cong. Globe, 31st Congress, part 2, p. 1859.)

Such is Mr. Fremont's *record of Statesmanship*. It shows his nomination by the *"Republicans"* to have been a hollow mockery—"a dishonest farce,"—an insult to the intelligence of the American people.

We shall hereafter pursue the record of this "remarkable man."

Bishop Hughes and Wm. H. Seward have been, for years, intimate personal and political friends. It is a part of the political history of New York, that Seward is alone indebted to Hughes for his reelection to the United States Senate. They are both now united in the support of Fremont, and they procured his nomination over Judge McLean, a pure and patriotic man—for many years a *Methodist Class-Leader*, and an officer of a *Protestant Bible Society*.

The coalition between Hughes, Seward and Fremont, is complete, and the evidence of the foul coalition and conspiracy will appear in full, in a few days, but not in time for us to get it into this work. We are right glad of it, as it narrows the contest down to one between Fillmore and Fremont, and especially at the North.

In some of the Northern States, it is now conclusive that a *Buchanan* ticket will not be run, while in every Northern State where such a ticket is run, it will be with no hope of success! Hughes and Seward will induce several States to drop Buchanan, and unite on Fremont, by *bargaining* with them, and obligating themselves to give the Democracy half of the spoils. Already several *Southern* Democratic papers are saying, that if they can't elect Buchanan, they prefer Fremont to Fillmore! This ought to open the eyes of all true patriots.

OLD LINE WHIGS, AND THE MOTIVES GOVERNING SOME OF THEM!

In this free country of ours, gentlemen have a right to support any Presidential or other ticket they may choose to support; and where they are governed by pure motives in differing from a majority of their neighbors and old political associates, no one has a right to complain.

Some few gentlemen, known as "Old Line Whigs," will not come into the support of the American ticket, but will even support the Democratic ticket; and do it from an honest (though mistaken) belief that they can most effectually serve the interests of the country by this course. With such, we shall be the last man to raise a quarrel—claiming the right to do as we please in matters of the sort. But there are some men in the ranks of the enemy now, who are governed by very different motives; and as these are quoted against the American party, or, as their refusal to act with the party is a matter of *boasting* in the Democratic ranks, it is due to the cause of truth, and of the country, that they should be understood, that their efforts may be *appreciated*.

Without intending to be tedious, we name JAMES C. JONES, of Tennessee, as at the head of the list of *Old Liners*, whose devotion to the *South*, and love of *liberty*, prevent him from supporting Fillmore and Donelson. This is the veriest *stuff* in the political world! Gov. Jones cannot excuse the matter of his opposition to Millard Fillmore upon the grounds he rests the case, in his Circular addressed to his constituents. The true secret of the matter must come to light, that old Whigs and new Whigs, Americans and Democrats, may appreciate his motives.

Last fall, at the Fair in Jackson, in West Tennessee, in the house and at the bedside of ANDREW GUTHRIE, on being inquired of as to his future course, the Governor became very much excited, and roundly asserted, that if the American party nominated *Fillmore*, he should go against him. [**hand pointing right ==>]*Because Fillmore, in his appointment of persons to office in Tennessee, did not consult him, but in many cases appointed his personal enemies!* Mark, he did not pause to inquire *who* might be the opposing candidate to Mr. Fillmore. He was not then, as he is not now, governed by any *principle* in the matter, but by *passion*. He is *against Mr. Fillmore*, under all circumstances, no matter who may oppose him! And why? Because Mr. Fillmore did not suffer him to put his numerous *active friends* into fat offices under the General Government; to many of whom he had made pledges while he was struggling for a seat in the United States Senate—where he ought never to have gone, and where the better portion of those who aided in his election now regret having sent him!

But it is true, Fillmore and his Cabinet did refuse the extravagant demands made for office by the Governor; and in no single instance did they appoint men to office from Tennessee without consultation with BELL, GENTRY, and WILLIAMS; all three of whom were offensive to *Jones*. They had proven themselves to be worthy of consultation; the Governor had not! This accounts, moreover, for the efforts of Jones at Baltimore to defeat the nomination of Fillmore, and to procure the nomination of Scott—efforts which, unfortunately for the country, were but too successful!

When the American party was organized in Tennessee, JONES had no objection to the creed, and would have fallen into the ranks, but then he beheld *Gentry* and *Brownlow* in the party—men whom he despised above all others. He tried to prevent the nomination of Gentry for Governor by letter-writing, and by seeking to get up a *Whig* Convention. Failing in these schemes, he threw himself into the arena, and *secretly* damaged Gentry all he could, and played into the hands of Johnson, who was only elected by a majority of some *two thousand votes*!

We are not informed as to the course Gov. Jones will pursue in this contest, further than this, he will go against Fillmore. We predict that he will support Buchanan. *Pride of character* may keep him from it—if he have any of that commodity left, after his five years' residence at Washington! The platform upon which Buchanan has been placed by the Cincinnati Convention, is a reiteration of violent and undying hostility to every measure of public policy that was advocated by HENRY CLAY and the Old Whig party. Jones still *professes* an equally undying devotion to Clay and his principles. Moreover, Jones has, on every stump in Tennessee, held up Buchanan as a *rank old Federalist*, a Pennsylvania *Abolitionist*, and as the *wicked traducer*, *violent calumniator*, and *malignant persecutor* of Henry Clay—even attributing his promotion to the Secretaryship of State, by Mr. Polk, to his *infamous agency* in fastening upon Mr. Clay the foul charge of "bargain, intrigue, and corruption." We confess that we are at a loss to see how Jones can fall into the support of Buchanan. The *nomination* of the man is a direct insult to Old Clay Whigs!

ALBERT G. WATKINS, the Representative in Congress from the First Congressional District of Tennessee, has gone over to Democracy, placing his change upon the ground of his *great concern for the South*! We take it that he will support Buchanan without hesitancy. This would place Watkins before the country in his true colors, and reflect the likeness of the man with *daguerreotype* accuracy!! With such a platform, and such a candidate on it, Watkins would have the appearance of a man walking in one direction, with his head turned completely around, and his face looking the other way! The incongruity of the platform, and the peculiar reputation of Buchanan for political inconsistency, are alike adapted to the history and incidents of Watkins's late canvass for Congress! The plain truth is, that the man so completely destroyed himself, and was so ruinously exposed by his competitor, COL. TAYLOR, whom he beat only some two hundred votes, (and that by means that make his seat in Congress one of *thorns*,) that he could but go over to Locofocoism. And although he has, in former days, held up Buchanan on the stump as an old Federalist, and as the reviler and persecutor of Henry Clay, he can advocate him now with a better grace than he can look his Know Nothing constituents in the face! We cannot say of this man as Pope said of Craggs:

> "Broke no promise, served no private end,
> Gained no title, and who lost no friend."

WILLIAM G. SWAN, of Knoxville, is next on the list of "Old Line Whigs" who have gone over to the Foreign Catholic Democratic party, and of whose conversion the Democrats at a distance boast. Here they do not brag; but on the other hand, some of the leaders, whose names we can supply, authorize us to state that they do not want him, and will not receive him. This man was twice beaten for the Legislature in this county—never elected by the people to any position outside of Knoxville—and became soured at the Whig party. He went for *Johnson and Sag Nichtism* last summer, and his loss is not regretted by the American party in this county.

But JOHN H. CROZIER, of Knoxville, has gone over to "Old Buck" and his admirers; and this is claimed as a change! This little man, *supremely selfish*, was turned out of Congress five years ago, by JOSIAH M. ANDERSON, with the people at his back, for *taking too much mileage*, by several hundred dollars per session, for four years! He afterwards desired the Whig party to run him for Governor; but they were not willing to undertake the *load*. He became soured, and last summer paid a visit to some of the counties below, to avoid, as was believed, voting for Gentry for Governor, and Sneed for Congress. He was formerly very bitter in his opposition to Democracy; and on many a stump has he denounced *Buchanan*, and all others concerned in the "bargain and intrigue" slander of Clay, besides holding up "Buck" as a Blue-light Federalist! At a recent Buchanan Ratification meeting in Knoxville, he made a bitter speech against the American party!

These two men, Swan and Crozier, were active in getting up an organization against us, in 1849, by heading a company which purchased the *"Register Establishment,"* of this city, at the head of which they placed one *john miller m'kee*, behind whom they and others concealed themselves and wrote violent and abusive articles, through a controversy of two years. Driving the whole of them to the wall, as we did, in the controversy, they determined to *mob and tear down our office*; and with a view to this, those concerned deposited their *guns*, and other "implements of husbandry," in the law office jointly occupied by these two men, who have operated as *twin brothers* for several years—each sympathizing with the other in his political defeats! Those concerned were deterred from this contemplated and well-arranged assault upon our office, by COL. LUTTRELL, the Comptroller of the State, and other gentlemen of nerve, arming themselves with shot-guns, pistols, and hatchets, and taking their stand at our office!

Nothing daunted by this defeat, these *gallant* lawyers, and *generous*—not to say *brave*—opponents betook themselves to the county of Anderson, in this Judicial Circuit, and with great difficulty got up an indictment against us, under an old statute, forgotten by gentlemen of the bar, for *advertising a Baltimore lottery scheme;* when they themselves, and their relatives, were dealing in the *Art Union lottery* in this city! They were most signally defeated in that indictment; and, together with the two Williamses, brothers-in-law of Crozier, sought to drive the business men of the place, and others, from advertising in our paper, or subscribing for it. Failing in this, they sought to prevent us from getting the Government advertising under Fillmore's administration; and in this they failed, though this is the ground of their hostility to Fillmore and his Cabinet, as well as to John Bell, M. P. Gentry, and C. H. Williams.

The *Register* fell through—was sold under the hammer for *twenty-two hundred dollars*—McKee ran away—and the company have had about FIVE THOUSAND DOLLARS to pay for him, which hurts prodigiously! Our WHIG has steadily increased in favor with the people, and its circulation is now THE RISE OF FIVE THOUSAND—being the largest circulation that any political or other journal ever attained in East Tennessee! Indeed, no political weekly in Tennessee now has, or ever did have, a circulation equal to "BROWNLOW'S KNOXVILLE WHIG."

A young man calling himself *Luther Patterson*, has been conducting a foreign Sag Nicht sheet at Kingston, called the "Gazetteer," and which has gone by the board for the want of patronage. This little eight by ten sheet has been editorially, and by means of anonymous communications, assaulting the writer of this work, and the editor of the *Register*, MR. FLEMING. Patterson paid a recent visit to this place; at which time Fleming met with him on the street, and publicly chastised him, applying the toe of a stiff boot to the *west end* of his person, with some force. Patterson turned about and boasted in his paper that he had the best of the fight. Our paper and Fleming's corrected this false version of the affair, and gave the facts; whereupon Patterson sued out a writ in the Circuit Court for Fleming, for damages done to his person in said rencontre, laying his damages at $5,000! Shortly after this he instituted a civil action against the publishers of the paper we edit, and another against us for the article we wrote against him; and these suits are now pending.

These two *gallant* attorneys, as we are informed, are employed as counsel by Patterson—a young man who has no visible means of paying lawyers, but the *eagerness* of these gentlemen to get after us would lead them to "work for nothing and find themselves." In addition to their several civil suits against several of us, they have sent their man before the Grand Jury of Knox county, and made a presentment against us for having *out-wrote* their Sag Nicht editor! The object of these suits against the editors and publishers of the American papers here, is to *gag* them, or to check their influence in this contest. But they have mistaken their men. Like other vipers, they will find, before these matters end, that they bite a file—a file of good *American* steel, and tempered to that degree of hardness that all their malignity, intense and active as it is known to be, will not be able to prevail against it!

When we came to this city of Knoxville, in 1849, we sold our office at Jonesborough, at private sale, to pay a *security debt*, and purchased a new press and materials on a credit. These we sent on to the care of WILLIAMS & Co., the brothers-in-law of Crozier, who kept about the only commission and forwarding house in Knoxville. We were detained at Jonesborough four weeks by close confinement to our bed; and our materials arriving here, these "Old Line Whigs," who had always professed friendship toward us, refused to give them house-room; and had not JAMES W. NELSON and others stepped forward and paid the charges, and procured a house for them, the steamboat captain would have sold them out for the carriage!

These *magnanimous* gentlemen, members of the learned profession of the law, next contrived, through certain influences they brought to bear, to turn us out of the only office we could rent in the city, and thus they drove us *without the limits of the Corporation*, and compelled us to erect a temporary office upon our own lot, which we had bought on a credit. They were now at the end of their row. One was a candidate for Congress, the other for a seat in the Legislature. We pitched into both, and they were both defeated; but we do not claim that it was through our influence. Like Cardinal Wolsey, however, they both had to bid "farewell, a long farewell, to all their greatness." From the pinnacle of Congressional and Legislative honors, they have been precipitated to the shades of private life, and to political obscurity. Their chief ambition now is, to play "fantastic tricks" in courts of justice, and before grand jurors, in the way of annoying those they have neither the *manliness* nor *courage* to call to an account upon their own hooks!

The established usage of *gentlemen*, when offended by a newspaper editor, is to exact personal satisfaction. To acknowledge that you are personally aggrieved, and then to retort in tricks behind the offender's back, or words behind your privileges at the Bar, is to acknowledge that one is either a *fool* or a *coward*—perhaps both. A chief object in this crusade against us is to gag us during this campaign, and kill us off from the stump and the press; but they have certainly studied our character to but little purpose. And whatever line of policy their prompters and associates of the Locofoco school may urge upon them, let them be assured that they cannot muzzle criticism of their personal or political delinquencies. It is a sacred duty to unmask the *renegade*, to expose the *traitor*, and to hold up the *demagogue* to public reprobation. That duty will be performed freely and fearlessly, by the author of this work, come weal or come woe. If these two "Knights of the Rueful Countenance" kill and eat a dozen Know Nothings, we know one member of the Order they will not affright into silence. For their cowardly assaults and their officious intermeddlings they may bare their backs to the lash. We will be with them to the bitter end, and will only forsake them in the *Gethsemane* of their retreat!

Had we come here with press and type, in 1849, and agreed to be controlled by these men and their particular friends, we could have been *the* man for the times. Had we stooped to flirt and coquette and fawn and dance around these men, we could have had their endorsement, their influence, and their money, to any reasonable extent. But we neither sought their friendship, nor coveted their adulations. We claim to have been made of such inflexible materials, as not readily to go through the transmutations necessary to secure the kind regards of these men. We are no office-seeker, and desire no reward beyond the consciousness of having performed our duty, and of having served our country to the best of our ability.

We take this occasion to repeat what we have heretofore said in our journal, that nearly every prominent man in the country, calling himself an "Old Line Whig," and now opposed to Fillmore and Donelson, is influenced by personal grievances, or a desire to get office—matters with which the people have not the slightest concern. Their opposition to the American ticket proceeds from personal hostility, either to the candidates, some of the electoral candidates, or certain prominent advocates of the ticket, and from no less unworthy motives. Of course there are exceptions to this rule.

The idea of an Old Clay Whig supporting the Buchanan ticket is both absurd and ridiculous. To say nothing of the foul and malignant charge of "bargain, intrigue, and corruption," Buchanan labored to fasten upon Clay, the Platform upon which the Cincinnati Convention has placed Buchanan repudiates every principle Clay contended for, and held as sacred to the day of his death. On the contrary, the American party has not ignored one political tenet held by the Whig party, but has added new ones; none of which are at war with the creed of Clay, or the Constitution of our country! To make short work of a long story, no man who ever was a *true Whig*, and acted with that party *from principle*, can consistently go over to the *bogus* Democracy of this day, and vote for Buchanan and Breckenridge!

Talk about a Clay Whig turning Sag Nicht! What an idea! What principle does this Foreign Democratic party hold, that an Old Line Whig, or a conservative man, North or South, does not disapprove? What principles have they ever held, the evil effects of which are not now standing out in bold relief as a monument of their shame, and to which they have added the unpardonable sin of making war upon Native American Protestants?

In conclusion, the reader will please allow a few remarks personal to the writer, and he is done—leaving the public to make their own comments, and their own disposition of both this book and its author. Our life has been a public life—our cause a public cause. We have our faults, as most men have; and we have committed some errors, as most men have. Our few acts of goodness and virtue, if any, we leave others to hunt up; our faults are subjects of criticism, and are viewed with a *jaundiced eye* by our opponents. Through a course of *eighteen years* of editorial invective, (whether right or wrong,) we claim to have been actuated by none other than the best of motives. We have never been prompted by ambition, malice, or a desire to make money. Our voice, which has echoed over many hills and through many valleys, has never been heard in extenuation of guilt; has never been heard to plead the cause of the gambler, the swearer, the drunkard, the robber, or the assassin. Wherever vice has lifted its "seven heads and ten horns"—wherever fraud has showed its thieving hand—wherever gambling has displayed its rotten heart—wherever demagogues have sought to impose on the honest people—there have we tried to be conspicuous; not as their aider and abettor, but as their scourge, their accuser, and their unrelenting foe. And among this class of men are our most bitter foes. What friends we have are to be found at the fireside of virtue—among sober, sedate, and thinking men, and among the brave and honorable. We have never been the slave or sycophant of any man or party, as our immense band of subscribers, numbering thousands, will bear us witness.

And now, Americans, while we look forward to the future with pleasing anticipations—while we rejoice in prospect of the final triumph of wisdom, of reason, and of virtue, over audacious ignorance, palpable corruption, canting hypocrisy, and caballing Democracy—God forbid that we should indulge the vain idea that we have nothing to do! Let every friend of American rights and Protestant liberties take a bold, a decided stand, vowing most solemnly that he will have no fellowship at the ballot-box with the friends of that unpitying monster, a DEMO-CRATIC PAPAL HIERARCHY! Be active, be vigilant, and persevering, and the day is ultimately ours!

> "Strike till the last armed foe expires;
> Strike for your altars and your fires;
> Strike for the green graves of your sires,
> God, and your native land!"

TO STEPHEN TRIBBLE—LETTER NO. 2.

Sir:—On the night of the 9th of June, 1856, you held forth in the Court-House in Charleston, Mo., taking myself, *Rev. Josiah McCrary*, the Methodist stationed preacher of that town, and Methodists generally, for your text. It would seem that the *touch* I gave you, and a letter of mine read before a large congregation in Charleston, on Sabbath evening, June 8th, *have fully developed all the latent black-guardism of your early training and corrupt nature!* I will now place the record of your *infamy* before the world in such a permanent form, and circulate it so extensively, that your low Billingsgate and vile blackguardism can never harm any man or sect. I will make such a showing of you that no persons of refined feelings or of any pride of character will hear you preach or entertain you in future! I will remind many readers of the showing up of your infamous character and conduct, by the editor of the Louisville Journal, ten or twelve years ago, and of the exposure of your villainous conduct by the *Rev. Mr. McNutt*, of Kentucky, through the Nash-ville Advocate, some eight or nine years ago.

I will only add the following article from my paper of the 21st June, 1856, as it completes your record, so far as Tennessee is concerned. I will only add, that you were driven out of McMinn County in East Tennessee, where you were preaching, lying, and drinking whiskey, years ago. There and then, too, the records of the Sullivan County affair, certified to by the Clerk, were produced against you! But to the article from my late paper:

STEPHEN TRIBBLE AGAIN.

This old hypocrite and scoundrel has been denying in the pulpit that he was ever convicted of manslaughter or branded! It turns out, also, that the old villain once joined the American party in West Tennessee! And last, but not least, it seems that he was turned out of both the Methodist and Presbyterian Churches before he became a Campbellite preacher. A pretty disciple to be abusing honest men! But to the law and to the testimony:

"Roane County, June 3d, 1856.

"Sir:—In your issue of the 14th of May, you notice *Stephen Tribble*, and ask for information concerning him. He came to the lower end of Roane county from one of the upper counties of East Tennessee, and passed himself for an Arian preacher. I objected to his preaching in a meeting-house, and came near getting myself into a scrape. About that time a gentleman came from our upper country, and said he had seen his father apply the branding-iron to Tribble, and the smoke rose ten feet high! I then began to play on a harp of one string against him, and that was *a tribble*, whereupon he left between two days for Kentucky! He was once expelled from the Methodist Church, and afterwards he was expelled from the Presbyterian Church. If Tribble disputes what I say, all I ask is a chance to prove it. I live ten miles south of Kingston, near Barnardsville. Yours truly,

"JOHN BLAIR."

THE SHERIFF BRANDING TRIBBLE IN THE HAND.

"PARIS, TENN., June 6th, 1856.

"DEAR SIR:—I see in a late issue of yours that you are after a Reverend wolf, Stephen Tribble. I am personally acquainted with him, as I lived in Sullivan county when he was in the Blountville jail. I have heard him preach here, and deny from the stand ever having been in jail, when he and I had talked the whole matter over the day before. He is now about forty-eight years of age—has a scar on his cheek. He preached here monthly in 1846, and here it was that he joined the American party. He now resides either in Graves or Fulton county, Kentucky. One of his brothers told me last week that he now preaches at one point in Kentucky, and the rest of his time in Missouri. One of their preachers told me that he gets drunk and cuts up largely. Yours, with respect,

"A. J. HICKS."

To the foregoing letters we add a certified copy of the records of the Circuit Court of Sullivan county, and after this we shall leave this *old clerical debauchee* to preach for such Sag Nichts as may feel edified by his ministry:

"MONDAY, Sept. 24, 1827.

"State of Tennessee, First Circuit, Sullivan County Court: met according to adjournment. Present, Honorable Samuel Powell, Judge, &c."

"FRIDAY, Sept. 28, 1827.

"STATE *VS*. STEPHEN TRIBBLE AND JOHN TRIBBLE.

"In this cause, the jury having retired yesterday to consider of their verdict, under the care of an officer, and the same jury, to wit: James Steele, Wm. Morgan, Joshua Miller, John Thomas, Wm. Hashman, John Wassum, Thomas Brown, Stephen B. Cawood, John K. Arnold, Thomas Fain, William Hughes, and William H. Biggs, returning to the bar, do say, they find the defendants not guilty of the murder, but they find them guilty of manslaughter as charged in the bill of indictment. Whereupon the defendants moved the Court for a rule to show cause why a new trial should be had, which rule is granted, and on argument said rule is discharged. It is therefore considered by the Court that for such offence the said defendants be imprisoned for the term of four calendar months: that they be branded with the letter M in the brawn of the thumbs of their left hands on to-morrow morning, and that they pay the costs of this suit or remain in custody until the same is paid."

"STATE OF TENNESSEE, SULLIVAN COUNTY.

"I, Jno. W. Cox, Clerk of the Circuit Court of Sullivan County, do hereby certify that the foregoing is a full, true, and perfect copy of the final judgment in the case of State *vs.* Stephen Tribble and John Tribble, as appears of record in my office.

"Given under my hand at this office, the 10th of June, 1856.

"Jno. W. Cox, Clerk,
"By A. J. Cox, Dep. Clerk."

In conclusion, *Stephen*, I take my leave of you now, having introduced you to the 5,000 subscribers to the Whig, the 7,500 subscribers to our campaign paper, and the *tens of thousands of readers* of this book—a work which will exist and be referred to when I am in my grave, and you are in the hot embraces of the Devil! You will at least agree with me that *that* was an evil hour for you when you travelled out of your way to assail me before a strange audience in Missouri.

I am, &c.,

W. G. BROWNLOW.

Knoxville, June 23d, 1856.

A SERMON ON SLAVERY.

Delivered by the undersigned in Temperance Hall in Knoxville, on Sabbath, 8th of June, 1856, to a large and attentive audience, composed of citizens and strangers—some from the North and some from the South—occupying one hour and a quarter in the delivery. It is published as it was delivered, without an omission or an alteration. Respectfully, &c.,

W. G. BROWNLOW.

TEXT.—"Let as many servants as are under the yoke count their own masters worthy of all honor, that the name of God and his doctrine be not blasphemed."—1 Tim. vi. 1.

Whoever reflects upon the nature of man, will find him to be almost entirely the creature of circumstances: his habits and sentiments are, in a great measure, the growth of adventitious circumstances and causes; hence the endless variety and condition of our species. That race of men in our country known as Abolitionists, Free-soilers, or Black Republicans, look upon any deviation from the constant round in which *they* have been spinning out the thread of their existence as a departure from nature's great system; and, from a known principle of our nature, the first impulse of these fanatics is to condemn. It is thus that the man born and matured in a free State looks upon slavery as unnatural and horrible, and in violation of every law of justice or humanity! And it is not uncommon to hear bigots of this character, in their churches at the North, imploring the Divine wrath to shower down the consuming fires of heaven on that great Sodom and Gomorrah of the New World, all that section of country south of Mason and Dixon's line, where this unjust practice prevails.

When an unprejudiced and candid mind examines into the past condition of our race, and learns the fact which history develops, as the inquirer will, that a majority of mankind were *slaves*, he will be driven to the melancholy reflection, that the world, when first peopled by God himself, was not a world of freemen, but of *slaves*!

Slavery was really established and sanctioned by Divine authority among even God's chosen people, the favored children of Israel. Abraham, the founder of this interesting nation, and the chosen servant of the Most High, was the owner of more slaves than any cotton-planter in South Carolina or Mississippi. That magnificent shrine, the gorgeous temple of Solomon, commenced and completed under the pious promptings of religion and ancient Free-Masonry, was reared alone by the hands of slaves! Egypt's venerable and enduring pyramids were reared by the hands of slaves! Involuntary servitude, reduced to a science, existed in ancient Assyria and Babylon. The ten tribes of Israel were carried off to Assyria by Shalmanezer, and the two strong tribes of Judah were subsequently carried in triumph by Nebuchadnezzar to end their days in Babylon as slaves, and to labor to adorn the city. Ancient Phœnicia and Carthage were literally overrun with slavery, because the slave population outnumbered the free and the owners of slaves! The Greeks and Trojans, at the siege of Troy, were attended with large numbers of their slaves. Athens, and Sparta, and Thebes—indeed, the whole Grecian and Roman worlds—had more slaves than freemen. And in those ages which succeeded the extinction of the Roman empire in the West, slaves were the most numerous class. Even in the days of civilization and Christian light which revolutionized governments, laboring serfs and abject slaves were distributed throughout Eastern Europe, and a portion of Western Asia—conclusively showing that slavery existed over these boundless regions. In China, the worst forms of slavery have existed since its earliest history. And when we turn to Africa, we find slavery, in all its most horrid forms, existing throughout its whole extent, the slaves outnumbering the freemen at least three to one. Looking, then, to the whole world, we may with confidence assert, that slavery in its worst forms subdues by far the largest portion of the human race!

Now, the inquiry is, how has slavery risen and thus spread over our whole earth? We answer, by the *laws of war, the state of property, the feebleness of governments*, the thirst for *bargain and sale*, the *increase of crime*, and last, but not least, *by and with the consent and approbation of Deity*!

These remarks may suffice by way of an introduction, and they will serve to indicate the course we intend to pursue, if the announcement of the text has not already done that. *Let as many servants as are under the yoke count their own masters worthy of all honor*, &c. The word here rendered *servants* means SLAVES, converted to the Christian faith; and the word rendered *yoke* signifies the *state of slavery* in which Christ and the apostles found the world involved when the Christian Church was first organized. By the word rendered *masters* we are to understand the heathen masters of those Christianized slaves. Even these, in such circumstances, and under such domination, are commanded to treat their masters with all honor and respect, that the name of God, by which they were called, and the doctrine of God, to wit, Christianity, which they had professed, might not be blasphemed, might not be evil spoken of in consequence of their improper conduct. Civil rights are never abolished by any communication from God's Spirit; and those fiery bigots at the North who propose to abolish the institution of slavery in this country are not following the dictates of God's Spirit or law. The civil state in which a man was before his conversion, is not altered by that conversion; nor does the grace of God absolve him from any claims which the State, his neighbor, or lawful owner may have had on him. All these outward things continue unaltered: hence, if a man be under the sentence of death for murder, and God see fit to convert him, he is not released from suffering the extreme penalty of the law!

The Church of Christ, when originally constituted, claimed no right, *as an ec-*

clesiastical organization, to interfere in any way with the civil government. This was the principle upon which the Church was founded, as announced by its immortal Head. When Christ was doomed by a cruel Roman law to its most ignominious condemnation, he did not so much as resist it, because *it was law*, nor did he complain of it as oppressive.

> "Then Pilate entered into the judgment-hall again, and called Jesus, and said unto him, Art thou the King of the Jews?... Jesus answered, My kingdom is not of this world: if my kingdom were of this world, then would my servants fight, that I should not be delivered to the Jews; but now is my kingdom not from hence.... To this end was I born, and for this cause came I into the world, that I should bear witness unto the truth." —John xviii. 33-37.

When Christ came into the world on the business of his mission, he found the Jewish people subject to the dominion of the Roman kingdom; and in no instance did he counsel the Jews to rebellion, or incite them to throw off the Roman yoke, as do the vagabond philanthropists of the North in reference to the existing laws of the United States upon the subject of slavery. Christ was, by lineal descent, "THE KING OF THE JEWS," but he did not assert his temporal power, but actually refused to be crowned in that right.

Under the Roman law, human liberty was held by no more certain tenure than the whim of the sovereign power, protected by no definite constitution. Slavery constituted the most powerful and essential element of the government, and that slavery was of the most cruel character, and gave to the master absolute discretion over the lives of the slaves. Notwithstanding all this, Christ did not make war upon the existing government, nor denounce the rulers for conferring such powers, although he looked upon cruel legislation in the light in which the character of his mission required. And although the *Church itself* was not what it should have been, in no instance did Christ ever denounce *that*. The only denunciations the Saviour ever uttered, were those against the doctors and lawyers, ministers and expounders of the Jewish code of ecclesiastical law.

But allow us to present the case of the Apostle Paul, as proof more palpable and overwhelming, on this very point. He had been falsely accused, cruelly imprisoned, and tyrannically arraigned; and that, too, before a licentious governor, an unjust and dissipated ruler, and an unprincipled infidel. The Roman law in force at the time arrested the freedom of speech, denied the rights of conscience, and even forbade the free expression of opinion in all matters conflicting with the provisions of the laws of the Roman government. In his defence before Felix, Paul never so much as speaks of Roman law, though well acquainted with it, but "he reasoned of *righteousness*, and *temperance*, and the *judgment to come*." Here was a suitable occasion to condemn the regulations and to question the authority of the villainous statutes of Rome; but instead of this, Paul plead his rights *under* the unjust regulations of the law. He charged Felix with *official* delinquency, with *personal* crime, and, as a *man*, he held him up to public scorn, and threatened him with the vengeance of God! He appealed *to the law*, and justified himself *by the law*. He claimed the rights of a *"Roman citizen"* —demanded the protection due to a Roman citizen—and he scorned to find fault with the law, cruel and unjust as he knew it to be. And the consequence was, that the licentious infidel who ruled, *"trembled."*

The views we have here presented are not at all new, but have been uniformly acted upon by evangelical Christians, in all ages of the world. Since the days of St. Paul and Simon Peter, no reformer has appeared who was more violent than that good and great man, MARTIN LUTHER. JOHN CALVIN possessed a revolutionary spirit—he fought every thing he believed to be wrong—he was unyielding in his disposition, and unmitigated in his severity. Yet neither of these great men ever made war upon the existing laws of their respective countries. JOHN WESLEY was the great reformer of the past century—he reformed the whole ecclesiastical machinery of the modern Church of Christ; and his doctrines, and manner of conducting revivals, are leading elements of American Christianity. But Mr. Wesley never made war upon the English government, under which he lived and died. On the other hand, it is a matter of serious complaint among sectarians not friendly to the spread of Methodism, that Wesley wrote elaborately against the war of the Revolution. He was devoted to law and order, and he deemed it a religious duty to oppose all resistance to existing laws. In his troubles at Savannah, Georgia, like Paul before the licentious governor, he appealed *to the law,* and sought by every means in his power to be tried *under* the law, asking only the privilege of being heard in his own defence! And it was, in all the instances we have mentioned, *"that the name of God and his doctrine be not blasphemed,"* to quote the expressive language of the text, that existing laws have been adhered to by the propagators of gospel truth.

The essential principles of the great moral law delivered to Moses by God himself, are set forth in what is called the tenth commandment, in the 20th chapter of Exodus: "Thou shalt not covet thy neighbor's house, thou shalt not covet thy neighbor's wife, nor his *man-servant,* nor his *maid servant,* nor his ox, nor his ass, nor any thing that is thy neighbor's." Now, the only true interpretation of this portion of the Word of God is, that the species of property mentioned are *lawful,* and that all men are forbid to disturb others in the lawful enjoyment of their property. "Man-servants and maid-servants" are distinctly *consecrated as property,* and guaranteed to man for his exclusive benefit—proof irresistible that slavery was thus ordained by God himself. We have seen learned dissertations from the pens of Abolitionists, saying, that the term "servant," and not "slave," is used here. To this we reply, that both the Hebrew and Greek words translated "servant," mean also "slave," and are more frequently used in this sense than in the former. Besides, the Hebrew Scriptures teach us, that God especially authorized his peculiar people to *purchase* "BONDMEN FOR EVER;" and if to be in *bondage for ever* does not constitute *slavery,* we yield the point.

The visionary notions of piety and philanthropy entertained by many men at the North, lead them to resist the *Fugitive Slave Law* of this government, and even to *violate the tenth commandment,* by stealing our "men-servants and maid-servants," and running them into what they call free territory. Nay, the *villainous piety* of some leads them to contribute *Sharpe's Rifles* and *Holy Bibles,* to send the *uncircumcised Philistines* of New England into Kansas and Nebraska, to shoot down the

Christian owners of slaves, and then to perform religious ceremonies over their dead bodies! Clergymen lay aside their Bibles at the North, and females, as in the case of that model beauty, *Harriet Beecher Stowe*, unsex themselves to carry on this horrid and slanderous warfare against slaveholders of the South! And English travellers, steeped to the nose and chin in prejudices against this government and our institutions, have written books upon the subject. The Halls, Hamiltons, Trollopes, and Miss Martineaus, *et ed omne genus*, all have misrepresented us! These English writers all denounce slavery, and eulogize *Democracy*; as if an Englishman could be a Democrat, in the modern, vulgar sense of the term, and be a consistent man!

But we do not propose, in this brief discourse, to enter into any defence of the African slave trade. Although the evils of it are greatly exaggerated, its evils and cruelties, its barbarities, are not justified by the most ultra slaveholders of this age. The vile traffic was abolished by the United States, even before the British Parliament prohibited it. All the powers in the world have subsequently prohibited this trade — some of the more influential and powerful of them declaring it *piracy*, and covering the African seas with armed vessels to prevent it!

This trade, which seems so shocking to the feelings of mankind, dates its origin as far back as the year 1442. Antony Gonzales, a Portuguese mariner, while exploring the coast of Africa, was the first to steal some *Moors*, and was subsequently forced by Prince Henry of Portugal to carry them back to Africa. In the year 1502, the Spaniards began to steal negroes, and employ them in the mines of Hispaniola, Cuba, and Jamaica. In 1517, the Emperor Charles V. granted a *patent* to certain privileged persons, *to steal exclusively* a supply of 4,000 negroes annually, for these islands!

African slaves were first imported into America in 1620, a century after their introduction into the West Indies. The first cargo, of twenty Africans, by a Dutch vessel, was brought up the James River, into Virginia, and sold out as slaves. England then being the most commercial of European nations, engrossed the trade; and from 1680 to 1780, there were imported into the British Possessions alone, TWO MILLIONS OF SLAVES — making an average annual importation of more than 20,000! And the annual importation into America has transcended 50,000! The States of this Union, north of Mason and Dixon's Line, commonly called the New England States, were never, to any great extent, *slaveholding*; their virtuous and pious minds were chiefly exercised in *slave-stealing* and *slave-selling*! To Old England our New England States owe their knowledge of the art of slave-stealing; and to New England these Southern States are wholly indebted for their slaves. They stole the African from his native land, and sold him into bondage for the sake of gain. They kept but few of their captives among themselves, because it was not profitable to use negro labor in the cold and sterile regions of New England. And when they enacted laws in the New England States abolishing slavery, they brought their negroes into the South and sold them before their laws could go into operation! This is the true history of slavery in New England. They stole and sold property which it was not profitable to keep, and for which they now refuse all warranty. And what few American ships are in the trade now, at the peril of piracy, are New

England ships.

The pious and religious portion of New England Abolitionists, we take it, are the better portion, and in these we have no sort of confidence. Take, for example, the case of that great man, and powerful pulpit orator, STEPHEN OLIN, who came into Georgia, and was introduced into the ministry by BISHOP ANDREW and his friends, and by this means married a lady owning a number of slaves. He sold them all for the money, pocketed the money, and returned to his congenial North; and when BISHOP ANDREW was arraigned before the General Conference of 1844, because he had married a widow lady owning a few slaves, this man OLIN appeared on the floor, and spoke and voted against the Bishop! Dr. Olin had washed his hands of the sin of slavery—had his money out at interest—and he was ready to plead for the rights of the poor African! May we not exclaim, "Lord, what is man?"

We are acquainted with many of the leading Abolitionists of the North connected with the Methodist Church; and although we suppose they are about as good as the Abolitionists of other denominations we have no confidence in them. The most of them would enter their fine churches on the Sabbath, preach for hours against the sin of slavery, shed their tears over the oppressions of the "servile progeny of Ham," in these Southern States; and on the next day, in a purely business transaction, behind a counter, or in the settlement of an account, cheat a Southern slave out of the *pewter* that ornaments the head of his cane!

There is much in the political papers of the country calculated, if not intended, to fan a flame of intense warfare upon the subject of slavery, which can result in no possible good to any one. Those politicians who are exciting the whole country, and fanning society into a livid consuming flame, particularly at the North, have no sympathies for the black man, and care nothing for his comfort. They only seek their own glory. This political disquiet and commotion is giving birth to new and loftier schemes of agitation and disunion, among the vile Abolitionists of the country, and to bold and hazardous enterprises in the States and Territories. And many of our Southern altars smoke with the vile incense of Abolitionism. We have scores of Abolitionists in the South, in disguise—designing men—some filling our pulpits—some occupying high positions in our colleges—some editing political and religious papers—some selling goods—and some following one calling and some another, who, though among us, are not of us, Southern men may rest assured!

We endorse, without reserve, that much-abused sentiment of a distinguished South Carolina statesmen, now no more, that "slavery is the corner-stone of our republican edifice;" while we repudiate, as ridiculously absurd, that much-lauded, but nowhere-accredited dogma of MR. JEFFERSON, that "all men are born equal." God never intended to make the *butcher* a judge, nor the *baker* a president, but to protect them according to their claims as butcher and baker. Pope has beautifully expressed this sentiment, where he has said:

> "Order is heaven's first law, and this confessed,
> *Some are*, and *must be*, greater than the rest."

We have gone among the free negroes at the North—we have visited their miserable dwellings in Philadelphia, New York, Boston, and other points; and, in every instance, we have found them more miserable and destitute, as a whole, than the slave population of the South. In our Southern States, where negroes have been set at liberty, in nine cases out of ten their conditions have been made worse; while the most wretched, indolent, immoral, and dishonest class of persons to be found in the Southern States, are *free persons of color*.

The freedom of negroes in even the Northern States, is, in all respects, only an empty name. The citizen negro does not vote, and takes good care not to do so. The law does not interdict him this privilege, but if he attempt to avail himself of the privilege, he is apprehensive of "apostolic blows and kicks," which the pious Abolitionists will administer to him. All the social advantages, all the respectable employments, all the honors, and even the pleasures of life, are denied the free negroes of the North, by citizens full of sympathy for the down-trodden African! The negro cannot get into an omnibus, cannot enter a bar-room frequented by whites, nor a church, nor a theatre; nor can he enter the cabin of a steamboat, in one of the Northern rivers or lakes, or enter a first class passenger car on one of their railroads. They are not suffered to enter a stage-coach with whites, but are forced upon the deck, whether it shall rain or shine—whether it be hot or cold. Industry is closed to them, and they are forced to live as *servants* in hotels, or adopt the professions of barber, or boot-black, or open oysters in saloons, or sell villainous liquors to the lower classes of German and Irish emigrants, who throng our large cities and towns. The negroes even have their *own streets*, and their own low-down kennels; they have their hospitals, their churches, their cars, upon which are written in large letters, "FOR COLORED PEOPLE!" Finally, they are forced to have their own *grave-yards*—the *yellow* remains of Northern Abolitionists, and pious white men, refusing to mingle with the bleeching bones of the dead negro! While, in the South, they crowd the galleries and back seats in our churches, travel in our passenger cars, and even *loan their money* to our white men at interest! Such is an outline of the contrast between free negroes at the North, and slaves at the South.

Let us turn again to the Holy Scriptures, and see whether or not they sustain or condemn the institution of slavery. The opposers of slavery profess to be governed alone by the teachings of the Bible, in their war upon this institution. It is vain to look to Christ or any of his apostles to justify the blasphemous perversions of the word of God, continually paraded before the world by these graceless agitators. Although slavery in its most revolting forms was everywhere visible around them, no visionary notions of piety or schemes of philanthropy ever tempted either Christ or one of his apostles to gainsay the LAW, even to mitigate the cruel severity of the slavery system then existing. On the contrary, finding slavery *established by law*, as well as an *inevitable and necessary consequence*, growing out of the condition of human society, their efforts were to sustain the institution. Hence, St. Paul actually apprehended a *"fugitive slave,"* and sent him back to his lawful owner and earthly master!

Having already appealed to the authority of the Old Testament Scriptures, we turn to that of the New, where we learn that slavery existed in the earliest days of the Christian Church, and that both *masters* and *slaves* were members of the same

Christian congregations. Slavery was an institution of the State in the Roman Empire, as it is in the Southern States of this confederacy, and the apostles did not feel at liberty to denounce it, if, indeed, they felt the least opposition to it—a thing we deny.

But, before we appeal to the irresistible authority of the New Testament, we will submit a few only of a great many passages from the Old Testament—not having quoted as extensively as may have been deemed necessary:

> "And he said, I *am* Abraham's servant."—GEN. xxiv. 34.

> "And there was of the house of Saul a *servant*, whose name was Ziba; and when they had called him unto David, the king said unto him, Art thou Ziba? And he said, *Thy servant is he.*"—2 SAM. ix. 2.

> "Then the king called to Ziba, Saul's *servant*, and said unto him, I have given unto thy *master's* son all that pertained to Saul, and to all his house."—Verse 9th.

> "Thou, therefore, and thy sons, and thy *servants*, shall till the land for him, and thou shalt bring in *the fruits*, that thy *master's* son may have food to eat, &c. Now Ziba had fifteen sons and TWENTY SERVANTS."—Verse 10th.

> "I got me *servants* and maidens, and had *servants born in my house*; also, I had great possessions of great and small cattle, above all that were in Jerusalem before me."—ECCLES. ii. 7.

> "And he said, Hagar, Sarai's maid, whence camest thou? And she said, I flee from the face of my *mistress* Sarai."—GEN. xvi. 8.

> "And the Angel of the Lord said unto her, *Return to thy mistress,* and submit thyself to her hands."—Verse 9th.

The only comments we have to offer upon these passages are, first, one individual acknowledges himself the owner of twenty slaves! Another was raising slaves, and having them born in his house!! And last, but not least, the angel of God ordered the fugitive slave to return to her lawful owner!! High authority, this, for apprehending runaway slaves!

In reference to bad servants, we read in Prov. xxix. 19:

> "A servant will not be corrected by *words*; for though he understand, he will not answer."

The Scriptures look to the correction of servants, and really enjoin it, as they do in the case of children. We esteem it the duty of Christian masters to feed and clothe well, and in cases of disobedience to *whip well.*

In the book of Joel, iii. 8, the *slave trade* is recognized as of Divine authority:

> "And I will sell your sons and your daughters into the land of the children of Judah, and they shall sell them to the Sabeans, to a people far off; FOR THE LORD HATH SPOKEN IT!"

> "Let every man abide in the same calling wherein he was called.

Art thou called, being *a servant*? Care not for it; but if thou mayest be made free, use it rather. For he that is called in the Lord, being *a servant*, is the Lord's freeman; likewise also he that is called, being free, is Christ's servant."—1 Cor. vii. 20-22.

"*Servants*, be obedient to them that are your *masters according to the flesh*, with fear and trembling, in singleness of your heart, as unto Christ. Not with eye-service, as men-pleasers; but as the servants of Christ, doing the will of God from the heart. With good-will doing service, as to the Lord, and not to men: knowing that whatsoever good thing any man doeth, the same shall he receive of the Lord, whether he be bond or free. And, *ye masters*, do the same things unto them, forbearing threatening: knowing that your Master also is in heaven: neither is there respect of persons with him."—Eph. vi. 5-9.

"*Servants*, obey in all things your *masters according to the flesh*: not with eye-service, as men-pleasers; but in singleness of heart, fearing God. And whatsoever ye do, do it heartily, as to the Lord, and not unto men: knowing that of the Lord ye shall receive the reward of the inheritance; for ye serve the Lord Christ."—Col. iii. 22-25.

"*Masters*, give unto *your servants* that which is just and equal: knowing that ye also have a Master in heaven."—Col. iv. 1.

"Let as many *servants as are under the yoke* count their *own masters* worthy of all honor, that the name of God and his doctrine be not blasphemed. And they that have *believing masters*, let them not despise them, because they are brethren; but rather do them service, because they are faithful and beloved, partakers of the benefit. These things teach and exhort."—1 Tim. vi. 1, 2.

"Exhort *servants* to be obedient unto their *own masters*, and to please them well in all things; not answering again; not purloining, but showing all good fidelity; that they may adorn the doctrine of God our Saviour in all things."—Titus ii. 9, 10.

"*Servants*, be subject to *your masters* with all fear; not only to the good and gentle, but also to the froward. For this is thankworthy, if a man for conscience toward God endure grief, suffering wrongfully."—1 Peter ii. 18, 19.

We have but a single word of comment to offer upon these passages of Scripture. The original words used by the Greek writers, both sacred and profane, to express slave; the most abject condition of slavery; to express the absolute owner of a slave, and the absolute control of a slave, are the strongest that the language affords, and are used in the passages here quoted. If the apostles understood the common use of words, and desired to convey these ideas, and to recognize the relations of master and servant, they would, naturally enough, employ the very words used. To say that they did not know the primary meaning and *usus loquendi* of the original words, is paying them a compliment we wish not to participate in! And to show that we are not singular in our views of the meaning expressed in the passages quoted, showing that they express in the one case slaves, and in the other masters or owners, actually holding them as property, under the sanction of the laws of the State, we quote from the following authorities:

That great commentator, Dr. ADAM CLARKE, on 1 Cor. vii. 21, says:

> "Art thou converted to Christ while thou art a slave—the property of another person, and bought with his money? *Care not for it.*"

The learned Dr. Neander, in his work entitled "Planting and Training of the Church," in referring to *Onesimus*, mentioned in the epistle to Philemon, says of him:

> "It does not appear to be surprising that a *runaway slave* should betake himself at once to Rome."

To the foregoing might be added other authorities of equal weight and importance.

It is a well-known historical fact, that slaveholders were admitted into the AP-OSTOLIC CHURCHES; nor would this assumed position of the advocates of slavery be at all denied by any intelligent and well-read men at the North, but for the fact that they think such an admission would decide the question against abolitionists. We have given much attention to this subject within ten years past, and we feel no sort of delicacy in expressing our views and convictions, as revolting as they may be to Northern men and Free-soilers, even among us. We believe that the primitive Christians held slaves in bondage, and that the apostles favored slavery, by admitting slaveholders into the Church, and by promoting them to official stations in the Church. And why do we believe all this? Because we are sustained in these positions by uninterrupted historical testimony!

Well, for the information of abolitionists and other anti-slavery men dispersed throughout the South, we assume that the fact of the apostles admitting into Church fellowship slaveholders, and promoting them to positions of honor and trust, shows that the simple relation of master and slave was no bar to Church-membership. Masters and slaves, in the days of the apostles, were admitted into the Church as brethren: they partook in common of the benefits of the Church: they held to the same religious principles: they squared their lives by the same rule of conduct: acknowledged the same obligations one to another; and worshipped at the same altar. This was true of the first and succeeding centuries, when the relations of master and slave, and the practice of the Church in reference thereto, were very much like they are in the Southern States of our Union at present. But to the proof that slaveholders were admitted into the apostolic Churches:

1. Historians all agree that slavery existed, and was general throughout the Roman empire, at the time the apostolic Churches were instituted. We have at our command the authorities to prove this, but to quote from them would swell this discourse beyond what we have intended. We will cite the authorities only; and anti-slavery men who deny our position can examine our authorities. See Gibbon's "Decline and Fall of the Roman Empire," vol. i. See "Inquiry into Roman Slavery, by Wm. Blair," Edinburgh edition of 1833. See vol. iv. of "Lardner's Works,"

page 213. See vol. i. of "Dr. Robertson's Works," London edition. Other authorities might be given, but these are sufficient, as they show that slavery was a civil institution of the State; that the Roman laws regarded slaves as *property*, at the disposal of their masters; that these slaves, whether white or colored, had no civil existence or rights, and contended for none; and that there were *three slaves to one citizen*—showing something of a similarity between the Roman empire and our Southern States! Gibbon says that slavery existed in "every province and every family," and that they were bought and sold according to their capacities for usefulness, and the demand for laborers—selling at hundreds of dollars, and from that down to the price of a beast of burden! Now, it is notorious that the gospel made considerable progress among the citizens of the Roman empire; and, as nearly every family owned slaves, it is certain that slaveholders were converted and admitted into the Church. It will not do to say that the poor, including the slaves, were alone converted to God, because the apostles make frequent allusions to the receiving into the Church of intelligent, learned, and opulent persons. The learned Dr. Mosheim, in his Church History, vol. i., relating to the *first three centuries*, settles this question most effectually. He says:

> "The apostles, in their writings, prescribe rules for the conduct of the rich as well as the poor, for *masters* as well as *servants*—a convincing proof that among the members of the Church planted by them were to be found persons of opulence and masters of families. St. Paul and St. Peter admonished Christian women not to study the adorning of themselves with pearls, with gold and silver, or costly array. 1 Tim. ii. 9: 1 Peter iii. 3. It is, therefore, plain that there must have been women possessed of wealth adequate to the purchase of bodily ornaments of great price. From 1 Tim. vi. 20, and Col. ii. 8, it is manifest that among the first converts to Christianity there were men of learning and philosophers; for, if the wise and the learned had unanimously rejected the Christian religion, what occasion could there have been for this caution? 1 Cor. i. 26 unquestionably carries with it the plainest intimation that persons of rank or power were not wholly wanting in that assembly. Indeed, lists of the names of various illustrious persons who embraced Christianity, in its weak and infantile state, are given by Blondel, p. 235 de Episcopis et Presbyteris: also by Wetstein, in his Preface to Origen's Dia. Con. Mar., p. 13."

A few reflections, by way of concluding, and we are through with our discourse, already extended beyond the limits we had prescribed:

First.—There is not a single passage in the New Testament, nor a single act in the records of the Church, during her early history, for even centuries, containing any direct, professed, or intended denunciation of slavery. But the apostles found the institution existing, under the authority and sanction of law; and, in their labors among the people, masters and slaves bowed at the same altar, communed at the some table, and were taken into the Church together; while they exhorted the one to treat the other as became the gospel, and the other to obedience and honesty, that their religious professions might not be evil spoken of!

Secondly.—The early Church not only admitted the existence of slavery, but in various ways, by her teachings and discipline, expressed her approbation of it, enforcing the observance of certain Fugitive Slave Laws which had been enacted by the State. And, in the various acts of the Church, from the times of the apostles downward through several centuries, she enacted laws and adopted regulations touching the duties of masters and slaves, *as such*. This, in our humble judgment, amounts to a justification and defence of the institution of slavery.

Thirdly.—Our investigations of this subject have led us regularly, gradually, certainly, to the conclusion that God intended the relation of master and slave to exist. Hence, when God opened the way for the organization of the Church, the apostles and first teachers of Christianity found slavery *incorporated with every department of society*; and, in the adoption of rules for the government of the members of the Church, they provided for the rights of owners, and the wants of slaves.

Fourthly.—Slavery, in the age of the apostles, had so penetrated society, and was so intimately interwoven with it, that a religion preaching freedom to the slave would have arrayed against it the civil authorities, armed against itself the whole power of the State, and destroyed the usefulness of its preachers. St. Paul knew this, and did not assail the institution of slavery, but labored to get both masters and slaves to heaven, as all ministers should do in our day.

Fifthly.—Slavery having existed ever since the first organization of the Church, the Scriptures clearly teach that it will exist even to the end of time. Rev. vi. 12-17 points to "The Day of Judgment," "The Last Day," "The Great Day," and the condition of the human race at that time, as well as the classes of persons to be judged, rewarded, and punished! A portion of this text reads, "And the kings of the earth, and the great men, and the rich men, and the chief captains, and the mighty men, and every BONDMAN, and every FREEMAN," etc., will be there; evidently implying that slavery will exist, and that the relations of master and slave will be recognized, to the end of time!

Lector House believes that a society develops through a two-fold approach of continuous learning and adaptation, which is derived from the study of classic literary works spread across the historic timeline of literature records. Therefore, we aim at reviving, repairing and redeveloping all those inaccessible or damaged but historically as well as culturally important literature across subjects so that the future generations may have an opportunity to study and learn from past works to embark upon a journey of creating a better future.

This book is a result of an effort made by Lector House towards making a contribution to the preservation and repair of original ancient works which might hold historical significance to the approach of continuous learning across subjects.

HAPPY READING & LEARNING!

LECTOR HOUSE LLP
E-MAIL: lectorpublishing@gmail.com

www.ingramcontent.com/pod-product-compliance
Lightning Source LLC
LaVergne TN
LVHW091146180726
843490LV00004B/1331